THE PROMISE OF
FRANCIS

THE PROMISE OF
FRANCIS

The Man, the Pope, and the Challenge of Change

DAVID WILLEY

G

GALLERY BOOKS
New York   London   Toronto   Sydney   New Delhi

G

Gallery Books
An Imprint of Simon & Schuster, Inc.
1230 Avenue of the Americas
New York, NY 10020

First Gallery Books trade paperback edition April 2017

GALLERY BOOKS and colophon are registered trademarks of Simon & Schuster, Inc.

For information about special discounts for bulk purchases, please contact Simon & Schuster Special Sales at 1-866-506-1949 or business@simonandschuster.com.

The Simon & Schuster Speakers Bureau can bring authors to your live event. For more information or to book an event contact the Simon & Schuster Speakers Bureau at 1-866-248-3049 or visit our website at www.simonspeakers.com.

Manufactured in the United States of America

10 9 8 7 6 5 4 3 2 1

Library of Congress Cataloging-in-Publication Data is available.

ISBN 978-1-4767-8905-7
ISBN 978-1-4767-8906-4 (pbk)
ISBN 978-1-4767-8907-1 (ebook)

For Judy

CONTENTS

—⁓⁓—

INTRODUCTION

The Challenge of Change

I once read that priests are like airplanes: they make news only
when they crash, but there are many that fly.
—POPE FRANCIS, DECEMBER 22, 2014,
TO THE ROMAN CURIA

Shortly after his election in March 2013, Pope Francis watched as an aide broke the seal on the front door of the papal penthouse apartment in the Apostolic Palace and handed him the key. For the past century, this ten-room apartment had been home to every successor of Saint Peter. As always when a pope dies (or as in this case, resigns), the doors of the official residence had been sealed with red ribbon and wax. The heavy window shutters had been closed, the electricity shut off.

The new pope was curious to see the home offered him. The Apostolic Palace inside the Vatican is the world's fourth largest royal palace complex, outclassing even the former residence of the emperors of China, the Forbidden City in Beijing, and the Royal Palace of Madrid, currently Europe's largest functioning palace.

But Francis was also apprehensive: the outward trappings of power had never interested the man known until only a few days previously as Cardinal, and often simply "Father," Jorge Bergoglio. At home in Buenos Aires, he had always lived frugally, rarely attending official dinner parties or receptions. He had shunned the comfortable and spacious official archbishop's residence in a posh suburb in favor of a couple of rooms in a church property adjoining the downtown cathedral. On weekends there he liked to cook his own meals. He dismissed his official chauffeur and preferred to travel around town by public transport, including the subway.

The papal apartment inside the Vatican is one of Rome's most desirable pieces of residential real estate. It has stupendous 360-degree views of the Eternal City, and among its amenities are a hidden roof garden, a private chapel, a studio equipped for emergency medical treatment and dentistry, and a state-of-the-art kitchen. In addition, it offers separate quarters for a female domestic staff of four.

Romans always liked it: on evenings passersby in St. Peter's Square would gaze upward and see a light burning in the second window from the left of the top floor of the papal apartment, well known to be the pope's private study. The sight was somehow reassuring, for it confirmed that the pope was at home and busy at his desk. For me as a Londoner, it was akin to seeing Queen Elizabeth's personal flag, the Royal Standard, aflutter above Buckingham Palace, confirmation that the queen is in residence.

Pope Francis peered inside the darkened rooms while aides fumbled for the light switches. When the lights were on he exclaimed in open dismay: "But there's room for two hundred people! I can't settle here." As he explained in a later interview, "When I saw the papal apartment, inside myself I distinctly heard a 'no.' Not that it is luxurious—it is old, large and tastefully decorated, but it is like a funnel. The entrance is so narrow that people could enter only in dribs and drabs. I cannot live without people. I need to live my life with others."[1]

As a result, so far during his papacy that apartment has remained shuttered and dark, save for when Francis appears at a window on Sunday morning to bless the pilgrims and Romans crowding into the square below. He also occasionally receives heads of state and other official visitors in its private library. (Larger delegations are received in spacious frescoed reception rooms on a lower floor.)

Instead Francis elected to live across the piazza in the more modest Casa Santa Marta. This Vatican guesthouse is run like a hotel with a public lobby and a restaurant with communal dining tables. During the weeks before electing a new pope and the actual balloting in the conclave, more than one hundred cardinals had occupied rooms there. Among its amenities is a modern chapel.

The new pope took up residence on the second floor in room number 201, the three-room suite previously reserved for VIP visitors. As this temporary arrangement became permanent, so did his routine. As he has for years, Francis rises every morning at 4:30 A.M. and prays in solitude before breakfast. Then he celebrates mass in the tiny, modern chapel of the Casa Santa Marta, where he delivers a short homily to forty or so specially invited worshippers.

During these early morning hours he sometimes wanders, often alone, around his new domain of one square mile, to chat with workmen, Vatican policemen, gardeners, firemen, and drivers. He learned that scores of homeless people were sleeping rough literally on his doorstep, sheltering in the embrace of Bernini's colonnades facing St. Peter's Basilica, or in doorways around the Vatican. So he asked his almoner, the Polish priest whose job it is to help the most needy in the Vatican neighborhood, to distribute hundreds of new sleeping bags, to install showers in the public toilets discreetly hidden behind the colonnades, and to arrange for a barber to give free haircuts once a week. He invited four of them (one insisted on bringing his dog with him) to share his birthday lunch at Santa Marta. He invited a group of 150 homeless for a free visit to view the artistic splendors of the Sistine Chapel, and offered front row seats at a Vatican charity concert to another.

In Argentina he had been known for taking public buses and the subway; now, snubbing the armor-plated Mercedes papal limousine used by his predecessors, he chose a small Ford Focus for his sorties into Rome.

The entire floor where he lives at the Casa Santa Marta is now reserved for his secretaries and main executive staff. And in the guest-house are a number of meeting rooms conveniently close to the Vatican's main audience hall, where he can hold private meetings with VIP visitors and discussions with heads of Vatican departments (that is, "dicasteries," in ecclesiastical jargon).

His admitted longing for company can startle outsiders, even when they are ranking clergymen. The Casa Santa Marta has two elevators, one in theory reserved for the pontiff, the other for "ordinary" individuals including cardinals and bishops. Pope Francis tends to shun his personal elevator. A few old-timers sink to their knees when finding themselves in the communal elevator with the pope. When one obviously terrified visiting bishop suddenly found himself standing close to the pope, a smiling Francis told him, "Don't worry. I'm not going to eat you!"

In its relatively severely decorated communal dining hall, where Pope Francis takes his meals in company, his table is separated from the others by a row of potted plants. A few of his fellow residents find that to run into a pope before breakfast, even behind potted plants, can be off-putting. As one Santa Marta guest confided to me, some make it a point to rise early enough to avoid that encounter, which they, if not he, view as extraordinarily formal, especially before morning coffee.

———

On the dark night of March 13 in St. Peter's Square, rain was pelting down. For two days the cardinals had been sequestered inside the Sistine Chapel to ballot for a successor to Pope Benedict. In our own way the media was also sequestered by radio and television producers. Initially I had been on a hillside TV position overlooking the Vatican, but now I was in St. Peter's Square high atop an open, windswept two-story scaffolding platform with plastic roofing that had been temporarily erected so that we could broadcast live around the clock, necessary to feed the differing time zones. Below us was a mass of flag-waving pilgrims (a third of the world's countries have religious symbols on their national flags) plus thousands of curious Romans protecting themselves from the downpour with umbrellas.

Beside the small army of resident Vatican reporters on the scaffolding were commentators flown in for the occasion. No one expected a decision before day three, and this was only day two. So during the long hours as we waited, we had little to do but to speculate upon who would be the next pope. In this guessing game, the prime candidates included, besides the Italian Cardinal Angelo Scola, Archbishop of Milan; the Canadian Marc Ouellet, a Vatican heavyweight in charge of the appointment of bishops worldwide; Cardinal Cláudio Hummes of São Paolo, Brazil; and, as a long shot, the African Cardinal Peter Turkson of Accra, Ghana, who was already occupying the influential curial post of head of the Justice and Peace Commission.

None of us recalled that according to secret diaries that surfaced after Benedict had been elected pope eight years previously, Jorge Mario Bergoglio from Argentina had been the runner-up to Joseph Ratzinger.

Now the great bell of St. Peter tolled, and white smoke spewed from the narrow copper chimney tube atop the roof of the Sistine Chapel. At that point we knew that a pope had been elected, but not who he was. Still invisible, Bergoglio retired to the so-called Room of Tears next to the chapel to be vested in one of three all-white outfits prepared by papal tailor Gammarelli: one for a pope who was short and thin; one for a man of normal size; and one for a large, corpulent man. More than an hour passed. As we learned only later, the new pope was Bergoglio. The delay came about first because he had insisted on informing personally by telephone the retiring Pope Emeritus Benedict, who was watching the proceedings on TV with his closest staff members at the papal summer villa at Castel Gandolfo, outside of Rome. Long minutes had passed before anyone heard the telephone ringing and bothered to pick up the call.

The new pope, elected after only five ballots, as yet unknown to the excited crowds outside in the rain, secluded himself to pray alone inside the Pauline Chapel. This was and is the pope's private chapel, only a few steps away from the Sistine Chapel. Aides had prepared a throne and kneeler there for the new pontiff. Instead Bergoglio seated himself in a back pew. Both Sistine and Pauline chapels had been decorated by Michelangelo, but in quite different moods. The Pauline Chapel, normally inaccessible to visitors, contains Michelangelo's last two huge fresco paintings, in which the artist openly advocated church reform; Michelangelo knew that a conclave was to be held there. Upset by such insubordination, Paul IV, the reigning pontiff in 1555 (who invented the Roman Inquisition), cut off the aging Michelangelo's pension for the rest of the artist's life.

While the newly elected pontiff prayed, we of the media perched on our fragile tower continuing the guessing game.

At last the white curtains at the window behind the loggia on the façade of St. Peter's Basilica were parted, and we could see a splash of red robe between two specks of white, the acolytes. When finally the man in red, French Cardinal Jean-Louis Tauran, spoke, he began in Latin: "Annuntio vobis gaudium magnum" (I announce to you a great joy), concluding with the famous words that everyone understood, "Habemus Papam" (We have a pope). As the crowd of over a hundred thousand roared, Tauran continued in Latin, Vatican workmen draped a huge dark red and white tapestry over the balcony, and finally we heard "Bergoglium," followed, though not immediately, by "Franciscum."

Now the great dark red velvet draperies were closed. Again we waited, in what was an extraordinarily prolonged theatrical moment, for the new pope to appear. From other balconies on the façade, cardinals in full regalia peered over. In this interval we were reminded of the fact that Bergoglio was the first-ever Jesuit to be elected pope, as well as the first pontiff from Latin America.

And then suddenly he was there in front of us, bespectacled and smiling broadly. His first words were stunningly simple: "Fratelli e sorelle, buona sera!" he said in Italian, not Latin. "Brothers and sisters, good evening!" It was a foretaste of his style of friendly familiarity. He continued: "It seems that my brother cardinals have gone almost to the ends of the earth to give Rome a bishop, and here we are."

As the anthems of Italy and the Vatican were played by the band of Italy's paramilitary Carabinieri, umbrellas were furled despite the rain, and the sea of flags waved. A galaxy of flashing mobile phones and tablets turned the piazza into a sparkling electronic firework display.

When the new pope had concluded his first blessing, he said, "Let us begin our walk together, let us pray one for another. We are a great brotherhood. I hope that this journey we begin together will be fruitful for the evangelization of this beautiful city. Let me ask you a favor," he said. "I would like you to pray for me as well, in silence."

At these words, total silence fell instantly over the crowded piazza, and he bent forward, in a gesture of unequivocal humility.

Elected pope, Francis immediately found himself facing conflictual differences that almost defy the imagination, and moreover are magnified upon a global scale. The Roman Catholic Church has been a global power for centuries; Jesuit missionary Matteo Ricci was in India in 1578 and in China by 1582, and other Jesuits were running missions in South America by the seventeenth century. But today's is a vast global church, whose reach is radically extended by rapid air travel and instantaneous communications.

This means that everyone knows what the other is doing. The persistent yet reliable reports of child molestation, from California to Ireland to Australia, and of polygamy practiced among the pope's rapidly expanding African flock—many of whose priests and bishops are themselves the sons of polygamous unions—cannot be swept under the carpet.

If we did not know, there was Pope Benedict XVI's butler to tell us, in the Vatican scandal that came to be known as "Vatileaks." Pope Benedict's butler and personal valet, Paolo Gabriele, had systematically stolen from Benedict's own desk top-secret documents, copies of which he handed over to Gianluigi Nuzzi, an Italian journalist. Gabriele actually believed that he was acting in the best interests of the church, but these copious leaks of documents had far-reaching consequences. Indeed, given the speed and globality of information about the church, the credibility of the entire institution was further harmed.

Popes don't normally get a full briefing on the problems afflicting the universal church from their predecessors. The previous pontiff has usually been safely embalmed and entombed, and a week of official mourning been observed before the vital business of electing a successor begins.

But Pope Francis, surprisingly—and quite rapidly—elected by his peers to take over the scandal-tainted Catholic Church on March 13, 2013, did not have to rely on secondary sources or to scour the written record to inform himself about the disastrous situation confronting him.

A fifteen-minute ride in a brand-new helicopter, graciously provided by the Italian government, brought Pope Francis from the Vatican to the papal palace at Castelgandolfo. Pope Benedict had tactfully retired there after his resignation at the end of the previous month. The former pope, wearing a white padded jacket, looking rather wan and leaning on a cane, was waiting in the garden to embrace Francis. It was an amazing photo-op, this first meeting between the two popes, one reigning, one retired, who henceforth were to cohabit, albeit somewhat uneasily, inside the Vatican walls.

On the surface there was immediate gracious cordiality. They grasped hands and went off to pray together in the private chapel of the sprawling Renaissance castle, where a white upholstered armchair and kneeler had been strategically placed for the new pope. "No, we are brothers, we pray together," insisted the new pope, kneeling side by side with Benedict.

They retired to a small drawing room where they sat facing each other. On a coffee table between them was a large white box with two white envelopes on top, which Pope Benedict had prepared for his successor. Here was the top-secret report that Pope Benedict had commissioned into the theft of some of his most private documents by his former butler. What is certain is that the former pope wanted to hand in person certain papers to his successor that were for his eyes only.

———

The Vatileaks scandal, which erupted in 2012, was not without precedent. When I was fresh out of Cambridge, I had gone to work for Reuters News Agency in Rome in 1956. There being no Internet nor smartphones, it fell to me to collect, even before Pope Pius XII spoke, a sealed envelope containing the text of his traditional Easter Sunday message to the world, "Urbi et Orbi." The pickup point was in the coffee bar opposite the main entrance to Vatican City. By secret agreement, a friendly but corrupted Vatican official had planted it there on a certain shelf. Rome's big four international news agencies paid him a retainer so that he would leak papal texts; but, most important, he guaranteed they would also have instant news of a papal illness or death; should the pope die on a Monday, the scoop went to Reuters; if a Tuesday, to the Associated Press, and so on.

Pope Pius XII did die the following year, but I did not have to return to the coffee bar, for by then I had moved on to other assignments in Brussels, then to North Africa, East Africa, and the Far East at the time of the Vietnam War.

I returned to Rome in 1972, this time permanently as a reporter for the BBC, and Paul VI was pope. Once more I was at St. Peter's—this time, at the Apostle's shrine, not the modest English church where as a cradle Catholic I used to attend mass with my mother as a child. From that point on I would cover the Vatican as well as Italian affairs. In so doing I would follow three successive popes on their foreign travels; with John Paul II alone I made fifty foreign trips covering every continent.

I looked back at my adolescent altar server days from a vastly more informed perspective. I may have "lapsed," in Catholic jargon, but over the years I became fascinated by the geopolitics of the world's longest enduring international organization. From Alice Springs to Zambia I saw the Catholic Church in action from the top, and became quite addicted to soaring above the Atlantic, Pacific, or Indian Oceans at thirty-six thousand feet in the company of the Vicar of Christ and his retinue as a member of the traveling Vatican Press Corps, or the VAMP as they are known today.

———

For Pope Benedict, his butler's betrayal, and the ensuing scandal, were the last straw. On February 11, 2013, he stunned the entire Catholic world by announcing his resignation. This was the first time in centuries that any pope had stepped down voluntarily from his high office, and no one had expected or prepared for it. His official reason was a "lack of strength of mind and body" due to advancing age—he was already seventy-eight when elected and eighty-six when he decided to step down.

Within two weeks the cardinals who had been summoned to elect a successor converged on Rome during the last days of February 2013. They could not ignore the fact that their church was living through desperate times. Desperate measures were required. For almost two decades the church had been rudderless. During the final decade of his pontificate, John Paul II had been seriously weakened by Parkinson's disease, and while he tried his best, his physical decline forced him to leave management of the church to others, some of whom took advantage of a de facto power vacuum. His successor was Cardinal Joseph Ratzinger, German theologian and long-serving aide to John Paul. During his eight-year reign as Benedict XVI, that aging pontiff found himself overwhelmed by an avalanche of intractable problems. Frustrated, he seemed to long to shrink back into the academic life to which he had been accustomed before becoming pope.

The Vatican bank stood accused of money laundering and was under investigation by the Italian judiciary. The clergy sex abuse scandal, and the extensive cover-up by bishops and by the Vatican itself, was making daily headlines worldwide. In Europe and North America, vocations were in decline, especially among women. American nuns were being accused of radical feminism, and stunned to learn that they were the subject of an official Vatican probe. The forty-year-old ban on contraception was simply ignored by the faithful in most countries, although not by the Vatican. The debate over same-sex marriages, abortion, and communion for the divorced simmered. Ever fewer faithful attended Sunday mass; in Latin America defections to evangelical Protestant churches soared. In the Middle East, assaults upon the already dwindling Christian presence, masterminded by radical Islam, were gathering speed.

Not least, there was a growing recognition that many of the reforms proposed and begun during the Second Vatican Council (1962–65) had never been fully implemented. Popes John Paul II and Benedict XVI had backpedaled (although neither would probably admit this). Cardinal Carlo Maria Martini, the Jesuit archbishop of Milan, once tipped as a possible future pope, wrote prophetically just before he died in 2012 (his words were published only posthumously), "The church is two hundred years behind the times."

"Our culture has aged, our churches are big and empty, our rites and customs are pompous," Martini said in his startlingly frank and prophetic deathbed interview: "The church must admit its mistakes and take a radical path of change, starting with the pope and the bishops."

Before the conclave was formally opened inside the Sistine Chapel, groups of cardinals met every morning and afternoon, and then often met again privately in smaller groups in the evening. A sense of panic permeated many of these tense meetings, as was clear not only from confidential whispers from cardinals but unwittingly from the media briefings by the official Vatican spokesman, Father Federico Lombardi.

These preconclave meetings proved to be decisive. On March 9, at the daily official gathering of all the cardinals (the General Congregation) in the Synod Hall within the Vatican, the Archbishop of Buenos Aires, Cardinal Jorge Mario Bergoglio, made a short but forceful speech that gripped the imagination of many in the assembly. The speech was "masterful and enlightening," said the cardinal from Cuba, Jaime Lucas Ortega y Alamino, to whom Bergoglio later gave his handwritten notes to keep.

From these notes it is clear that Bergoglio's two main points were, first, that "the Church must come out of herself and go to the peripheries" [marginal areas of the world] in both a geographic and existential sense.[2] Second, the church must beware of "theological narcissism"—that is, must stop looking inward; "spiritual worldliness is the great evil," he said. Cardinal Bergoglio concluded by suggesting that the next pope be one to carry out "possible changes and [the] reforms that must be made."

"Reforms"—this was the key word that many, but not all, wanted to hear.

But whether or not they wanted to hear it, behind the ritual pomp and circumstance key questions were being posed. What was the significance of the election of the first Jesuit pope in history? And what would it mean to have the first-ever pope from South America? Pope Francis was not only a bishop who had come from the end of the earth. He was an outsider come in from the cold.

More than two years have passed since then. The popularity of Pope Francis has soared beyond the imaginable; in 2013 he drew 6.6 million visitors to the Vatican in only nine months. During 2014 nearly six million people attended his general audiences, masses, and private meetings. In 2015 an estimated seven million attended his final mass in a park in Manila during his pilgrimage to the Philippines. It may have been the largest crowd to gather in human history.

Pope Francis is admired by atheists and Protestants as well as by Roman Catholics. He is perceived as a rare moral leader on the world stage and, for many, the only point of moral reference in an era of strife and brutality unprecedented since World War II. Pew Research polls show that he ranks among the world's most popular political leaders, second only to President Barack Obama. Polls in Italy show that he is the sole leader who is admired without qualification.

Much of this worldwide admiration derives from his frugal lifestyle, in sharp contrast with that of some other princes of the church whom he has not hesitated to criticize for their worldly ways.

Not even former Pope Benedict is immune from criticism on this score. Once a nun's convent, his retirement home lies on the far side of the Vatican Gardens. It had been entirely restructured to accommodate Joseph Ratzinger several months before the shock announcement of his abdication. Residing with him in it is the former pope's longtime secretary, Archbishop Georg Gänswein, and the four consecrated women who perform domestic chores—those same four women who occupied their own top-floor quarters in the papal apartment within the Apostolic Palace.

Other large Vatican homes are traditional perks for those who have held or hold top Vatican jobs. Cardinal Tarcisio Bertone, who was Benedict's secretary of state, occupies a huge, 4,306-square-foot penthouse apartment that, like Ratzinger's, was also newly restructured specifically for him. (Bertone has since complained that his bedroom roof leaks.)

Cardinal Pietro Parolin, the successor to Ratzinger's foreign affairs chief Bertone, resides in a magnificent Renaissance apartment, while retired Cardinal Giovanni Battista Re occupies another penthouse with an astonishing view over Rome. Another palatial apartment is occupied by the governor of Vatican City; its past occupants included deceased Vatican financial luminaries like the Marchese Giulio Sacchetti, a layman from the noble Florentine banking family that had tended papal finances for centuries. It was so large that when occupied by Cardinal Rosario Castillo Lara from Venezuela, he was ironically nicknamed "Cardinal Settebagni" (Cardinal Seven Bathrooms).

Other desirable Vatican lifetime "grace and favor" homes include a villa on the Janiculum hill overlooking St. Peter's Basilica. Its occupant is the cardinal in charge of the foreign missions dicastery, Propaganda Fide. And other very comfortable residences belonging to the Vatican lie within an extraterritorial enclave in the heart of Trastevere.

———

During the first months after his election, Pope Francis made it known among his aides that he had no intention of imitating the unprecedented worldwide travel program of John Paul II, who made 105 foreign trips during a quarter century. But gradually as invitations came pouring in from countries in Africa, Asia, and Latin America, Francis changed his mind. During 2015, apart from his weeklong January visit to Asia and another, slightly shorter one, in September to the United States and Cuba, he made a day trip to Sarajevo in June, and plans a July visit to Ecuador, Bolivia, and Paraguay, not to mention a separate short stay in two African countries, the war-torn Central African Republic and Uganda in November. In 2016 he is already planning his first return trip to his native Argentina since his election, which will also include side trips to Chile and Uruguay.

Surprisingly, Francis had never visited the United States before his 2015 visit to Washington, New York, and Philadelphia. Nor had he ever traveled extensively in the Middle East. He had been unexpectedly marooned in Jerusalem by the outbreak of the 1973 Yom Kippur war during his first visit to the Holy Land, long before his official pilgrimage as pope to Jordan, the Palestinian territories, and Israel in May 2014. During his enforced stay at the American Colony Hotel in Jerusalem amid the 1973 hostilities while Syria and Egypt attacked Israel, he most likely met his reform-minded Jesuit colleague Father Carlo Maria Martini, the future cardinal archbishop of Milan, at the time rector of the Jesuits' prestigious Pontifical Biblical Institute.[3]

The recalibration of the College of Cardinals quickly became one of his top priorities. Pope Francis wants the electors of his successors to be more representative of the worldwide church, and particularly of the southern hemisphere, where most of the world's Catholics now live.

In his first batch of new cardinals' appointments in 2013, Pope Francis had already started a trend toward giving poor countries in the southern hemisphere more and fairer representation in Rome. Bishops and archbishops from some of the poorest countries in the world— from Haiti in the Caribbean, Burkina Faso and Ivory Coast in West Africa, and Nicaragua in Central America—were promoted to the highest ranks in the church. In February 2015, a second group, including the first-ever cardinals from the remote Pacific island of Tonga, as well as prelates from New Zealand, Vietnam, Ethiopia, Myanmar, and Thailand, received their red hats—together with a discreet papal admonition not to hold too many expensive or alcoholic celebration parties for their friends and supporters to mark the occasion.

Pope Francis tactfully advised each cardinal-elect how to respond to his appointment: "Accept it with humility. Only do so in a way that, in these celebrations, no spirit of worldliness creeps in to intoxicate one, even more than would a glass of grappa sipped upon an empty stomach."

Although the weight and influence of existing Italian, other European, and North American cardinals still dominates the Sacred College, gradually the electoral body is being transformed for the first time in its long history into a mirror of the new and varied Catholic world of the twenty-first century. It will take some years for Pope Francis' nominees to become the majority, but the new pattern of command in the Universal Church is already apparent in Rome. No new American cardinals figure among Pope Francis' first appointments, and bishops in charge of Italy's major dioceses (Italy is split up into 225 dioceses, more than in any other country in the world) can no longer take it for granted that they will receive a red hat to mark the final stage of their ecclesiastical careers as in the past.

———

What is already clear from the pontificate of Pope Francis is that he is a pope in a hurry. He does not intend to reign for an extended period. His eightieth birthday falls in December 2016. Indeed he may well decide to follow the rule he has already imposed upon all existing and future Vatican appointments, that when an office holder turns eighty, all official appointments lapse. He has twice hinted that he may decide to follow the example of his predecessor, Benedict, and retire at eighty. There is also a precedent for this age cutoff among his own Jesuit order; for this reason the current superior general, sometimes nicknamed "The Black Pope" from the color of his normal ecclesiastical dress, has announced his forthcoming retirement two years ahead of time.

Before becoming pope, Cardinal Bergoglio had already made arrangements to live at the end of his career in a priests' retirement home in Flores, Buenos Aires, a few blocks from his childhood home, when he was unexpectedly called to Rome in 2013. His room reservation there, as far as I have been able to ascertain, has never been canceled, and he may well decide to follow the new Vatican retirement rules that he himself invented. If so, he could step down just as his predecessor Benedict did, irrespective of whether he remains healthy enough to complete his ambitious plans of church reform.

He has never hidden his desire for normality in his life. He does not enjoy being the object of a personality cult. In an interview with the editor of one of Italy's leading dailies a year into his pontificate, he criticized the "mythmaking" that he detected growing up around him.[4]

"Portraying the pope as a kind of Superman, a sort of star, seems offensive," he said. "The Pope is a man who laughs, cries, sleeps tranquilly and has friends like everyone. A normal person."

It is also clear that Francis' papacy is not only about lifestyle. The Vatican bureaucracy—the Curia—is composed of nearly three thousand cardinals, bishops, priests, and laymen, plus a scattering of women. It has always been dominated by Italians, although increasingly clergy from other countries are being called to serve at the headquarters in Rome.

After twenty months of close observation of their work, Pope Francis decided four days before Christmas 2014 to present the senior staff of the Curia not with a joyful homily, but with a devastating catalog of its shortcomings. "A Curia that is outdated, sclerotic, or indifferent to others is an ailing body," he declared. He went on to list fifteen ailments afflicting those who run the church. Among his most serious criticisms were these:

- "Existential schizophrenia: the sickness of those who lead a double life." Such people, he said, "create a parallel world of their own where they set aside everything they teach others with severity, and live a hidden, often dissolute life."

• "The sickness of chatter, grumbling and gossip. The sickness of the cowardly who, lacking the courage to speak directly to people, speak instead behind their backs."

• "The sickness of the funereal face, or rather that of the gruff and grim who believe that in order to be serious it is necessary to paint their faces with melancholy and severity, and to treat others—especially those they consider inferior—with rigidity, harshness and arrogance."

• "The sickness of rivalry and vainglory: when appearances, the color of one's robes, insignia and honors become the most important aim in life."

• "The sickness of closed circles, when belonging to a group becomes stronger than belonging to the whole body. It becomes a cancer."

• "The sickness of worldly profit and exhibitionism: a disease of those who seek insatiably to multiply their power and are therefore capable of slander, defamation and discrediting others."

As an exchange of Christmas greetings, this litany of complaints about Vatican managers was without precedent. It shows the extent to which Pope Francis felt that his aims at reform were being frustrated by internal opposition. Judging from the tepid applause and the expressions on the faces of his listeners, the cardinals, bishops, and monsignors seated around the palatial audience hall were surprised and shocked by this public outburst of papal displeasure.

With this, the lines were drawn. Pope Francis is not only organizing a radical reform of the Vatican's written constitution, and the way in which the central government of the church is administered, but has called for a profound change of heart among those who claim to be devoting their lives to the good management of the church. The process of appointing new key figures in the Vatican administration is necessarily slow, and the effectiveness of Pope Francis' revolution may depend upon the time available for its execution. He seems to want to avoid creating enemies inside the Curia, but at the same time realizes he has a rapidly diminishing window of active life ahead of him during which he will have the necessary energy to bring about the changes he desires.

The aim of this book is not spiritual improvement, nor to present a catalog of inspiring papal quotes, but to assess—to the extent that this is possible—the chances of success of this groundbreaking stewardship of Pope Francis at St. Peter's.

Cardinal Jorge Bergoglio's sudden elevation from his relatively obscure post as archbishop of Buenos Aires to the leadership of 1.3 billion Catholics worldwide aroused unusually high expectations. Here was the promise of a change of direction by a church faced with multiple problems in retaining believers in both the developed and the developing worlds. War and civil strife in the Middle East were threatening the very survival of the church in the lands where the Christian religion itself was born.

How far is it reasonable to assume that the election of Latin America's first-ever pope can be the harbinger of radical change in the whole church? In the following chapters, I shall catalog some of the complexities of the situations faced by Cardinal Bergoglio as he took over the command of the world's longest enduring international organization.

Several new biographers of Pope Francis have spoken of a "miracle" or a "revolution" in describing his initial attempts at reform inside the Vatican during the first years of his pontificate. Others have called him a "radical." I prefer a less dramatic approach in analyzing the "Francis effect."

Every year the Vatican publishes a statistical yearbook on the state of the church—the latest figures refer to past history, to the situation up until two years ago. So there is no official statistical report yet on the

"Francis effect." The latest edition, which gives details of the number of seminarians, priests, and faithful worldwide, shows continuing but very uneven growth.[5]

The Catholic population of the world increased by 57 percent to over 1.25 billion between 1980 and 2012 but the number of priests declined by 17 percent. The number of men studying for the priesthood dropped for the second year in succession in 2013 after a period of previous steady growth. But the number of priests ordained each year in both Africa and Asia—the continents of major growth—has more than doubled since the 1980s.

There is a huge difference between Catholic population growth in Europe (6 percent), the Americas (56 percent), Asia (115 percent), and Africa (238 percent), mainly attributable to diverging fertility rates.

The distribution of parishes is strikingly lopsided and has not kept up with the increase in world population. Europe still has more priests and parishes than most of the rest of the world combined. The replacement of an aging and mainly European priestly workforce, one of the biggest immediate problems facing Pope Francis, seems further away than ever.

I shall examine his prospects of success in reforming the way the Vatican handles its money, in cutting away the deadwood inside the clunky headquarters bureaucracy known as the Roman Curia, and in dealing with the accountability of diocesan bishops in the Americas and in Europe who have been covering up clerical sexual abuse for decades. I shall also examine his attitude toward women. Does he really promise a greater role for women in running what has until now been a totally male-centered church? I shall assess his success as an international leader committed to the cause of peace and reconciliation.

I shall look at Francis' promise of greater collegiality and outside consultation in governing the church—that is to say, in strengthening the role of the Vatican's Synod of Bishops, hitherto more of a debating society than a "parliament of the church." I shall try to understand why he continues to insist that his church is neither a democracy, whose policies should be set by majority decisions, nor comparable to an NGO (nongovernmental organization) or major international business corporation.

For Pope Francis, the church is not a moral border post or control point, but rather a place where he can help to bind the wounds of the marginalized poor. He sees the church as a "field hospital after battle," as he told his fellow Jesuit Father Spadaro in an extended interview in 2013.

"It is useless to ask a seriously injured person if he has high cholesterol and about the level of his blood sugars!" said the pope. "You have to heal his wounds. Then we can talk about everything else. Heal the wounds, heal the wounds . . . And you have to start from the ground up."

The pope's vivid language is unlike anything heard coming out of the Vatican during recent papacies. It may not please some Catholics, and it is certainly causing a degree of consternation among Vatican administrators accustomed to running things their way.

"The dogmatic and moral teachings of the church are not all equivalent," Pope Francis concluded. "We cannot be obsessed with the transmission of a disjointed multitude of doctrines to be imposed insistently. We have to find a new balance; otherwise even the moral edifice of the church is likely to fall like a house of cards."

The promise of a radically different future for the Catholic Church at the beginning of the second millennium is there, but can Francis deliver on his promises?

1

The Bishop of the Slums

The work of the priests in the Buenos Aires slums is not ideological, it's apostolic, and therefore part of the church of Rome. Anyone who thinks it's a different church doesn't understand how priests work in slums.

—POPE FRANCIS, RADIO INTERVIEW,
BAJO FLORES, ARGENTINA, MARCH 13, 2014

The first time I saw Pope Francis in person and heard his gentle but powerfully convincing slow tones in the Vatican's cavernous audience hall just days after his election, he made it crystal clear that he had no sympathy for the external trappings of a rich church. He had extensive firsthand experience of real poverty in his years of ministry in the teeming slums, the *villas miserias*, of his native city, Buenos Aires. He was the first pope ever elected from a megacity, a metropolis inhabited by more than ten million people.

"How I would like a church of the poor, for the poor," he told us.

As head of the Catholic Church in Argentina, he had never kept a set of custom-tailored cardinal's formal red robes handy at the Vatican for ceremonial occasions, like some of his fellow princes of the church. Nor had he ever fastened around his neck the "Cappa Magna," the long red silk ceremonial train still worn by some fashion-conscious senior clerics who enjoy parading in costly ecclesiastical finery. As pope, he has publicly deplored clerics who are "unctuous, sumptuous and presumptuous."[1]

In fact during one of his 2015 local parish visits as bishop of Rome, he was spotted wearing a white cassock with cuffs seriously frayed from hard use.

Italy's leading daily *La Repubblica* commented: "After the plastic watch and the iron cross, now it's the fraying tunic. In a photo taken during the visit of Pope Francis to Ostia, on the Roman coast, the Pope's vestment is visibly getting worn."

It was not the first time that his lack of interest in sartorial matters had been noticed. His scuffed black shoes and his black socks peeping out from under his white cassock attracted media attention immediately after his election. Former Pope Benedict used to favor expensive custom-made red slippers more in line with Vatican tradition.

The mass-circulation Italian Catholic weekly *Famiglia Cristiana* (Christian Family) wrote:

> *A small detail, certainly. But indicative of the pastoral style of Bergoglio. The black shoes he has worn since his election, the simple cross of metal, the ring of the fisherman in silver and a very simple watch on his wrist: a Swatch, a basic model, giving the date but with no other special function. It costs about 50 euros. It is said that when the watch broke, it was not easy to convince him to buy a new one. He wanted to change only the strap, and "gave in" to buying a new one only after he was assured that a new one, identical to the old one, would not cost more than changing the watch-band.*

He hailed from a country, Argentina, that by the second decade of the twenty-first century had turned into an economic basket case, unable to repay its international debt. It had been a dramatic shock for gaucho pride, after enjoying the status of being one of the wealthiest countries in the world during earlier economic booms, for Argentina to descend slowly toward international penury at the end of the twentieth century. In 2015, the country suffers under the burden of 40 percent annual inflation.

At home, the cardinal from Buenos Aires who liked to be called "Father Jorge" had already espoused poverty as a virtue, just like his namesake Francis of Assisi. After promotion to the leadership of the church in Argentina, he refused to move into the large suburban mansion occupied by his predecessor, and lived simply in two rooms in a property next to his cathedral church.

So Francis' first promise was to transform the popular image of the Vatican as a place that flaunted its wealth and its artistic riches to a place where the poor and even the homeless would not feel out of place. He refused to move into the ostentatious palace where all popes in living memory had resided, chose to take his meals in a cafeteria, slept in a guesthouse, and used a Ford Focus service car, not the Vatican's official papal limo, for his sorties into Rome.

Bumping into a bishop one day in the guesthouse lobby, he asked the prelate what he was waiting for. "My driver," the prelate replied.

"Shouldn't you be walking, like I do?" was the new pope's startling reply.

———

In 1964, the future Pope Francis, twenty-eight-year-old Father Jorge Mario Bergoglio, was still completing his studies to become a full member of the Jesuit order. He was doing a two-year teaching stint at one of the oldest and most prestigious high schools in all Argentina. Among his teenage students at the Immaculate Conception College in Santa Fe de la Vera Cruz, three hundred miles from Buenos Aires, was Jorge Milia, then age fifteen.

"We were rebel adolescents, full of hormones, and thirsty for nov-
elties," Milia recollected in a recent interview.[2] "We couldn't play any
instruments, since we had none—no drums, no electric guitars—but it
was the sixties, and we all wanted to be Beatles."

Seeking help, they turned to the priest who was teaching the boys
literature, psychology, and art history. "Within a short time he helped
us find electric guitars, a room to rehearse in, and an amplifier." Father
Bergoglio also located for the boys, who now called their Beatles-style
band The Shouters, an English-speaking student who could transcribe
the words of the Beatles' songs. "Father Jorge never refused a request for
help. If he saw that people became involved, he continued to support
them."

During those same two years of high-school teaching, Father Bergoglio introduced his pupils in literature to the works of the already
famous Argentinian short-story writer and novelist Jorge Luis Borges.
Through a family connection—his own former piano teacher who
became personal secretary to Borges—Father Bergoglio contacted
Argentina's most famous literary celebrity and invited him to visit the
school. Borges came and stayed five days. To encourage the students'
appreciation of the novelist's work, Bergoglio had his students emulate
Borges by writing their own short stories. The best were sent to Borges,
who wrote an introduction to a book that was later published—and
became a local best-seller.

On yet another occasion, Bergoglio arranged a showing in the
school cinema of the Ingmar Bergman movie *The Seventh Seal*. His
point was to illustrate literary connections with the dance of death, a
common theme in Spanish literature. Theater as well as cinema was
important; for a high-school performance in 1964, a historical play was
staged about battles between Spanish and indigenous tribes, set in what
is today's Uruguay. In such all-male church schools the female roles
were usually played by boys dressed as girls. Bergoglio, producer of the

play, complained that this damaged the image of women and encouraged the mothers and sisters of some of the actors to take the female parts.[3] They did; in its way, this was revolutionary.

From the beginning, as these incidents suggest, Bergoglio showed a particular sense of creativity—a capacity to think outside the box.

Asking myself where this began, and where he had begun, I traveled to Argentina in the summer of 2014, where I was startled to see a sign in a travel agency offering a three-hour bus tour called "The World of Pope Francis." All the better that the tour was free, subsidized by the city of Buenos Aires. For it, our guide, Daniel Vega, wore a smart black blazer. Before we left he helped the driver attach to the side of the bus a large banner proclaiming CIRCUITO PAPAL.

Our tour began outside the Church of St. Joseph of Flores, a twenty-minute subway ride from the city center. This was the parish church in which the young Bergoglio and his family used to attend Sunday mass, and where, at age seventeen, he had a mystical experience during confession—"a moment of truth," he later recounted—that made him decide to become a priest. The church interior was dilapidated, and restoration work under way on the cupola intimated a risk of collapse.

This was the church opposite a small park in Flores, at the time a relatively modest suburb or barrio, where the Bergoglio family made their home: his father, Mario; his mother, Regina; his two brothers, Alberto and Oscar; and his sisters, Marta and Maria Elena. Born December 17, 1936, Jorge was the eldest sibling. His grandparents, who had six children, had sold the coffee shop they owned in Turin and migrated to Argentina in 1929.

Argentina had been a Spanish colony since the 1580s and gained independence from Spain at the end of the Napoleonic wars in 1816. Italian émigrés had already been arriving in Argentina in increasing numbers since the second half of the seventeenth century. Today it is estimated that of its population of twenty million, 50 percent to 60 percent have some Italian ancestry. The Bergoglios and their only child, a son, Mario, who had been working for the Banca d'Italia in Turin, made the five-week Atlantic crossing on board the liner *Giulio Cesare*, arriving in January 1928.

At that time Argentina boasted the world's eighth largest economy, but with the onset of the Great Depression, the country was about to plunge into a severe economic crisis. The newcomers were able to join relatives in Parana, a river port upstream along the River Plate, who had arrived seven years earlier and had set up a company that sold road building materials; the relatives had built a four-story building that they called Palazzo Bergoglio, which had the only elevator in town.

Five years later, Mario Bergoglio, trained in Italy as an accountant, married Regina Maria Sivori, a young Argentinian woman also of Piedmontese origin. The family had by then moved to Buenos Aires, where the two had met in a church. Jorge, their first child, spent considerable time at the home of his grandmother Rosa, now living nearby. Jorge was particularly close to his grandmother, whom he has mentioned many times since his election to the papacy as his guide and source of religious inspiration; together they used to recite the rosary, and to this day Pope Francis keeps a letter from his grandmother in his breviary.

During a meeting at the Vatican with leaders of the now-worldwide Protestant Salvation Army, Pope Francis, speaking in Italian, recalled an incident from his childhood that set him on his lifelong quest to encourage reunification with the Christian churches that separated from Rome—first the Orthodox church at the time of the Great Schism in the eleventh century, and then again the Protestants during the sixteenth-century Reformation.

"It was 1940—I suppose none of you were even born then," he told the sixty-year-old Salvation Army general André Cox with a smile. "At that time the general idea was that all Protestants went straight to hell!

"I remember as clearly as if it happened yesterday. There were two

Salvation Army women with that special bonnet that they wear walking on the other side of the road and I asked my grandmother: 'Who are they? Are they nuns?' 'No,' she said, 'they are Protestants! But they are good Protestants!' So I received my very first lesson in ecumenism from your people."

"Thank you very much," he added emphatically, in his halting English.

Because the grandparents continued to speak with each other in Italian, albeit in the Piedmontese dialect, Jorge became bilingual in Italian as well as Spanish. (He can, in addition, get by in Latin, German, French, Portuguese, and English, though he is uncomfortable when speaking anything but Spanish and Italian.)

The first stop made by our tour bus was in front of the childhood home of Jorge Bergoglio. This was at 531 Calle Membrillar, a modest two-story dwelling just seven blocks from the parish church at Flores, in what was in his time a lower-middle-class suburb of Buenos Aires. Its two- and three-bedroom row houses were mostly of brick, and many, including the Bergoglio home, had small gardens or patios. Reflecting the Spanish style, theirs and many of their neighbors' sported ironwork balconies. After the deaths of Jorge's parents, the family home was rebuilt in the 1970s, but its leafy street must always have had dignity and charm.

Money was short; Mario Bergoglio worked as a bookkeeper in a factory that made hosiery, and, to make ends meet, he took on extra jobs. They had no luxuries, no vacations, no car, but there were records of grand opera playing in the background to the traditional Italian game of *briscola*. After the birth of her last child, his mother suffered from a form of paralysis, and, as the elder son, Jorge stepped in, learning to cook.

So one can imagine the scene in the Bergoglio home, with teenager Jorge hovering over a frying pan. Typically, Bergoglio insisted on installing a hot plate in his modest three-room suite in his Santa Marta residence in Rome. While in seminary he would cook for his fellow future priests on the Sundays when the official paid cook had a day off.

Our next stop was nearby: the playground where young Jorge kicked soccer balls with his friends after school. "He was never without a ball at his feet," one of his teachers recalled. It was a close-knit family, and his father took Jorge to see matches in which the local San Lorenzo soccer team played.

The bus made a zigzag course through the sprawling city, stopping briefly at the places where the future pope had studied: his elementary school; the technical high school where he had studied chemistry; and the Immaculada Concepción Seminary where, after working in a chemistry lab on foods for a time, he began his studies for the priesthood at age twenty-one. He had told his mother that he planned to study medicine. But when she found in his room no medical textbooks, only numerous volumes of theology including many in Latin, she expressed surprise.

After he acknowledged that he intended to pursue seminary studies full time, his mother was initially distressed (so say his early biographers).

"I thought you were studying medicine," she reportedly said.

"I did not lie to you. I am studying medicine, but medicine of the soul," he replied—so goes the legend, at any rate.

The bus passed through the broad streets of downtown Buenos Aires, where on Saturday afternoons couples gather to dance the tango right in the middle of the street. Here our guide informed us proudly that Jorge, in his late teens, used to dance the tango or the somewhat less slinky milonga *con mucho gusto*.

The image of a tango-dancing future pontiff captured the imagination of believers and nonbelievers alike. On December 17, 2014, hundreds of tango dancers gathered in streets around the Vatican to celebrate, with music and movement, the pontiff's seventy-eighth birthday.

"I liked the tango very much as a young man," said the pope in an interview in 2010.[4] "My favorite singers were Carlos Gardel and Ada Falcon. She later became a nun."

It was not all fun and tangos. In 1957, when he was twenty-one, Jorge fell ill with pleurisy. The illness lasted at least three months, and surgeons had to remove a portion of his upper right lung. On her own initiative, a nursing sister tripled his doctors' prescription of antibiotics. He has credited her boldness with helping him to survive what risked being a fatal illness. Now in his late seventies, he admits that he still feels the effects of this early and permanent impairment of his health.

From the venue of street dancing the bus now took us to the Jesuit seminary, the imposing but rather stark neoclassical Villa Devoto. Jorge entered here in 1958 for training as a future priest. He decided not to become a diocesan priest based in a parish, but to join the elite Society of Jesus, the Jesuits. In 2013, Pope Francis, reflecting upon his experience in that seminary, described the environment of his training as "closed and rigid thought, more instructive-ascetic than mystical." His teachers left little space for innovation, he said.

On the other hand, the Jesuits attracted him; he knew that in undertaking the rigorous, fourteen-year training and series of vows demanded to join the order, he would be living in a deeply committed Catholic community. The order was founded nearly five hundred years ago by St. Ignatius of Loyola, a town in the Basque country of northern Spain, and is among the most prestigious within the Catholic Church. An aristocrat and soldier, Ignatius turned to the life of the spirit after suffering a wound in battle, and in the 1530s wrote a classic book of meditations, prayers, and contemplative practices called *The Spiritual Exercises*. That book remains extraordinarily influential for many Catholics today, and for Jorge Bergoglio, its spiritual insights became a handbook for life. The impact of St. Ignatius is reflected in Pope Francis' keynote teaching document, *Evangelii Gaudium* (*The Joy of the Gospel*), which he wrote in 2013.

As an order, the Jesuits were formally recognized by Pope Paul III—that same pope who would be a protector and benefactor of Michelangelo—in 1540. From the outset they were missionaries, with about a thousand Jesuits already working in Europe, Asia, Africa, and the New World by 1556, when Ignatius died. In 1632, Jesuit missionary Paul Le Jeune sent his first report of missionary work in the New World back to his superiors in France. From Paraguay the order spread into Brazil, Bolivia, and Argentina, in order to convert to Christianity native American peoples within Spain's empire.

The Jesuits first set foot on the River Plate in Argentina over four centuries ago, in 1585. There, as the 1986 British film *The Mission* showed dramatically, they found the seminomadic indigenous people, the Guarani, in pitiful conditions, exploited by the Spanish colonists. The Jesuits organized the Guarani into stable communities called *reducciones* (reductions) and eventually created fifteen missions in Argentina.

They were teachers, but also learners. When the Jesuits found local customs in contradiction with Christian teachings, they tried to understand why. For instance, they were troubled that the Guarani killed their sickliest children upon birth, but learned that it was because, as a nomadic tribe, they could not tend to them.

Given their missionary work, the Jesuits also became skilled teachers and even businessmen. They were the guardians of the colonies' know-how: "Astronomers, botanists, pharmacists, printers, zoologists, cartographers, and architects, as well as theologians and jurists, they were admired not just for their knowledge and accomplishments, but also for their discipline and personal austerity," according to Austin Ivereigh, an historian of church-state relations in Argentina.[5] They learned to run successful ranches and plantations, akin to the medieval European monasteries; the accumulated wealth from these paid for construction of Jesuit colleges in all Argentina's major cities, including Buenos Aires.

Although the Jesuits protected the indigenous people in Spanish South America from slavery, the advent of Portuguese colonization in Argentina resulted in what came to be known as the Guarani wars, fought against the Guarani, who were defeated by the Portuguese in 1756.

Back in Europe, the monarchs of Spain, Portugal, and France had become deeply suspicious of Jesuit teachings and power; to them, the Jesuits appeared subversive because of their support for the rights of ordinary people rather than the divine right of kings. A decade later all the Jesuits were expelled from the Americas as well as from Europe, in what is known as the "Suppression," which took place everywhere on the same day, April 2, 1767. Ordered by Pope Clement XIV, the Suppression lasted until the end of the Napoleonic era, when the Jesuits were able to return to their missions and schools, including in the Americas.

They had already returned to Argentina in 1814, just after the country achieved independence from Spain. But when the new dictator, Juan Manuel de Rosas, demanded that they preach against his political enemies and place his picture upon their altars, the Jesuits were again expelled from Argentina. They returned only after de Rosas was ousted in February 1852 and fled into exile in England, where Queen Victoria welcomed him at Plymouth with a twenty-one-gun salute.

During the second half of that century the Jesuits once again became one of Argentina's largest and most influential religious orders. Still, by comparison with their first generation of Jesuits, rather than frontiersmen, they acted defensively in their dealings with the secular powers.

Given their centuries of far-flung missions, their knowledge of languages, and grasp of the subtleties of other cultures, the Jesuits came to be considered overly cosmopolitan, highly politicized, and interfering. Their leader was often called the "General," reflecting the order's military origins, but sometimes also the "Black Pope," not always a compliment. Even today some despise the Jesuits, and the Internet harbors various hate sites, like the one offering "Free Anti-Jesuit Papacy PDF Books," with such titles as *Engineer Corps of Hell* and *The Jesuit Conspiracy*. Another site discusses "Jesuits Devil Worship" (the grammar is theirs).

———

In 1969, Bergoglio, on the eve of his thirty-third birthday, was ordained a priest by the retired bishop from Córdoba in the chapel of the Colégio Máximo. Just four years later, he took his final vows against a background of civil war on the streets of Buenos Aires. In a promotion that came with exceptional rapidity, only three months after those final vows he was made provincial superior, or head of all the Jesuits in Argentina. He succeeded Father Riccardo O'Farrell, a sociologist who had supported all the changes introduced by Vatican II. O'Farrell had gone further, to embrace liberation theology, a Catholic movement in several Latin American countries that sought to redress unjust economic, political, and social conditions in underdeveloped regions. It was to be the "preferential option for the poor," in the words of Peruvian theologian Gustavo Gutierrez.[6] Their goal was to create Christian-based communities run by socially committed Catholics.

Back in Rome, Pope John Paul II and his bureaucrats were deeply suspicious of the movement. In their eyes it was basically Marxist and supported class struggle. This was the height of the Cold War, and in the Vatican there was fear that that the more extreme liberation theologians were in effect justifying armed struggle between rich and poor. In Rome, liberation theology became identified with the political expansionism of Soviet Communism and of Fidel Castro's Cuba.

O'Farrell's years in charge of the Jesuits in Argentina coincided with a dramatic decline there of religious vocations. Between 1961 and 1973, the year of Bergoglio's promotion, new vocations had slipped from twenty-five to just two; every year during that same period between ten and fifteen seminarians deserted. O'Farrell's six-year term in office was abruptly cut short after just four years.

Taking his place, the thirty-six-year-old Bergoglio, until that time a professor, banned such elements of Vatican II as guitar-strummed songs played at mass, returning the Jesuit churches to traditional hymns and Gregorian chants. O'Farrell had allowed the Jesuit students and priests to wear nonclerical clothing. Bergoglio insisted upon clerical collars and cassocks. He also steered the order's seminary students away from some studies that O'Farrell had encouraged, such as politics, sociology, anthropology, and engineering.

At the same time, Bergoglio encouraged his students to seek contacts with the poor. On weekends, students were urged to visit parishes in the big city slums, while discouraged from contact with potentially political organizations: trade unions, cooperatives, and even Catholic NGOs. According to Father Rafael Velasco, a former student of Bergoglio, now rector of the Catholic University of Cordoba, the Bergoglio of those years was "very pastoral, but also a bit patronizing—more interested in relieving the effects of injustice or poverty than in empowering the poor."

Others have described the Bergoglio of the 1970s as deeply conservative and authoritarian; some also criticize him as inexperienced.

In 1976, a military junta seized power in Buenos Aires. Immediately it began a crackdown on anyone perceived to be a political opponent. Tens of thousands of people disappeared in a systematic campaign of kidnappings, torture, and murder.

That very year, Bishop Enrique Angelelli of La Rioja in northeastern Argentina died in a faked automobile accident. The son of Italian immigrants like Bergoglio, the bishop was a strong supporter of agrarian reform, which meant tackling the ownership of giant plantations. When he tried to protect farmworkers, local landowners had marched straight into the church where he was preaching and had thrown stones at him. (Thanks to documents found in Vatican archives on the instructions of Pope Francis, his murderers, who were in the military, were finally brought to justice exactly forty years later; knowing he was on the death list, one month before his murder Angelilli had written of his fears to Papal Nuncio Pio Laghi, who had forwarded his letter to the Vatican, where it was archived and forgotten until it was brought to light again in 2014.)

Theirs was the era of the *desaparacidos* (the disappeared), among them hundreds of nuns, lay Catholic teachers, and 150 priests. Some therefore make the case that Bergoglio's view—that priests should not be involved in politics—was the better part of wisdom, for in this way some lives may have been saved; these were divisive times, and there was no easy way to exercise spiritual leadership during what amounted to civil war.

Following his six-year term as provincial superior, in 1979, Bergoglio became rector of the Colégio Máximo, the most important Jesuit university conferring degrees in philosophy and theology in all Latin America. This was the year after Karol Wojtyla had been elected pope as John Paul II, the first non-Italian pontiff in 450 years. John Paul interpreted political strife in Latin America through strictly Polish spectacles. Having lived through Nazi and then Communist-led dictatorships in Poland, he found Latin American politics and Peronism hard to fathom. Not surprisingly, therefore, Bergoglio found himself facing a cruel, right-wing military dictatorship at home and, in the Vatican, hostility toward anything smacking of Marxism, which in Argentinian terms meant pressure on the part of radical priests to commit the church as a spearhead for social and economic reform.

Shortly after the military junta seized power, two Jesuit priests who had been working in the slums were kidnapped and tortured by the regime. Bergoglio had ordered them to stop their work, but they had refused, and he came under harsh criticism from some in the Jesuit order for having failed to protect them. A further complication was the 1982 Falklands War, which pitted Argentina against Britain.

By 1986, Bergoglio had been walking that tightrope for a decade, and he found himself in trouble with his superiors in Rome. For them, his fifteen years of leadership of the Argentinian Jesuits had become divisive. As a benign form of punishment they relieved him of his post and dispatched him into temporary exile in Germany, where he was to carry out "research" for a doctorate.

And this is why our next bus stop was at San Jose del Telar, a small modern church in a somewhat upmarket suburb called Agronomeia. We were there to see, in the church, a reproduction of an eighteenth-century baroque painting of the Virgin Mary, whose original Jorge Bergoglio had admired while in Germany. The painting in the Church of St. Peter Am Perlach in Augsburg shows Mary, flanked by two angels, untying a long and tangled ribbon; underfoot she crushes the head of a serpent, representing the devil. Behind the painting, whose formal title is *Mary, Undoer of Knots*, was the true story of a Bavarian aristocrat. Seeking advice for his failing marriage, he was told by a Jesuit priest to bring him the long white ribbon that Bavarian brides traditionally carry to their wedding. Supposedly it represents Eve's knot of disobedience in the Garden of Eden; as a symbol, Mary's unraveling of the knot refers to her power to resolve all of life's tangles.

The painting left a deep emotional mark upon Bergoglio, a stranger in a distant land, and when he returned temporarily from Augsburg to Buenos Aires six months later, he brought with him a postcard of the painting. (His poor relations with his fellow Jesuits meant that for two years, 1990–92, he would be sent to cool off in Cordoba, a city 250 miles from Buenos Aires.)

Times changed, and by 1992 the military dictatorship and "dirty war" had ended. That year Bergoglio was ordained auxiliary bishop of Buenos Aires, and, at the ceremony, he distributed prayer cards showing the painting of *Mary, Undoer of Knots*. To honor their new bishop, the San Jose church parishioners then raised money to commission an Argentinian artist to make a full-sized copy of the painting.

Thanks to its association with Bergoglio, the little church became a popular shrine to Mary, drawing pilgrims from all Argentina and even from abroad; on the Feast of the Immaculate Conception, tens of thousands now converge there every December.

The events of these years gave Father Jorge, as he preferred to be called despite his important new role, a different focus. He became actively involved with the poor and the marginalized, to the point that he was becoming known as the Bishop of the Slums. By 1998, he had quadrupled the number of priests working in the *villas miserias* (shantytowns), in which some three million inhabitants of the Argentinian capital lived.

As our guide also reminded us, after he was promoted to archbishop and primate of Argentina in February 1998, Father Jorge shunned his predecessor's palatial residence in an exclusive neighborhood fourteen miles away. He moved into a very modest apartment next door to the cathedral; of its four rooms he could use three, one being a chapel. In the same way, he decided after his election as pope not to live in the huge papal apartment on top of the Vatican's Apostolic Palace.

Exactly as he would when he became pope in 2013, he adopted a lifestyle and system of church government that represented a sea change by comparison with that of his predecessor. His frugality became legendary: he cooked his own meals, and, to visit city parishes, used the bus and subway. He had so few personal belongings that when a friend gave him a present of classical CDs, he asked him to record them on cassettes because he had no CD player. When he was made a cardinal in 2001, he chose not to order new robes, but had the hand-me-downs of his late predecessor altered to fit him. He told fellow clerics planning to fly to Rome to see him receive his red hat that they should instead save the price of the ticket and distribute the money to the poor.

This was a difficult time for Argentina. Bergoglio's promotion to cardinal happened to coincide with the country's virtual bankruptcy. Between 1998 and 2002, Argentina suffered from a severe economic depression that reportedly reflected financial crises in both Brazil and Russia. In four years the economy shrank by one-fifth, and the government defaulted on its foreign debt. Poverty soared; demonstrators in the Plaza de Mayo died in clashes with the police.

At last our bus headed to its final destination: the neoclassical Metropolitan Cathedral in the now-notorious Plaza de Mayo in the heart of the business district. Just across the square is the Casa Rosada, the palatial pink mansion that serves as the official residence of the Argentinian president. In his cathedral the new cardinal called upon priests and laypeople to work together; care of the poor and the sick would be a priority.

It was winter and 4:30 P.M. Already the sky had turned dark. The official tour was over. Now my own would begin.

It began with a walk through the gardens of the vast Plaza de Mayo. Groups of aging army veterans from the Falklands War were standing outside a camp they had erected. Banners lit by candles were looped between lampposts, and bore protests that these veterans had been abandoned by the Argentinian state and left destitute after having fought for their country against the British.

On the façade of the cathedral was the new pope's coat of arms and the crossed keys of St. Peter in stucco. In the foyer stood a large portrait of a beaming Pope Francis (he is the first pope in history to choose that name) and the text of Saint Francis' famous prayer:

> *Lord, make me an instrument of your peace. Where there is hatred, let me sow love; where there is injury, pardon; where there is doubt, faith; where there is despair, hope; where there is darkness, light; where there is sadness, joy.*

Inside the dim cathedral a few dozen worshippers, mostly women, were praying.

I recalled that during the years when Bergoglio was archbishop, for an annual ceremony marking Argentina's national day, he received here a delegation representing the highest authorities of the state, but with important exceptions: for years he had been boycotted by the country's populist president Cristina Kirchner, who resented his political influence. Far worse, her entourage alleged that he had been an accomplice of the military dictatorship, and even tried to lobby among Argentinian bishops against his election to the papacy.

But after his election, when the polls showed that two-thirds of Argentinians admired him (today, 95 percent), in a surprising about-face, Kirchner called upon him four times altogether in Rome, where on one occasion the two had lunch together in his home in the Casa Santa Marta. On her return, posters popped up on walls declaring WE SHARE HOPES, with her photo next to the pope as she offered him a set of porcelain cups for drinking the traditional Argentinian herbal tea, "mate."

The next morning I went where the bus tour had not—to one of the most notorious of the multiple slums of Buenos Aires. This one near the port was called Villa 31, but changed its name, as we shall see. It was and is considered a dangerous area for outsiders to visit, but I had an introduction to Father Eduardo Drabble, a worker priest who had been ordained by Father Bergoglio.

Villa 31 was a far cry from downtown Buenos Aires. The city had been one of the world's major capitals at the end of the nineteenth century, when Argentina was the world's fourth wealthiest country—a booming frontier land, attractive to immigrants. The papal bus tour had taken us down spacious boulevards and through European-style middle-class neighborhoods that still reflect that prosperity. The turn-of-the-twentieth-century Colón opera house, built in lavish art deco style, is one of the world's largest, and still hosts top international performers.

In Villa 31, the poverty-stricken, drug-infested slum I was now entering, Father Eduardo was carrying on the work begun under the then Father Jorge. By telephone he had warned me not to take a taxi: "It is too dangerous unless someone from here accompanies you. Phone me and I'll pick you up." As I later learned, neither taxis nor police cars would enter Villa 31.

We were to meet in front of an auto dealership, which boasted a row of gleaming secondhand Porsches and Mercedes-Benzes in its window. Within minutes of Father Drabble's arrival in his beat-up red pickup truck we entered a warren of boxlike shanties and ramshackle two-story buildings, and then quickly arrived at his tiny Christ the Worker church, built of cement block and brick. On its outside wall was a touching memorial plaque dedicated to the memory of Father Carlos Mugica, murdered by a right-wing paramilitary death squad after saying mass in his slumland church of San Francisco Solano in 1974.

Father Mugica is today celebrated as a martyr of the church in Argentina. His story is akin to that of Archbishop Óscar Romero of San Salvador, who was similarly gunned down in 1980 by a murder squad while saying mass. Just the day before, from the pulpit he had urged the Salvadoran military, as Christians, to stop their violations of basic human rights. Romero had been outspoken against poverty, injustice, and the torture inflicted by his country's military regime, and his funeral attracted an astonishing quarter of a million mourners. His statue already stands in Westminster Abbey in London. He is venerated as "Saint Romero" in El Salvador, but efforts to put him on the road to official sainthood had been sidetracked by Pope John Paul II because his name had been linked to liberation theology, feared in Rome to be inspired mainly by Marxist ideology. Romero was finally beatified— putting him one step away from full sainthood—at a ceremony in San Salvador in May 2015. He was formally declared a martyr for the Catholic faith, and his canonization can be expected to follow shortly.

———

Father Mugica was born into a wealthy Buenos Aires family and grew up in spacious surroundings with plenty of servants. He played tennis, soccer, and rugby, and at age twenty, during a visit to Rome in 1950, discovered his vocation to be a priest. Returning to Argentina, he became one of the first politically active Argentinian priests, and was deeply committed to fighting for the rights of the poor. He lived in fear of being banned by the hierarchies of the church of his time because of his political activities. "Nothing and no one will stop me from serving Jesus Christ and his church, fighting together for the poor and their liberation," he once wrote. This quote became the motto for the 2014 celebrations of the fortieth anniversary of his death.

Father Eduardo Drabble is cut of similar cloth. He too was from a privileged family; his great-grandfather was English and, from Scotland, brought shorthorn cattle to Argentina. After studying for a law degree, Eduardo worked as an attorney in Buenos Aires for three years, but then abandoned the law to become a priest, ordained in 2009 by Cardinal Jorge Bergoglio himself.

Seated in his tiny office, we observed the ritual often shared with Father Jorge: to sip through a straw the rather bitter lukewarm brew, maté. Drabble is a handsome, bearded man of thirty-six, and as he spoke his face lit up.

"I'd thought the law was a way to help people, but you can help them more by being a priest," he said. "To me, Jorge Bergoglio's finest intuition was to realize that we don't change people; people change us. We grasp that our system is unjust, and as priests we have an authoritative voice. With the strength of our organization we can and do support the people."

He explained to me how Villa 31 is physically detached from the city of Buenos Aires. On the divided highway between the international airport and the high-rises of the downtown, I had already noticed huge screens erected to try to conceal or camouflage the existence of some of the worst slums along the route. Similarly, the road to Villa 31 was a broad superhighway soaring above the barrio, making access to it difficult, and indeed invisible to those traveling overhead in the fast lane. In this way few foreign visitors to Buenos Aires come face to face immediately with the reality of the *villas miserias*.

Home to fifty thousand people, Villa 31 has open sewers and potholed mud roads. It has no hospital, not a single public school, apart from the one small religious school maintained by Drabble's church. "We are in a desperate environment, where no one else wants to be. For us, this is heaven: being in the *villas miserias* is a blessing. You don't learn it at Harvard or Cambridge. The streets teach you the Gospel," Father Drabble enthused.

Forty percent of those living in Villa 31 are under sixteen years of age, he went on to explain. "The government distributes free condoms, but this seems to have no effect, and we often see young women alone with three or four children."

Drugs are its cancer. I saw children, some of whom looked no more than ten, squatted by the roadside with the blank eyes of drug addicts. "You can buy a dose of *paco* [cocaine residue] for only $1," said Father Drabble.

Some months after my own visit, Cardinal Mario Poli, who succeeded Bergoglio as archbishop of Buenos Aires, visited the barrio to launch yet another appeal for action by both the church and society to deal with the problem of drugs. "Addictions are a challenge," said the cardinal in December 2014. "In this misery, which all Argentinians share, we need a serious drugs policy and a strong approach to health care."

Father Pepe Di Paola, a famous shantytown priest in Buenos Aires and close friend of Pope Francis, was more forceful: "The social fabric here is unraveling. We can set up thousands of centers run by the best professionals, but it is all pointless if the rest of society fails to join us in trying to resolve these problems. The rest of society—meaning the police, the government, the wealthy landowners, the industrialists."

Just one week after his election, Jorge Bergoglio telephoned Father Eduardo Drabble from the Vatican to ask for news of the barrio. Half a world away, Pope Francis never forgets the world he left behind to govern his whole church.

———

In Rome, the Polish Pope John Paul II died after a lingering illness in April 2005, and a conclave was summoned to elect his successor. The German Cardinal Joseph Ratzinger was elected with the necessary two-thirds majority of votes.

But there was a surprising footnote. Argentinian Cardinal Jorge Bergoglio, as it was later learned, had been the runner-up in the election. Despite the fact that Bergoglio's opponents at home launched a campaign to halt his candidacy, he is reported to have received forty votes in the final balloting, although he was relatively little known to those outside Latin America.

In 2007, he traveled to Aparecida in Brazil to participate in the fifth Latin American Episcopal Conference (CELAM). The bishops gathered there elected him to chair the committee that would draft the final document of the meeting, which was particularly important because Catholicism in Latin America was changing drastically. Despite such valiant efforts as those of Father Drabble and Father Di Paola, Argentinian Catholicism is seriously challenged. Latin America is home to 40 percent of the world's Catholic population, and from 1900 through the 1960s, at least 90 percent of Latin Americans were Catholic.

But countless Latinos have either turned their backs on religion altogether or converted to evangelical Protestantism for such reasons as "enjoyment of the style of worship" (69 percent of converts), "greater emphasis on morality" (60 percent), and "found a church that helps members more" (58 percent). During the twentieth century, the 90 percent of Latin Americans who used to belong to the Catholic Church at the beginning of the century shrank to under 70 percent, according to a November 2014 Pew Research survey.

The conference at Aparecida therefore had particular importance for the future of the church, and it was a tribute to Bergoglio that he was chosen to draft its final report, in which social outreach played a key part. From that document's chapter 8:

> *We pledge to work harder, so our Latin American and Caribbean Church may continue to accompany our poorest brothers on their journey, even to martyrdom. Today, we want to confirm and promote the option of preferential love for the poor which was expressed in previous conferences. . . . The Latin American Church is called to be a sacrament of love, solidarity and justice in our countries."*

For the *Economist*, this document amounts to a "refined version of liberation theology."[7]

"Preferential love for the poor": these were the words of the man who became pope in March 2013. His intimate knowledge of the lives of the poor, and his commitment to all those he had known and cared for personally, came as a surprise to many veteran Vatican watchers, more accustomed to the remote pomp and circumstance of church ritual than to the friendly and frugal lifestyle of Jorge Bergoglio.

This lifestyle was illustrated by the arrival of Father Pepe Pinto, who suddenly appeared in the Casa Santa Marta one Saturday afternoon shortly after Bergoglio became pope bearing a large suitcase filled with gifts donated by the people of the *villas miserias*. In it too were personal objects to be blessed by the pope: rosaries, statuettes, photographs.

He cried for his Argentina. In April 2013, when he had been pope for barely a month, he sent a letter to the Association of the Mothers of

Plaza de Mayo to say that he shared their sorrow and their fight for justice for "the tragic loss of their loved ones at this moment in Argentina's
history." The association had been created in 1977 to denounce the
disappearance of tens of thousands of Argentinians during the military
dictatorship. The military forcibly but secretly gave out for adoption the
infant children of murdered parents. For decades Bergoglio had been
accustomed to seeing them demonstrate every Thursday in front of the
Casa Rosada, near the cathedral.

And when Estela de Carlotto, the president of the Association of
the Grandmothers of the Plaza de Mayo, called upon him in Rome in
November 2014, she was received, together with her grandson, Ignacio,
whom she had only recently met for the first time. His mother, Laura
Carlotto, had been killed shortly after his birth in 1978, and Ignacio's
identity had just been confirmed by DNA testing.

As all this shows, Pope Francis had long since changed from the
young conservative he had been in his early years in the church. When
he was catapulted into a leadership role with the Jesuits at age thirty-six,
just when his country was plunged into a military dictatorship, he was
not yet prepared to walk such a difficult path. During that era he had
censored books of liberation theology. He had long since admitted that
this was an error—and not only; now, as pope, he began corresponding
with the Franciscan theologian from Brazil, Leonardo Boff.

For a pope, this was a radical change, and not only in style. In 1985,
the then-Cardinal Ratzinger, later Benedict XVI, initially silenced Boff
for one year for having published his seminal work, *Church, Charism and
Power: Liberation Theology and the Institutional Church*.[8] After Ratzinger
accused him of "religious terrorism," Boff was deeply insulted. He left
the Franciscan order in 1992 but continued as an academic, teaching
theology, ethics, and philosophy at the University of Rio de Janeiro, and
as a visiting lecturer all over the world, including in Italy.

In a recent interview with the German Deutsche Welle, Boff said,

"I think this pope will create a new dynasty of popes from the Third World. Only 24 percent of the world's Christians live in Europe, while 62 percent live in Latin America, and the rest, in Asia and Africa. Today Christianity is a religion of the Third World, which originated in the First World." Boff believes that these churches bring new life into Christianity, and that the Third World church has its own heroes, martyrs, and prophets, including "the people's saint, Óscar Romero."

In that same interview, the formerly discredited Latin American theologian heaped praise upon Pope Francis for his readiness to discuss hitherto taboo subjects. "When he heard that a priest in Rome would not baptize an illegitimate child, he said, 'There are no illegitimate daughters or sons—there are only children.'" For Boff, "Francis has already started to reform the papacy."

Not only are Boff's teachings no longer censored, but Pope Francis asked Boff for suggestions while drafting his new encyclical on the protection of the environment.

As pope, Francis is a reflection of his Latin American origins and experiences. He appears unlikely to renounce this heritage in his papacy or in his private life. John Paul II was quick to celebrate his election by a triumphal return to Poland and indeed made multiple return visits there. By contrast, Pope Francis has shown remarkable restraint. He could easily have carried out a side visit to his homeland when he attended World Youth Day in Brazil, just three months after his election, but chose not to do so. Although he visited three other Latin American countries during 2015, his first trip back home to Argentina is not scheduled until 2018.

However, he remains strongly attached to his origins. Although he has four times received Argentine President Cristina Kirchner and hosted a private luncheon for her, he indicates that he prefers not to welcome politicians. He receives many other visitors from Argentina, particularly close personal friends such as Rabbi Abraham Skorka, rector of the Latin-American Rabbinical Seminary in Buenos Aires, and Omar Abboud, the soft-spoken former head of the Islamic Center, now director general of the Institute for Interreligious Dialogue in Buenos Aires. Both these old friends from Argentina were invited to accompany Pope Francis on his visit to the Holy Land in May 2014.

Earlier that year Pope Francis had aroused curiosity when news was leaked that he had telephoned the Argentine consulate in Rome to ask for renewal of both his passport and his identity card. Within days the consul general hand-delivered the new documents to the pope at the Vatican. Simultaneously, the pope felt it necessary to let it be known that he had no intention of an immediate return to Argentina.

On the other hand, do these documents suggest that the pope has an exit strategy? Possibly. In Buenos Aires, Father Eduardo Drabble had confided to me, "When the pope realizes he can do no more, when he realizes that his mission is finished, I believe he will retire. He may well return here to live in a home for retired priests."

I was reminded that, before his election, Jorge Bergoglio had already reserved a place in a retirement home for clergymen at Flores, his birthplace.

———

Meanwhile Argentina continues to come to the pope. In November 2014, Argentine artist Alejandro Marmo brought to Rome two giant statues made of scrap iron—one a crucifix called *Cristo Operaio* (Christ the Worker)—which were placed in the garden of the papal villa at Castel Gandolfo, where they were blessed by the pope. "The sculptures are a sign of the creativity of which we are capable, even using abandoned raw materials," said the pope during the blessing ceremony. "They symbolize the genius that God has wished to place in the mind of an artist."

The statues reflect the "culture of waste," the artist explained, because they are made of such recycled materials as iron chains and gates abandoned to rust decades ago. The sculptures were constructed by a group of young Argentinians with drug problems, "those excluded from society," said Marmo in an interview with the Italian press agency ANSA. For him, the use of recycled materials in art serves as a metaphor for social recovery.

There is a special reason behind Marmo's gift and the pontiff's words. In Argentina, Pope Francis had been profoundly shocked when, during the severe economic crisis in Argentina after 2001, he saw men and young boys in rags poking through the garbage dumps of Buenos Aires looking for recyclable materials and also collecting cardboard to sell. Bergoglio is an activist, and he helped the more than three thousand ragpickers, called *cartoneros*, form an association. He also became their chaplain, supporting them, marrying them, and baptizing their children. He regularly deplores what he, like the artist Marmo, calls "the throwaway culture."

Visitors from Argentina have also brought lighter moments to Rome. To celebrate the pope's seventy-eighth birthday in December 2014, a horde of tango dancers, mindful of the pontiff's early passion for their national dance, converged in the Via Della Conciliazione, the street leading up to Saint Peter's, for a dance-in. The languorous tones of the tango belted out from loudspeakers in the square, which normally amplify Pope Francis' voice, as pilgrims of all ages—from teenagers to grandparents—tried out their paces on the uneven cobblestones of the square, not the most friendly of dance floors.

In Buenos Aires, Bergoglio had quickly come to grips with a financial scandal involving his predecessor as archbishop. A powerful local Catholic banking family, the Trussos, had been financing the travel program of Cardinal Antonio Quarracino and paying his credit card bills. The archdiocese held a number of accounts in their bank, Banco de Credito Provincial (BCP), which had collapsed in 1997. Some family members went to jail.

On taking over the top job in the Argentinian church in 1998, Bergoglio quickly hired a firm of international accountants to sort out the mess he inherited in his diocesan finances and began to enforce for the first time strict accountability and transparency procedures. So there was promise too that one of Pope Francis' first priorities on his arrival in Rome would be to find out the truth about long-standing rumors about the Vatican Bank; that it had for years been functioning as a convenient offshore money-laundering center, fiscal paradise, and tax haven for unidentified account holders in the heart of the Italian capital.

Two years into the new papacy the situation has changed drastically. All account holders, cardinals included, have had their finances examined in detail by professional scrutineers from the United States, and rigid new transparency and money management rules have been imposed on every Vatican department.

But there are increasing grumbles inside the Roman Curia that the new teams set up by Pope Francis to monitor Vatican finances are prying too deeply into long accepted procedures. Serious budgeting and accounting rules are relatively new concepts at the Court of the popes. What exactly has been going on at the Vatican Bank?

2

Peter's Pence

If money and material things become the center of our lives,
they seize us and make us slaves.
—POPE FRANCIS' TWEET @PONTIFEX,
OCTOBER 29, 2013, 3:29 P.M.

Pope Francis set the example: upon his election he continued to wear the same simple metal cross that he had worn as archbishop in Buenos Aires, rejecting the papal gold cross. He also declined to wear the ermine-bordered mozzetta, or short shoulder-cape worn tradition-ally over the white papal cassock. He rejected the gold-embroidered papal ceremonial stole. Setting to his task, he wore ordinary black trou-sers under his cassock, in a papal first. He refused to wear the traditional papal cummerbund, hand-embroidered with his coat of arms at a cost of over thirteen hundred dollars. Instead of the expensive handmade scarlet silk slippers favored by former Pope Benedict and his predeces-sors, Pope Francis wore, and continues to wear, scuffed black loafers and plain black socks instead of the papal white. Responding to comments, he retorted succinctly in what can be called papal sarcasm, "Mardi Gras is over."

It may at first seem like a simple cosmetic shift, but Francis' footwear is emblematic of a sea change in the shadowiest part of the Vatican: one with a long history of troubles and a recent record of scandal.

Since the early Middle Ages, popes have struggled to keep the Vatican financially afloat. The annual collection taken in Catholic churches around the world each year at the end of June is still called "Peter's Pence," after a levy first collected in England in Saxon times. The proceeds, worth nearly $80 million in 2013, are now devoted by the pope to charitable works. The United States is the biggest donor, providing more than a quarter of the total, followed by Italy, Germany, Spain, France, Ireland, Brazil, and South Korea, in that order.

Whether Peter's Pence was a voluntary offering to Rome by pious Catholics or an obligatory church tax is not clear from the earliest records, but the threat of withholding payment proved a useful weapon against uncooperative popes more than once in the hands of early English kings. Peter's Pence was abolished by act of Parliament after the Reformation in 1534, and then revived again as a worldwide voluntary offering by Pope Pius IX toward the end of the nineteenth century.

The amount of money collected each year for the pope's charities provides a useful barometer of the current pope's power as a fund-raiser. In June 2012, when many American Catholics rallied to the support of American nuns who had been placed under Vatican investigation by Pope Benedict for alleged "radical feminism," the proceeds registered a significant dip. Catholics were urged by the nuns to send their contribution directly to them, rather than to Rome.

The total current worth of the Vatican according to latest published accounts is $3.2 billion, a much smaller amount than might be assumed by outsiders. Complete financial transparency has been ordered by Pope Francis, but Cardinal George Pell from Australia—whom he put in overall charge of sorting out the Vatican's tangled finances in 2013—admits that this is proving difficult to achieve. Briefing the assembled cardinals of the church at a closed-door Vatican meeting in February 2015, Pell revealed that he had discovered some $500 million in Vatican accounts that were inexplicably left off the 2013 balance sheet, plus another $1 billion that should have been included but had been "mistakenly" left out.

The $3.2 billion figure does not include the $10.2 billion assets belonging to religious orders and Catholic dioceses around the world and reported to be under the management of the Vatican Bank in 2014. To put all this into perspective, however, the declared assets of a typical major global institution such as Microsoft for example (which reported a total of $172 billion assets in 2014) make the fabled wealth of the Catholic Church, while hardly small change, much less impressive when it is analyzed on paper.

An independent auditor-general, reporting directly to Pope Francis, with sweeping powers to audit the books of any Vatican office he chooses, was appointed for the first time in June 2015. He is Libero Milone, an Italian accountant with widespread international experience and an expert in corporate risk management.

Francis met considerable opposition in trying to push his financial reforms through the Vatican bureaucracy. Cardinal Wilfrid E. Napier of Durban, South Africa, one of the eight cardinals and seven lay financial experts appointed during 2014 to devise appropriate coordinated policies and best practices for all the economic activities of the Holy See and Vatican City State, painted a mixed picture of reluctant cooperation and outright internal opposition when he briefed Vatican journalists during February 2015. The Vatican department in charge of the church's worldwide missionary activities, the Congregation for the Evangelization of Peoples, with offices in downtown Rome, has been accustomed to running its own budget for centuries, he said.

For this reason, it was among those putting up the stiffest resistance to the new financial reporting rules. "It's a culture shock to have to report to somebody other than themselves," he added.

In Europe by far the wealthiest diocese is that of Cologne, Germany, which encompasses two million Catholics. Publishing its accounts (for 2013) for the first time in 2015, it revealed total assets of $3.8 billion—greater than those of the Vatican. Cologne was one of only four of Germany's twenty-seven bishoprics to make its accounts public. Among real estate it owns are some twenty-four thousand apartments, some of which are rented to low earners. The reason why the German church is so wealthy is that it benefits from a long-established 8 percent church tax on income payable by every registered Catholic. In 2013, this amounted to a whopping $6 billion. In 2014, the tax was extended to include income from capital gains as well as wages and salaries. This led to an exodus of about two hundred thousand German Catholics from their church during that year, the largest number in two decades. Catholics who deregister in order to save on their tax bill can still attend mass, but they can be refused access to the sacraments of confession and communion and can even be denied a church burial.

One German bishop became the subject of a widely reported spending scandal during 2014. Franz-Peter Tebartz-van Elst, the fifty-five-year-old bishop of Limburg, remodeled his official residence to the tune of $40 million in 2013 (installing walk-in closets costing $480,000 and a bathtub for $20,000). A senior Vatican official traveled to Germany to carry out an official inquiry into the financial affairs of the "Bishop of Bling" as he became nicknamed in the international media. The prelate was suspended from his office by Pope Francis but was later quietly rewarded with a new job in Rome, a minor post involving religious education. The leniency with which Pope Francis treated the "Bishop of Bling" caused eyebrows to be raised among observers of the Roman scene in the light of the simplicity and frugality practiced and propagated by Francis himself.

"The entire Catholic Church in Germany has been immensely damaged," Cologne Cardinal Rainer Maria Woelki said.

The Vatican's own cash flow is handled by its own bank called the Istituto per le Opere di Religione (Institute for Works of Religion), usually known as the IOR. It is housed in a round, fortresslike medieval tower named after its builder, Nicholas V, who became pope in 1447. The tower, situated just behind St. Peter's Square, lies squeezed between the massive walls of the august Apostolic Palace and the more mundane building that houses the Vatican printing press.

Directly in front of the tower—the Torrione, it is called—are barracks where the 120 members of Pope Francis' elite Swiss Guard live. Thanks to this proximity, bank employees are occasionally serenaded by the mournful notes of guards playing the alpenhorn, a crazily elongated wind instrument, an eight-foot-long traditional wooden Swiss horn, which produces melodies much beloved by inhabitants of the Swiss Alps.

Centuries ago the Torrione had served as a papal prison. To enter it today is, in its way, akin: the visitor must pass through a double barricade of circular sliding security doors of the kind found in Italian banks today, and then exhibit a plastic Vatican ID card with an electronic chip.

Its managers like to remind the faithful and anyone else who asks, "It is not a bank in the normal sense of the word." Indeed it is not: it clings to its peculiarities.

Some are innocuous. Today's IOR Bank account holders can get immediate cash from one of the three modern ATM machines inside Vatican City—they include one conveniently located just inside the bank. Instructions are in Italian and English, plus a notice in a third language advising the account holder: *Inserito scidulam quaeso ut faciundam cognoscas rationem*—Latin, that is, for, "Insert your card to carry out the desired operation."

Up a flight of stairs you enter a semicircular banking hall. Tellers sit behind armored glass screens as nuns, priests, bishops, and a handful of nonclerics quietly deposit funds or withdraw cash; about 25 percent of the bank's transactions are in cash—a much higher proportion than in any normal bank—because church funds to finance distant foreign missions often have to be hand carried.

When Francis inherited control of the bank, the secretive tower was in the process of having its dirty laundry very publicly aired.

In what came to be known as the Vatileaks scandal, in 2012, Italian investigative journalist Gianluigi Nuzzi revealed corruption and money laundering at the highest level in the IOR. *Der Spiegel*, the German news magazine, said the Vatileaks documents exposed Pope Benedict's "frail leadership" of the Vatican.[1] On the very eve of his retirement, Benedict took the opportunity to make a change in the leadership of the bank. The IOR's new president was to be the aristocratic Ernst Conrad Rudolf von Freyberg, a prominent lawyer who had worked with the Bemberg Group of financiers in New York and London, and later with the German Blom+Voss Group in his native Germany. The full significance of this appointment—one of the last Benedict would ever make—would become clear only later, but the problems facing Von Freyberg began decades before.

———

In 1971, the year before my arrival in Rome, Pope Paul VI had appointed an American prelate named Paul Marcinkus to run the Vatican Bank; for another eighteen years he would continue to hold that office. From Cicero, Illinois, Marcinkus was the son of an immigrant window washer from Lithuania. After being ordained a priest in Chicago at age twenty-five, he had studied at the papal university in Rome and then enrolled in the Vatican's school for papal diplomats. Diligently working his way up the international ecclesiastical ladder, he served in papal embassies in Canada and Bolivia.

Returning to Rome, he came to know Cardinal Giovanni Battista

Montini from Milan, the future Pope Paul VI. Thus Marcinkus became Montini's principal English translator in the Vatican's Secretariat of State. After Montini was elected pope in 1963, Marcinkus played a prominent role in organizing the pontiff's foreign trips, beginning with the historic first visit by a pope to Jerusalem the following year. Apart from his language abilities and experience in the diplomatic service of the Holy See, Paul Marcinkus was tall and burly, and he became a trusted papal bodyguard.

The IOR job was thus a reward for years of faithful service to the Holy See, first as a translator, then as a bodyguard.

Marcinkus lacked experience in international banking. Despite a six-week crash course at Harvard University upon his appointment, he was soon wading in deep waters. He signed deals and issued promissory notes in favor of various dodgy international financiers, including the shady Sicilian businessman Michele Sindona, who ended up dying in prison after drinking a poisoned cup of espresso coffee. He also connived with Roberto Calvi, an Italian banker who met an even grislier end, dangling from a rope, with stones in his pockets, under Blackfriars Bridge in London, in a murder disguised as a suicide.

By then elevated to archbishop, Marcinkus was subsequently sought by Italian prosecutors seeking to question him in connection with the bankruptcy of Italy's biggest private bank, the Banco Ambrosiano, headed by Roberto Calvi. A board of laymen eventually assumed control of the IOR, and the Vatican was obliged to pay $240 million in a settlement with creditors.

Marcinkus meanwhile took refuge behind the curtain of Vatican diplomatic immunity and, retiring, left Italy to live in Sun City, Arizona, where he became a familiar figure on local golf courses. In 2006, Archbishop Marcinkus died in Arizona at the age of eighty-four.

He never admitted wrongdoing, nor was Marcinkus ever charged with any crime under Italian law. Twenty years before he died he revealed a certain degree of world-weary philosophical cynicism by reportedly observing that "You can't run the Church on Hail Marys." He later claimed that he had been misquoted; his exact words, he said, were: "When my workers reach retirement they expect a pension, and it's no use my telling them, 'I'll pay you 400 Hail Marys.'"

The archbishop accompanied Pope John Paul II on a pilgrimage to Portugal in May 1982. Exactly one year had passed since the pope survived the attempt on his life by Mehmet Ali Agca in St. Peter's Square, and the pontiff was visiting the Catholic shrine at Fatima to give thanks for his recovery. Near the altar where he was praying a deranged man lunged at the pope with a knife. As we learned only many years later from the pope's secretary, the assailant came close enough to draw blood.

The sturdy Marcinkus, who was standing as usual next to the pope, threw himself upon the intruder and wrestled him to the ground. The assailant, who turned out to be an ultra-right-wing Spanish priest, was arrested by police, and the religious ceremony resumed as if without a hitch.

We of the Vatican press corps had not been included in the visit to the shrine, and were in our Lisbon hotel when reports of this new attempt on the pope's life arrived. We raced to telephones, demanding information. Archbishop Marcinkus personally reassured us that no incident whatsoever had taken place.

Shortly afterward, Portuguese television showed in close-up the actual attack on the pope. The following day I managed to corner Marcinkus and asked him why he had denied what we had seen, live, on television.

"You can't always believe everything you see on TV," was his casual retort.

In the larger sense, the story of Archbishop Marcinkus is emblematic for the church. His crash course at Harvard University hardly qualified him for a career at the Vatican Bank. Few Italian bank officers ever become priests, and even fewer get senior accounting jobs inside the Vatican.

When this author asked the outgoing president von Freyberg in 2014 how many skeletons he had found in the IOR closet during his one-year term of office, "Much smaller ones than you might believe," he replied tactfully. "We have already closed four hundred accounts, and a further four hundred will be closed shortly. Nonclerics with only a loose relationship with the Vatican have traditionally been allowed to keep accounts at the Vatican Bank. We must put a stop to that."

Under von Freyberg's management, some three thousand customer relationships were terminated, leaving about fifteen thousand current accounts active. Among the accounts closed were those managed by the ambassadors to the Holy See of Iran, Iraq, and Indonesia; during the summer of 2011 bank officials had noticed that large sums of money were moving in and out of accounts these embassies held at the IOR.

Von Freyberg arranged for a renowned financial adviser to review the bank's operations. Founded by Washington lawyer and banker Eugene Ludwig, *Promontory* enjoys a reputation as a trusted financial consultant to both the U.S. government and international banks. Ludwig had been tapped by President Bill Clinton to head the Office of the Comptroller of the Currency (OCC) back in 1993. He is among the highest paid financial CEOs in the world, earning a reputed $30 million a year. *Promontory* operates from a brand-new office building two blocks from the White House, and Ludwig lives in one of Washington's most expensive mansions in northwest D.C.

Inside the Vatican, Ludwig's *Promontory* team toiled for more than a year. About two dozen auditors sat behind computer screens and systematically reviewed every account held at the bank. With their hourly billing rate at fifteen hundred dollars, this transparency exercise cost the Vatican about $10 million in consultancy fees.

Von Freyberg says it was money well spent. The only alternative was even more expensive: total closure of the bank, apparently something Francis had been seriously considering.

Pope Francis threw open the Vatican's finances to external scrutiny in a way that had no historical precedent. For some Vatican cardinals, to have allowed a group of foreigners to penetrate the inner sanctum of the Vatican bank, to pry into the financial secrets of the papacy, was anathema. It was as if the Holy See had voluntarily renounced a significant part of its sovereignty in the name of financial transparency. Furthermore, the digitization of secrets heretofore preserved by a handful of invisible "gnomes" meant that they could now be stolen in order to attack or to destabilize the Holy See from outside.

Moneyval, a monitoring committee of the Council of Europe based in France, had already been called in by Benedict, Francis' predecessor, to clean up the tarnished image of the bank. They reported in 2012 that there was "a lack of clarity about the role, responsibility, authority, powers and independence" of the AIF, the body set up by Pope Benedict to monitor the bank's operations. More recently, a number of other prestigious financial watchdogs were also hired. In December 2013, the Vatican announced that McKinsey & Co., the international management consultants, would advise Pope Francis on communications strategy. The U.S.-based accounting firm KPMG was brought on board to harmonize accounting procedures throughout the Vatican, and to bring these procedures up to international standards. Yet another accounting firm, Ernst and Young, headquartered in London, was retained to examine the accounting procedures of the Vatican City State.

For the first time, moreover, the IOR published its consolidated balance sheet on the Internet in 2013, showing it currently controls assets worth about $8 billion. "But we are smaller than most small-town savings and loans banks," von Freyberg insisted.

But these so-called "reforms" by past committees of cardinals with no real experience merely tinkered with the problem. Before Francis, popes have always reasoned that the less outsiders are permitted to know, the fewer questions they can raise and the less risk there is of causing scandal.

———

In February 2014, Pope Francis handed over authority for running the whole of the Vatican's muddled finances to Cardinal George Pell of Sydney, Australia, a member of what has come to be called the "Group of Eight" (later increased to nine) cardinal advisers who act as a sort of "kitchen cabinet," to help him sort out the sclerotic central administration of the church. Most important, the Group is parallel to the traditionally omnipotent Roman Curia. Among today's Vatican top administrators the burly Cardinal Pell is a new heavyweight—literally. His father had been a heavyweight boxing champion, and he himself had been a keen football player for many years in Australia.

Cardinal Pell, whose official new title is prefect for the Secretariat of the Economy, initially set up new offices in another Vatican tower, the Tower of Saint John, a medieval building on the far side of Vatican City that had been refurbished by Pope John Paul as a temporary residence for VIPs. The tower had previously housed, for a short period, Cardinal József Mindszenty, the famous Hungarian cardinal of the Cold War, sentenced to life imprisonment by the postwar Communist regime. Mindszenty had sought refuge in the American Embassy in Budapest to avoid rearrest by the Communists during the 1956 uprising, and was then released to Rome through the intervention of President Richard Nixon in 1971.

At his first public appearance in the Vatican's press office in July 2014, Cardinal Pell sketched out his plan, approved by Pope Francis, to install new checks and balances in the Vatican's accounting system and to ensure that the malpractices revealed in the Vatileaks scandal during the final years of the Benedict papacy are not repeated.

Both senior clergy and laypeople will sit on the various regulatory bodies set up by Pope Francis, Cardinal Pell explained, and external auditors have been appointed to provide an annual report in addition to new internal controls. Conflict of interest statements will have to be signed by everyone sitting on Vatican boards.

"We want to create a model of financial management rather than be seen as a cause for scandal," he reiterated.

A detailed spending review was launched. Shortly after Francis' election, blatant and embarrassing examples of waste surfaced. For the daily *La Repubblica*, Italian journalist Filippo Di Giacomo dug into the high cost of the elaborate gear worn by upper-echelon clergy. Some cardinals and bishops forked over almost $3,000 for a floor-length, hand-sewn cassock of finest wool, plus another $600 for the cummerbund; a surplice cost another $1,000. According to Di Giacomo, one prelate boasted that his surplice, adorned with hand-sewn lace, had cost almost $12,000.[2]

The full rollout of Pope Francis' financial reforms is expected to take at least two years, but in the meantime Cardinal Pell reassured the paid employees of the Holy See (2,880) and of Vatican City State (1,930) that their pensions were safe for the next twenty-five years.

The facts and figures that trickled out during the release of balance sheets in 2014 and 2015 set out the Vatican's financial situation in greater detail than ever before. For the first time, the public was able to look into the finances of one of the most secretive organizations in history.

In its latest report published in May 2015, the AIF (Financial Information Authority), the Vatican's new financial watchdog agency, revealed that there had been a slight decline in the number of suspicious financial transactions detected during 2014. Out of 147 potentially problematic transactions flagged, only seven were forwarded for further action by Vatican prosecutors. Most concerned fraud, tax fraud, or tax evasion.

During 2015, for the first time a tax information sharing agreement was signed with Italy. The Vatican now has similar financial information sharing agreements with some twenty countries including the United States. Previously the Vatican had declined to help foreign investigators track down money-laundering operations through the IOR using the curious argument that this in some way would have infringed Vatican sovereignty.

The IOR reported a twentyfold increase in earnings for the year ending December 2014, showing a net profit of $78 million by comparison with only $3.2 million the previous year, according to its publicly released Annual Report for 2014.[3]

Medals and precious coins are kept in the IOR's own vaults, but the main depository for the Vatican's gold is the U.S. Federal Reserve. The value of the Vatican's gold reserves fell to $26.8 million in 2013 from over $37.5 million in 2012, due to a "significant decline" in the gold price during the year.

The IOR invests 99 percent of its share and bond portfolio in funds that have their legal headquarters in Europe, while the remaining 1 percent is based in the United States.

In terms of expenditures, the largest single item in the Holy See budget is for wages and salaries, which in 2014 cost a total of $140 million, or an average of forty-eight thousand dollars per annum per employee, including pension contributions.

To shave costs, Cardinal Pell forecast a big shakeup in Vatican communications to favor greater use of the new social media, YouTube and Twitter. By his estimate, only about 10 percent of the world's Catholics are at present being reached by the traditional Vatican media, including Vatican Radio and the 150-year-old Vatican daily newspaper *L'Osservatore Romano*, which also runs weekly and foreign-language editions.

A new Vatican Media Committee was set up under the chairmanship of Lord Patten, former governor of Hong Kong, British Cabinet minister, and head of the BBC Trust, to advise Pope Francis on how to enhance the numbers of Catholics reached by the Vatican PR machine. But as we shall see in chapter 9, after several months of meetings he had to admit that it is easier to talk about reshaping the Vatican's media reach than to have to deal with a clerical bureaucracy that actively opposes any changes in established working methods. Another sign of the new times: Pope Benedict had never written in anything but longhand, and never used a computer. Pope Francis, with the help of his close aides, understands and uses the Internet freely, although he has admitted that he himself is "hopeless" with machines.

Using the hashtag *@Pontifex* he has tweeted to over twenty million faithful "followers" in nine different languages almost once a day every day since his election. An example: "When one lives attached to money, it is impossible to be truly happy."

Francis' reforms go above and far beyond footwear. In early June 2014, Pope Francis sacked the entire board of the Financial Intelligence Authority (all Italians, and all male), a watchdog group set up by Benedict. In their stead, Francis appointed a new panel of international experts in anti–money laundering including—and this was a first in Vatican banking—a woman.

And at least one recent case of attempted money laundering did not go undetected. In late June 2013 Monsignor Nunzio Scarano, a senior Vatican accountant, was arrested by Italian police on charges of currency smuggling and contravening Italy's tax laws.

He had first come under suspicion in January 2013 after reporting to Italian police a multimillion-dollar theft of valuable paintings and furniture from his palatial seventeen-room residence in Salerno, near Naples. Italian prosecutors could not understand how he had accumulated real estate and artworks valued well beyond his net worth as a mid-level Vatican employee.

Italian tax police released a video showing details of the Monsignore's luxurious home. According to Italian prosecutors, Scarano had two accounts at the Vatican bank: his personal account and another, named "Fondo Anziani" (Old People's Fund), purportedly used to receive charitable donations.

Paolo Cipriani and Massimo Tulli, the IOR's former director and deputy director, were forced to resign on Pope Francis' instructions shortly after Scarano's arrest. Both have now been ordered to stand trial in an Italian court on charges of violating anti–money laundering norms.

Scarano was incarcerated in Rome's Queen of Heaven prison on charges of plotting to smuggle $20 million into Italy from Switzerland in a scheme to help rich friends avoid Italian taxes. The tall, gray-haired, and distinguished-looking prelate was known inside the Vatican as "Monsignor 500" from his habit of flashing 500-euro banknotes every time he opened his wallet. He was a well-known guest at Roman dinner parties and seemed to have an easy entrée into Roman society.

Scarano was suspended from his Vatican job in July 2013 and his personal accounts at the Vatican Bank were frozen. He wrote a personal letter to Pope Francis protesting his innocence. Later, pleading ill health, he was released to house arrest.

His trial began in Salerno in December 2013 and is still going on. Additional charges were filed in January 2014 when Scarano was indicted, together with another Italian priest, Father Luigi Noli, of having laundered millions of euros through his bank accounts at the IOR. Prosecutors said there appeared to be a closer relationship between the two priests than "mere spiritual fraternity and affectionate friendship." They shared a home, and several bank accounts.

When his trial resumed in Salerno in April 2015 the court ordered Monsignor Scarano to undergo a psychiatric examination. The Monsignore was having visions, his lawyers said.

Nunzio Scarano had been ordained as a priest after two decades of experience as an Italian bank officer. He rose to the post of chief accountant in a key Vatican department known as the Administration of the Patrimony of the Holy See (APSA). This extremely secretive body had been set up under the Lateran Pacts of 1929 between Mussolini and Pope Pius XI to administer the funds in bonds and cash, which the Italian State transferred to the newly established Vatican City State—funds worth at that time some $50 million.

The APSA had two sections: one of them handled the Vatican's liquid assets, and the other, administration of the Vatican's extensive property portfolio.

That portfolio is massive, but APSA, unlike the IOR, has never published its accounts, so the exact extent is still unknown. Among properties said to belong to the Vatican are prime real estate and office blocks in some of London's most expensive districts including Pall Mall and New Bond Street. Other valuable investment properties are owned by the Vatican in the center of Paris, in the Rue de Rome.

But according to the Italian weekly *L'Espresso*, which claims to have seen a copy of the APSA balance sheet for 2013, the fabled wealth of the Vatican accumulated over centuries is barely sufficient to cover the ever-increasing running expenses of the Holy See.

The Vatican City administration, or the "Governatorate" in church jargon, managed to turn a modest profit of $29.5 million on income of $332 million and expenses of $302 million in 2013. Vatican City's chief source of income is entrance fees and merchandising from the Vatican Museums, where the number of visitors has peaked to over five million per annum since the election of Pope Francis.

APSA itself showed a small surplus of $11 million with income from properties and investments amounting to $260 million and expenses of $249 million.

But running a worldwide organization does not come cheap. One of the biggest expenses Pope Francis has to bear is the cost of running the Catholic Church's diplomatic service. The Vatican has established diplomatic relations with 180 different states. Office accommodations, communications, and travel costs for the Vatican *nuncios* or ambassadors in charge of permanent diplomatic missions abroad cost $33.5 million.

Vatican Radio further drains the pope's annual budget with expenditures of $36 million. It is burdened with a large number of retirement-eligible staff contracts. Much of its short-, medium-, and long-wave equipment is now obsolete. The station was originally set up by the Italian wireless pioneer Guglielmo Marconi in 1931. It has been taken to court by families living near its tall aerials—situated on a large agricultural estate on the outskirts of Rome—who suspect an alarming increase in cancer cases among their children may be due to electronic pollution by its transmitters. Vatican Radio has trimmed its electricity bills by reducing the power of some of its transmissions. It now routinely sends out all its signals on the Internet for rebroadcast by local Catholic radio stations around the world.

And, of course, the 120 members of the Pope's Swiss Guard, who provide security at all papal ceremonies and twenty-four-hour guard duties at all the entrances to Vatican City, cost nearly $8 million in wages and equipment.

In other words, there is only so far reform can go before the institutions and traditions of the church itself are threatened.

―――――

In his attempt to restore credibility and normality to the Vatican's financial operations, Pope Francis has been called a "turnaround CEO," comparable to IBM's Lou Gerstner, Fiat's Sergio Marchionne, or Apple's Steve Jobs.

"He rebranded RC Global" in barely a year, the *Economist* opined.[4]

Of course the Vatican will argue that the comparison is not valid, for the same reason that officials pretend a papal interview is not an interview "in the normal sense of the word" and insist that the Vatican

Bank is not a bank "in the normal sense of the word." There is truth
to their adherence to the idea that nothing is normal in Vatican City.
Geographically, Vatican City covers an area not much bigger than your
average small town or village, yet it has to operate in the real world, and
it therefore has to have all the external trappings of a normal sovereign state: post office, fire station, power plant, newspaper, police force,
supermarket, duty-free gas station, radio transmitter, plus its famous
monuments including the Vatican Museums, the Sistine Chapel, and
St. Peter's Basilica. The Vatican issues no GDP figures, partially because
it is difficult to estimate the statistical effect of prayer, which is the city-
state's main raison d'être.

But the Vatican does have a duty-free shop. The former railway
station—which still bears the pockmarks of the only Allied bomb to fall
inside Vatican territory during the Second World War—has been converted into a rarely publicized three-story Vatican luxury department
store open only to employees and their friends and family members.

You will find no reference to it on any Vatican website, but if you
want the latest sixty-five-inch flat-screen TV, or a box of the best Cuban
cigars, and you work for the pope in Rome, you will not be able to buy
them cheaper in any Roman discount store.

Other commercial activities inside the Vatican include a Philatelic
and Numismatic Office. Sales of stamps, coins, and medals account for
millions of dollars of papal income. A special limited-edition postage
stamp was recently issued to help pay for the $18 million restoration
of the attractively curving Bernini colonnades in St. Peter's Square, one
of the architectural glories of Rome. The Vatican has become expert
in attracting corporate sponsors for its restoration works, but since the
worldwide recession after 2006, it has become more and more difficult
for Vatican administrators to fund the maintenance of the fabric of the
Holy See.

On at least one point the *Economist* got it wrong. Pope Francis is
more committed to reform than his predecessors, but his priorities are

first and foremost concerned with religious faith, and differ from those of most CEOs.

Most priests do not understand basic financial practices. They don't know the right questions, let alone the right answers. At the same time, clericalism means that they have to be in charge of everything. Even if they want to delegate these financial responsibilities to laypeople, they don't know enough to appoint competent people. The temptation is always to appoint someone who is deferential or appears pious and trustworthy.

Clericalism and secrecy have been the causes of most of the Vatican financial problems. The highest authority for the Vatican bank used to be a board of cardinals with no expertise in finances, let alone banking. They did not know how to supervise a bank. The president of the bank was usually a layman, and a part-time appointment. Until recently, everything about the bank was secret.

The Catholic Church is still by no means safe from future scandal— on the contrary, in the immediate future more scandalous revelations can be expected as the adoption of new procedures flushes out those who have until now exploited the church. It is still uncertain to what extent Pope Francis will give the green light to criminal prosecutions of Vatican employees, including clerics.

As a pope who stresses compassion and mercy, it may be difficult for him to punish offenders. On the other hand, punishing wrongdoers would act as a deterrence to future crime and show that the Vatican is serious about financial reform.

———

In March 2014, Pope Francis convened an unusual summit of treasurers of thousands of Catholic religious orders around the world, whose assets are of course quite separate from those of the Vatican itself. He wanted them to reevaluate the management of their money and assets, especially some of the empty monasteries and convents that in recent years have been turned over to nonreligious activities, such as hotels, bed-and-breakfasts, and restaurants.

"Empty convents do not serve the church so that they can be turned into hotels for earning money," Francis said during a meeting in Rome with refugees from Africa and Latin America. "Empty convents are not ours, they are for the flesh of Christ, who are the refugees."

The idea that Pope Francis is promoting of the Catholic Church's divesting itself of its riches and handing its assets over to the poor does not automatically go down well inside the Vatican or among the many religious orders around the world that are facing dwindling numbers and declining incomes.

Since January 2015, draconian new accounting rules have been introduced by Cardinal Pell for every Vatican headquarters department. Total financial transparency is the order given by Pope Francis. An eighty-four-page rulebook has been prepared by the cardinal's small staff. New financial management policies and practices said to be based on the best international accounting and reporting standards have become mandatory. Vatican sources said some department heads had resisted the new rules, which involve some heavy form filling and the preparation of detailed individual annual budgets. Cardinal Pell described the state of the Vatican's finances before his arrival as "sloppy, inefficient and open to being robbed."

He told the U.K. Catholic weekly *The Tablet* that he had been on a committee supposed to be overseeing the Vatican's finances for eight years, yet "the only thing that was absolutely clear was that we didn't know what was going on."

Pope Francis' former private secretary Monsignor Alfred Xuereb, from Malta, has been put in permanent charge of implementing the Vatican's new financial management policies. A regular financial training program has been introduced to educate today's Vatican monsignori more thoroughly into the arcane secrets of modern management accounting. It is a very far cry from Archbishop Marcinkus' six-week crash course in international banking at Harvard, which led church finances into such disaster in the 1970s and 1980s.

———

Meanwhile, in the autumn of 2014, another financial scandal surfaced, this time concerning the leading Catholic religious order, the Franciscans, after whom Jorge Bergoglio chose his papal name. Brother Michael Perry, the American monk who is the elected head of the fourteen-thousand-strong order of Friars Minor announced he had called in the police and instructed lawyers to investigate losses amounting to tens of millions of dollars. Brother Perry admitted there had been a failure of financial controls. The Franciscans, who take vows of poverty and who in theory reject material possessions, risk bankruptcy unless they can repay what the head of their order describes as "significant debts." Pope Francis was immediately informed of the fraud and embezzlement charges.

He gave the Franciscans a severe rap on the knuckles when he addressed leaders of the order at the Vatican in May 2015. He warned them that they had better return to the spirit of their founder St. Francis—or else.

> If you are attached to the goods and riches of the world, and become dependent upon them for your safety, the Lord will strip you of this spirit of worldliness in order to preserve the precious heritage of minority and poverty to which you have been called through St. Francis. Either you freely embrace poverty and your lowly calling, or you'll end up stripped of your worldly goods.

If the pace of financial reform at the Vatican under Francis' reign has been constant, if sometimes slow, the promise of change in the church's attitude toward a greater role for women under the pope from Argentina has remained largely unfulfilled.

3

A Deeper Theology of Women

They [women theologians] are the strawberry on the cake, but
there is need for more of them.

—POPE FRANCIS, DECEMBER 5, 2014, ADDRESSING
THE INTERNATIONAL THEOLOGICAL COMMISSION

In the third year of his reign, Pope Francis scored a historic first. A
woman archbishop entered the Apostolic Palace for the first time.
On May 4, 2015, he warmly welcomed the female head of Sweden's
Lutheran church on an official visit to the Vatican. Archbishop Antje
Jackelén of Uppsala happens to be the first woman elected to lead what
until recently was Sweden's state church. The Swedish church is known
for its liberal positions, particularly on homosexuality; it consecrated the
first openly lesbian bishop in the world in Stockholm in 2009.

Francis greeted his guest as "Esteemed Mrs. Jackelén, esteemed
sister . . ." The Protestant Church in Sweden may be steadily losing
members, just like most other Christian denominations, but it still
claims over 60 percent membership of the Nordic nation. Catholics and

Lutherans are already planning joint ceremonies to mark the five hundredth anniversary of the Reformation, which falls in 2017.

"Division among Christians is still a scandal to the world," Pope Francis said promisingly.

Archbishop Jackelén was enthusiastic about the prospect of greater understanding between the two churches, but she also had some slightly barbed remarks. Growing in communion, she said, means learning—sometimes the hard way—about "sharing the richness of traditions rather than building fences around one's own turf," and about "empowerment rather than about power."

But curiously, Vatican officials played down what could have been promoted as a historical event. The meeting was deemed to merit only a brief mention down page in the official Vatican newspaper of record, without a photograph of their handshake. It was another example of the mixed messages we have increasingly become accustomed to receiving from the Vatican: a surprise step from Pope Francis himself, demonstrating a new openness on his part, followed by an apparent attempt at damage limitation by the overcautious officialdom of the Roman Curia, anxious to play safe and to limit any shock to traditionalist Catholics.

Few of Pope Francis' words have been taken quite so out of context as his comparing female theologians to a "strawberry" topping on a cake. The strawberry simile came during his speech at the inaugural session of the Vatican's International Theological Commission on December 5, 2014. For the first time ever, among the twenty commission members were seven female theologians. Because a strawberry is a luscious tidbit, some understood his words as trivializing the work of these women.

The commission was created by Pope Paul VI in 1969, and is composed of Catholic theologians. During their five-year term they are expected to help the Holy See, and especially the notoriously conservative Congregation for the Doctrine of the Faith, in its examination of current issues of doctrine. So what does this have to do with strawberries?

Just three months prior to that inaugural meeting, Francis himself had appointed five women theologians to the commission. In so doing he had boosted its female contingent to seven, or 16 percent of its membership. It already had two veteran female members, a nun, Sister Sara Butler, representing the United States, and a laywoman, Prof. Barbara Hallensleben of the University of Fribourg. Both owed their appointments in 2004 to the intervention of Joseph Ratzinger, who reportedly persuaded John Paul II that "omitting women from the whole of theology signified denying the creation and the election—the story of salvation—and hence [was] to suppress Revelation."[1]

The December meeting thus brought together for the first time, inside the Vatican, these two plus the five new female members. The first two are religious: Sister Prudence Allen, R.S.M., of the United States, and Sister Alenka Arko, Com. Loyola of Slovenia-Russia; the other three are laywomen: Moira Mary McQuenn of Canada; Tracey Rowland of Australia, and Marianne Schlosser, representing Germany and Austria.

At the meeting the pontiff declared that the commission, and for that matter the church in general, needs more women theologians. "They are the strawberries on the cake," he said. "But there is need for more [women theologians]." Their presence, he went on to say, "is a call to reflect upon the role women can and must play in the field of theology."[2] Then the pope advised the theologians that "by virtue of their feminine genius, [female] theologians can detect, for the benefit of everyone, some unexplored aspects of the unfathomable mystery of Christ. I invite you, therefore, to take the best advantage of this specific contribution of women to the intelligence of faith."

Pope Francis had intended these words as praise, but his comparing women theologians to a strawberry topping, combined with his use of phrases like "feminine genius," struck a negative chord among many for its overtones of chauvinistic male paternalism. Style trumped substance as criticism for dated gender words overshadowed the fact that it was Francis who had just appointed the five women theologians to the commission, and that his words were intended as compliments.

Said one woman theologian who was part of a group at the Vatican on International Women's Day in March 2014: "One thing we really hope is that he will sit down with women theologians, and there are many, and listen to them, rather than base his thoughts on stereotypes of feminist theology that some in the church have successfully perpetuated."

The most authoritative and oft-repeated attack came from David Gibson, biographer of Pope Benedict XVI and a regular contributor to various Catholic publications. His commentary, carried by the Religion News Service agency on December 11, 2014, was headlined "Lost in translation? Seven reasons why women wince when Pope Francis starts talking." Gibson's view:

"When he speaks about women, Francis can sound a lot like the 78-year-old Argentine churchman that he is, using analogies that sound alternately condescending and impolitic, even if well-intentioned."

Indeed, Francis has spoken repeatedly of the "feminine genius" and the need for a church to develop "a deeper theology of women," and of his determination to promote women to senior positions in Rome. He also points out that some of his remarks are meant as jokes, the fruit of a sense of humor that is part of his appeal.

Gibson's views were picked up all over the globe, including by the *Huffington Post*. In it he listed seven papal phrases he considered demeaning to women, beginning with Francis' telling delegations of visiting nuns from all over the world on May 8, 2013, that "the consecrated woman is a mother, must be a mother, and not an old maid."

Gibson's second example of why women wince on hearing pope-speak came from his interview published September 30, 2013, in the Jesuit magazine *America*: "A woman has a different makeup than a man, but what I hear about the role of women is often inspired by an ideology of *machismo*." Never mind that in the course of that interview the pope also said that the church needs a "stronger presence of women."

Item three on Gibson's list of papal-style gender irritations came from another interview, this in Italian, speaking on July 2, 2014, with Franca Giansoldati, Vatican correspondent for the Rome daily *Il Messaggero*. At one point the pope remarked that "women are beautiful, church is a feminine word, and we need to work on a new theology of women." Giansoldati reacted by suggesting that this statement hinted at misogyny. At this the pope laughed, responding, "The fact is that woman was taken from a rib. Oh, I am kidding; that was a joke!"[3] Perhaps—but Gibson for one was not laughing.

The fourth item on Gibson's strikeout list came during that same interview and was, in its way, perhaps the most gender-offensive. Giansoldati asked the pontiff when a woman might take over as head of a Vatican department. Until that time, no woman was permitted to a post above that of undersecretary in any Vatican department, and only two female undersecretaries existed. One was a nun, Sister Nicoletta Vittoria Spezzati, who served as undersecretary for the Vatican department for religious orders; the other, a laywoman, Flaminia Giovanelli, undersecretary for the Pontifical Council for Justice and Peace.

In response to Giansoldati, the pope dismissed the question with a tasteless quip: "Well, pastors often wind up under the authority of their housekeeper."

Commenting on that interview, Dr. Phyllis Zagano of the Department of Religion at Hofstra University wrote in the U.S. *National Catholic Reporter*: "I can't believe that a world class person like Francis who seems so much in touch with individuals and their suffering is capable of remarks like this. Yet I know he lives in a society where the ordinary needs of clerics are often taken care of by unmarried women or religious sisters who cook, clean, do laundry, order supplies and serve as receptionists, often on nights and weekends. Just like Mom."

That still seems to be the case in much of the clerical world. Do an Internet search for "rectory housekeeper" and you will find job descriptions from coast to coast. Even new rectories have a room with a bath or a suite just off the kitchen or laundry room for the woman who runs the rectory household and, if Francis is to be believed, the priests.[4]

Be that as it may, just one month after that interview, Pope Francis appointed Sister Maria Melone, a Franciscan nun born in La Spezia, Italy, to be the first woman rector of a pontifical university, the Antonianum. The post is the equivalent of the head of a Vatican department, and it may not be hazardous to suggest that, even as he quipped about a "housekeeper," Pope Francis had already scheduled Sister Melone's appointment.

Fifth on the wince-ometer: while addressing the European Parliament on November 25, 2014, the pontiff declared that an aging, wearied Europe has now become "a 'grandmother,' no longer fertile and vibrant. . . . The great ideas which once inspired Europe seem to have lost their attraction." As do grannies, seemed to be his implication, dull gray and infertile.

Sixth was the women-theologians-as-strawberries comment.

And seventh was Francis' comparing the church itself, in a homily spoken at his daily morning mass on December 9, 2014, in the Santa Marta Chapel inside the Vatican, "to a sad, anxiety-ridden spinster, closed in upon herself albeit well organized, with a perfect organizational chart." When the church fails to evangelize, it becomes mummified, a museum, he added. Instead the church should be a mother, for its joy is "to give birth."

Doubtless the pope was seeking to be homey and understood by the multitudes, but Gibson's listing of these elements of style ignited a firestorm of criticism. For these critics, the pontiff had come across as an old fuddy-duddy unaware of contemporary issues of gender, at least in language, that are now taken for granted by many Catholics, particularly in the English-speaking world.

This was spelled out in the *Washington Post* by Melinda Henneberger, former *New York Times* reporter and author of *If They Only Listened to Us*. Her commentary focused upon Francis' cautioning nuns not to become spiritual old maids. "I am at a loss to see how this could be other than insulting to women who've already given up having families of their own to serve God," she wrote.[5]

Joining the fray were biblical scholars from Notre Dame and Yale University, who dismissed the pope's words as "crass chauvinism." Other English-language critics called them "highly patriarchal."

And yet not everyone reading the pope's words interpreted them in the same way. Some understood the pontiff's words about machismo as exactly the opposite of Gibson's point two—that is, the pontiff's rejection of machismo and of the patriarchy that continues to marginalize women.[6]

Even the remark about strawberries had its supporters. What the pope actually said was this:

> Within the increasingly diverse composition of the Commission, I would like to note the increased presence of women—still not too many . . . they are the strawberries on the cake, but we need more—a presence that becomes an invitation to reflect on the role that women can and should play in the field of theology. Indeed, the Church acknowledges the indispensable contribution which women make to society through the sensitivity, intuition and other distinctive skill sets which they, more than men, tend to possess. . . . I readily acknowledge that many women . . . [offer] new contributions to theological reflection.

(The quote was from his Apostolic Exhortation *Evangelii Gaudium*.)

In her online blog called "Catholic Cravings," the Australian Catholic writer Laura McAlister adorned her interpretation of papal strawberries with luscious photos of strawberries tucked into desserts with rich whipped cream. For this young theology student (she is completing an MA in theology), the pontiff's words raised the more general question of how women in theology are seen today.

> *To me, it seems that female theologians are valued in terms of their femininity but male theologians in terms of their individuality. No one stops to wonder what distinctive gifts men bring to theology or how their masculine genius helps them to uncover other unexplored aspects of the mystery of the Faith. (Don't try to tell me there aren't any either. I know there are.)*
>
> *When we see women's contributions as primarily gendered and men's as not, we inevitably tokenize women. We make them into a few strawberries on an otherwise unaltered cake.*

In order to avoid this "tokenization," McAlister suggests that one must be more aware of "what we can only call the masculine genius. We need to emphasize and explore more fully the distinctive gifts of men as men, and not merely as the normative human beings. . . . Without a rigorous theology of masculinity, we will not truly appreciate the distinctive gifts of either men or women."

She also quotes Sister Mary Malone, that first female rector of a pontifical university in Rome, who had said in an interview with the Vatican's semiofficial Vatican daily *L'Osservatore Romano* that

> *The reference to female theology does not really fit with my vision of things: all that exists is theology. Theology as research, as a focus on mystery, as a reflection on this mystery. But precisely because this requires different sensitivities. A woman's approach to mystery, the way in which she reflects on this mystery which offers itself and reveals itself, is certainly different from that of a man. But they do not contrast.*
>
> *I believe in theology and I believe that theology created by a*

woman is typical of a woman. It is different but without the ele-
ment of laying claim to it. Otherwise it almost seems as though I am
manipulating theology, when it is instead a field that requires hon-
esty from the person who places him/herself before the mystery.

McAlister's conclusion: "All theology is women's theology, just as all theology is men's theology. . . . As thrilled as I am at the increasing rec-ognition of women in theology, I will be far more excited when the most newsworthy thing about these women isn't that they are women—but that they are thoughtful, insightful and faithful theologians. Because then we will truly know that the Holy Spirit is cooking up a storm."[7]

Her readers' comments were positive. "A generation ago 'women in management' were expected to be more cooperative, verbal and what-ever. Now we all have had female bosses and we all know it's not that simple," wrote one. "It's just part of being newer and fewer."

For Megan W., McAlister's post was "wonderful." A Catholic con-vert from Protestantism, she pointed out that "the idea of 'women theo-logians' is almost a distinctly Catholic view. . . . [and] that women that study theology are something 'different' from men is something that I have never come across."

And there are other ways to analyze Francis-speak. Besides his mention of theological strawberries, which evoke trifles, and old maids, who are left on the shelf because they are implicitly unattractive, Francis has advised Catholics to observe responsible parenting and not to mul-tiply like "rabbits."

He has also remarked, presumably in jest, that if anyone insulted his mother, he would give the offender a "punch."

————

In consideration of these references and his many other folksy words that excite media attention all over the world, we sought analysis of

Pope Francis' use of language from scientific linguist Nora Galli de' Paratesi. Born in Italy, Galli is herself multilingual and is a retired professor and author, including of a sociolinguistic study of the language spoken in Tuscany.[8]

Her opinion is that Francis' colorful phrases echo his growing up as the child of immigrant parents, who probably spoke at home not what is accepted as standard Italian, but the dialect of their native Piedmont; his grandmother, with whom he spent a good deal of time, seems to have spoken only Piedmontese.

"Like all dialects, the Italian dialects including Piedmontese are characterized by informality," said Galli. This implies a certain amount of family-style joshing.

In addition, it is known that in his past Pope Francis, raised in a lower-middle-class home in Buenos Aires, spent many years communicating in first person with very poor parishioners; even as cardinal he made regular visits to Argentinian slum homes. Few pontiffs have had a similar background of direct dealing, including in terms of language, with the *villas miserias*, or shantytowns, which he visited frequently enough that he became known in Buenos Aires as the Bishop of the Slums. Even today a park area in the city that has been taken over by three hundred families of squatters living in makeshift tin sheds is named *Villa Papa Francesco*, after Pope Francis.

Pope Francis actually speaks several languages, each with dialectal differences. In addition to the colloquial, dialect-influenced Italian of his childhood, he would have spoken the specific dialect of Buenos Aires known as *porteño* or *Español rioplatense*, referring to the city's position on the Río de la Plata. But at the same time the pontiff, who is known to be a serious scholar and deep thinker, in his formative seminary years in Buenos Aires and later as a professor of theology in a seminary at San Miguel, would have spoken a more standard Latin American Spanish.

He still appears comfortable while using a joshing tone, even when speaking from the papal throne. This remarkable family-style informality has played no small role in helping build his popularity, despite criticism from some who find this linguistic lightheartedness inappropriate. The informality of his spoken words is also a reflection of social class, and the critics of his use of language tend to represent an intellectual elite of English speakers.

On the other hand, misogyny is an integral part of the historical culture of the Roman Catholic Church, no less than of the historical culture of the secular states of the entire world. Consider the behavior of the male clergy toward women in sixteenth- and seventeenth-century Italy.

Concubinage was so common and taken for granted among the clergy of the day that the latest historical research into ecclesiastical and civil court records of the period following the Counter-Reformation shows that prosecutions of priests for sexual misbehavior with the opposite sex were rare. Yet, according to a recent study, one in every four or five defendants brought before a court was a member of the clergy. Charges of murder, sodomy, usury, contraband, and extortion were frequent. Then, as now, what counted was the honor of the church, which had to be preserved at all costs. Frequently, just as in the twenty-first century, bishops ordered priests convicted by ecclesiastical tribunals to return to their ministry, ignoring their criminal behavior.[9]

Historians of religion like Giulia Galeotti, journalist with *L'Osservatore Romano*, remind us, however, that for centuries the church was actually more open toward women than was the secular world. In her view, for centuries the church gave women opportunities that the secular world did not: it permitted women religious to study, and hence to emancipate themselves intellectually, as well as to rule over convents as managers even in the Middle Ages. Women who would later be elevated to sainthood had challenged bishops and even popes, according to Galeotti; and in the nineteenth century they founded congregations, traveled freely, and handled notable amounts of money. "Prior to the eighteenth century nowhere else in European society nor in the American colonies were women given so much authority," she said.[10]

Late-twentieth-century attitudes were far different, and by then a large number of its religious women began to see the church as backward and unjust toward women.

The decline in vocations is particularly visible in the United States, where the number of female religious peaked at 181,421 in 1966, then dropped to under 55,000 in 2014, or roughly the same number as a century ago, when the U.S. population was just 99 million, compared with today's 322 million.[11]

"Nuns are an endangered species," Jo Piazza wrote in a report in *Time* magazine in August 2014. "They are dying and not being replaced." In fact, the steady decline in their numbers is bound to increase because those remaining tend to be elderly; one out of ten is over ninety. Similarly, barely one out of ten is under fifty.

In the year 2012, the church could still lay claim to no fewer than 702,529 consecrated women worldwide, according to the Vatican statistics, but women's vocations differ radically by geographical area: in Asia women comprise 70 percent of the workforce of the church; in Africa, 58 percent; and in the United States and Europe, 57 percent.

Curiously, more women than men continue to give their lives to the church; the all-male church was comprised in 2012 of 5,133 bishops; 414,313 priests; and 55,314 other consecrated men, for a total of 424,760 males, meaning that the workforce remains predominately female.

If women in the West continue to desert vocations, their lack will present huge problems to the church. Preaching and saying mass remain male prerogatives, but women already tend some parishes in the West where there is no priest. Everywhere, without receiving a salary, nuns offer prayers, they teach on every level of schooling from infant to university, they look after prison inmates, they tend the dying in hospices, and, yes, they are housekeepers for the priests. A few also staff church press offices, and a rarefied few, as we have seen, are theologians.

When Ms. Piazza wrote that nuns are a "dying species," Donald R. McClarey, JD (an expert in canon law), objected strongly:

Nuns have thrived from the earliest ages of Catholicism because living a life in service as a bride of Christ is a magnificent way for women to make their paths through this Vale of Tears. Since Vatican II, hordes of female religious orders have abandoned this vocation to embrace every trendy lefty cause rolling down the pike. Their orders are dying off, not because of any action of the Vatican, but because being a trendy leftist does not require being a nun. Orthodox female religious orders, completely invisible in the blinkered universe of Ms. Piazza, are doing well with vocations because being a bride of Christ does require being a nun.

Some of McClarey's quarrel was implicitly with the Leadership Conference of Women Religious (LCWR), a network of some fifteen hundred Catholic sisters representing about eight out of ten American nuns. Because their median age is seventy-four, one can hardly expect them to be radical feminists. Nevertheless, the LCWR bounced into fame (or perhaps notoriety) in Catholic circles in 1979, when Sister Theresa Kane, a former LCWR president, seized the occasion of his U.S. visit to ask John Paul II to provide women the possibility "as persons being included in all ministries of the church." *All ministries*—that would include their being ordained as priests.

A later president, Sister Laurie Brink OP, a biblical scholar, touched off another storm when she said during a formal lecture to the conference members in 2007 that, while Jesus remains at the core of her being, "I've also moved beyond Jesus." Her twenty-eight-page paper was pro-

vocatively (to some) entitled "A Marginal Life: Pursuing Holiness in
the 21st Century." Years later, the meaning of her words "beyond Jesus"
was still being hotly debated in the U.S. Catholic press as well as back
at the Vatican. Cardinal William Joseph Levada, an American and the
former head of the Congregation for the Doctrine of the Faith (CDF,
also known as the Holy Office), expressed concern at the "beyond Jesus"
phrase, while the CDF itself called the movement Dr. Brink reflects
"incompatible with Catholic theology, and incompatible with religious
life."[12]

During the spring of 2012, the ever more alarmed CDF issued
a statement accusing the conference of promoting "radical feminist
themes" and the sort of "corporate dissent" that outraged Catholics all
over the world. That April the Vatican acknowledged that it had opened
an investigation into the LCWR because the American nuns had a
"secular mentality" and had strayed too far afield from Vatican traditional teachings. The members were guilty of theological speculation,
said the doctrine watchdogs.

The investigation was without precedent. To oversee the inquiry,
Pope Benedict appointed a committee of three U.S. men of the church,
under the direction of J. Peter Sartain, archbishop of Seattle.

The wiliest argument against the rebellious American nuns came
from Cardinal Gerhard Müller, who said that the Vatican wanted to
help the LCWR congregations to "rediscover their identity" because
otherwise these orders risk dying out from a lack of vocations.[13]

Not only nuns had troubles with the Vatican. In 2007, Lesley-Anne
Knight was elected secretary-general of the worldwide Catholic charity
Caritas Internationalis. As such Knight gained theoretical entry into
the inner sanctums of the church in Rome. But she became quickly
disillusioned by the lack of cooperation she encountered from inside
the Rome Curia.

With headquarters in Rome, Caritas Internationalis was founded in 1897 in Germany as simply Caritas, then expanded in 1951 into the broader world. Today it brings together 160 relief and social service organizations operating in as many countries, and is charged with tending "to the suffering of the poor and giving them the tools to transform their lives."

Knight, born in Zimbabwe, is an attractive, smart, and sunny woman, but after her four-year term at the helm of Caritas expired, she was ousted quite brutally in 2011 after she publicly criticized the Vatican in an interview with the *National Catholic Reporter* magazine for being in her view out of touch with Caritas itself and of having only one-way communications.

"Does the Holy See actually know what Caritas is doing?" she asked. "Dialogue is a two-way street."

Monsignor Giampietro Dal Toso, secretary of the Pontifical Council agency that oversees Vatican charities, took objection. Knight's "declarations on the lack of communion (!) with the Holy See might seriously damage the prestige of Caritas Internationalis, especially among the faithful," he declared. He said that Knight had no business informing the press about her concerns, and that her term would not be renewed.[14]

In her farewell speech at Caritas on June 4, 2011, Knight made a sharply pointed comment suggesting that part of the reason for the nonrenewal of her four-year contract was because she is a woman, and a laywoman at that:

> [*We must*] *work towards a more equitable balance between women and men in the leadership of Caritas organizations. We should not forget that lay women make up a huge proportion of Caritas workers. They deserve respect and recognition. My appointment as the first woman Secretary General in 2007 was a courageous step. You know that we can do the job—only fear, misogyny and prejudice stand in your way.*

Knight's replacement at Caritas was a French layman, Michel Roy.

In January 2013, Lesley-Anne Knight was made chief executive officer (CEO) of The Elders, an international organization of elder statesmen and human rights advocates brought together by Nelson Mandela in 2007 and chaired by Kofi Anan. Among its members are former U.S. President Jimmy Carter, South Africa's Archbishop Desmond Tutu, Norway's first woman prime minister, Gro Harlem Brundtland, and Mary Robinson, first woman president of Ireland and former UN Commissioner for Human Rights.

———

Pope Francis made it clear early in his papacy that he has no intention of modifying church teaching on the ordination of women priests. "The church has spoken and says no. . . . That door is closed," he told journalists on the plane back to Rome from his first foreign visit to Brazil. He then quickly qualified the ban by remarking "the church cannot be limited to altar girls or the president of charity, there must be more." But he went on to justify the ban by quoting his predecessor Pope John Paul, who stated definitively in 1994 that the church has no authority to ordain women.

Theologians have argued ever since about the difference between "definitive" and "infallible." The future Pope Benedict clarified that John Paul's document *Ordinatio Sacerdotalis* was not an infallible teaching. A September 2013 editorial in America's *National Catholic Reporter* optimistically speculated that Pope Francis had not talked about a barbed wire fence or a concrete barrier, but merely a "closed door"—to which he in fact holds the keys.

It's worth noting, however, that the church's official position on any attempt by a bishop to ordain a woman as a priest still ranks as one of the worst crimes that any ecclesiastic can commit—on a par with the sexual abuse of a child, heresy, or schism.

Despite the fact that the Vatican considers them excommunicated, the Association of Roman Catholic Women Priests (ARCWP), a U.S.-based organization that extends into South America, claims that there are already today more than 124 female priests and 10 bishops worldwide.[15]

Their support comes from Catholic men as well as women. A poll conducted by Univision of twelve thousand Catholics in twelve nations on five continents and in nine languages indicated that a goodly proportion favored women priests. In Europe, 64 percent of those polled approved, and in Latin American, 49 percent vs. 47 percent who disapproved. In the United States, 59 percent registered approval and only 36 percent disapproval. Showing geographical distinctions, in Africa those in favor were only 18 percent, with 80 percent disapproving.[16]

The poll also showed Catholics strongly in favor of the church changing its position on contraceptives. Again the figures showed geographical divergence, with the greatest percentage in favor (91 percent) from Latin America, including 91 percent of Catholics in Argentina and 93 percent in Brazil. The approval rating in Europe was 90 percent in Spain, 84 percent in Italy, while slightly lower in the United States, but still almost eight Catholics out of ten (78 percent). Only in two countries, Uganda and the Congo, did the Catholics polled register disapproval (44 percent).

In 2012, four hundred Catholics belonging to an organization called FutureChurch, headquartered in Cleveland, Ohio, launched a U.S.-wide campaign to promote discussion of the shortage of priests; the question of optional celibacy for priests; and the possibility of women deacons in the church. Contacts with bishops in forty-two dioceses indicated that eleven bishops "expressed some level of openness to dialogue about women deacons." Six said they are in favor, and five were willing to discuss it. Three more would discuss it, though in Rome. Of them all, only one bishop and one diocesan official "registered no support for women deacons."[17]

Back in Rome, the Congregation for the Doctrine of the Faith (CDF) went on the warpath against this, placing U.S. nuns under formal investigation on charges of allegedly failing to abide by Vatican instructions in 2008. Known as an Apostolic Visitation, the investigation was ordered by Cardinal Franc Rodé. Now retired, he was a senior official of the Curia. The investigation was the largest of its kind ever undertaken by the Vatican. Some 350 communities of religious women were formally queried, and official investigators personally visited ninety.

Both Catholic men and women registered opposition to the crackdown imposed by the Congregation for the Doctrine of the Faith, which they nicknamed the "Nunquisition." Even in the Vatican, opinion softened somewhat, and in 2011 Rodé was replaced by Brazilian Archbishop João Bráz de Aviz, who spoke in more conciliatory tones of dealing with the American nuns "without preemptive judgment, and listening to the reasons."

After Pope Francis was elected, the dialogue was further modified, in tone if not in substance. In late 2014, a cardinal considered particularly close to the pope, Seán O'Malley of Boston, admitted on a CBS-TV news show that the investigation had been "a disaster."

The previous April, sixteen progressive U.S. Catholic organizations had sent a letter to Pope Francis in which they complained that "faithful Catholic female leaders are disrespected and discounted in our church." In the letter the group, which called itself The Nun Justice Project, asked for a public apology from the Vatican's archconservative chief doctrinal overseer, CDF Prefect Cardinal Gerhard Müller, whom they accused of delivering "unjust mandates" and refusing dialogue with the American contingent.

But Cardinal Müller was still having none of it. "Above all we have to clarify that we are not misogynists. We don't want to gobble up a woman a day," he told a journalist from *L'Osservatore Romano* in early September 2014. If this sounded remarkably jovial, he still went on to clarify his view that the LCWR "do not represent all U.S. nuns, but just a group of North American nuns who form part of an association. We have received many letters of distress from other nuns belonging to the same congregations who are suffering a great deal because of the direction in which they [LCWR] are steering their mission."

This rather wantonly ignores that the organization represents 80 percent of American nuns. And in the end Müller lost, for in mid-December 2014 the Vatican called off the six-year investigation of the U.S. sisters, initiated under Pope Benedict XVI. Pope Francis then celebrated mass with some of the nuns and clergymen who had conducted the investigation. The result "will likely be seen as a major olive branch from the Vatican for American nuns as well as another sign of a more conciliatory approach under Pope Francis," commented John L. Allen, associate editor of the online magazine *Crux*, on December 16, 2014.

"The sisters deserve an apology," headlined an editorial in the *National Catholic Reporter*. "The investigation can now be seen for the sham it was, and we as a church should be ashamed of the abuse these faithful women suffered because of it."[18]

––––––

While the women religious were taking matters into their own hands, the church has struggled to deal with the question of women's ordination, with varying shifts in emphasis under different papacies.

In April 1976, the Pontifical Biblical Commission opened a door to the possibility, agreeing in unanimity that, "It does not seem that the New Testament by itself alone will permit us to settle in a clear way and once and for all the problem of the possible accession of women to the presbyterate." The commission then voted, twelve to five, in favor of the view that the Bible does *not* exclude the ordination of women, and that women can be ordained to the priesthood without going against the original intentions of Christ.

To this the Congregation for the Doctrine of the Faith objected. In its statement called *Inter Insigniores* of October 15, 1976, it decreed that "the Church, in fidelity to the example of the Lord, does not consider herself authorized to admit women to priestly ordination."

Pope Paul VI then stepped in, declaring—though not without a hint of ambiguity—that, although "a very large number of Christian communities are already benefiting from the apostolic commitment of women," the church does not consider herself "authorized to admit women to priestly ordination." Whereas "a few heretical sects in the first centuries, especially Gnostic ones, entrusted the exercise of the priestly ministry to women . . . this innovation was immediately noted and condemned by the Fathers, who considered it as unacceptable in the Church." Besides, "Jesus Christ did not call any women to become part of the Twelve."

Still, this could be read by some as a reluctance to slam the door completely on women priests. But then Pope John Paul II drew a sharper line in the sand by making the ban placed by the church on women priests definitive. As he wrote in his *Apostolic Letter Ordinatio Sacerdotalis*, of May 22, 1994, addressed to the bishops,

> *Priestly ordination, which hands on the office entrusted by Christ to his Apostles of teaching, sanctifying and governing the faithful, has in the Catholic Church from the beginning always been reserved to men alone. This tradition has also been faithfully maintained by the Oriental Churches. . . . The Church has no authority whatsoever to confer priestly ordination on women and that this judgment is to be definitively held by all the Church's faithful.*

To say "*no authority whatsoever*" amounts to a rebuke to Paul VI, who had made the less harsh statement that the church "*does not consider herself authorized.*"

Another apostolic letter called *Ad Tuendam Fidem*, which was drafted for John Paul by the then-Cardinal Joseph Ratzinger, followed shortly afterward and outlawed any further discussion on the ordination of women.

Delegates from Ireland, the United States, U.K., and Australia attended an international Catholic meeting in County Louth, Ireland, in September 2014. Among them was Erin Saiz Hanna of the U.S. Women's Ordination Conference. In an interview with the daily *Irish Independent*, Saiz Hanna protested that "it is very clear they [the Vatican] are saying that women are defiling the Eucharist in the same way as men have defiled the Eucharist by abusing children." A British woman attending the meeting protested that the identity of women religious in the U.K. desiring female ordination had to be kept secret to avoid Vatican punishment. "It feels like the Soviet Union," said one.

Defying the Vatican ban, Oliva Doko, seventy-one, was ordained a priest in 2006 and a bishop in 2010. "I am tired of men deciding that women cannot be ordained and blaming God for it," she told *Irish Independent* reporter Sarah MacDonald. A former priest from Australia, Paul Collins, of Catholics for Ministry & WATAC in Australia, said, "There is a ministerial revolution going on, and the hierarchical church doesn't even know."

During the final months of Benedict's papacy, he had Father Roy Bourgeois sacked because the priest had participated in the ordination of a woman (more on his case follows). Three months later a Jesuit priest in Wisconsin was similarly dismissed for having celebrated a liturgy with a woman who purported to be a Catholic priest. And in Rome a spokesman for the Redemptorist order confirmed to journalist Francis X. Rocca that one of its members was under Vatican investigation for alleged ambiguities "regarding fundamental areas of Catholic doctrine." The fundamental area in question was the question of women's ordination.

Inside the Vatican the situation has changed little since then.

An eminent Vatican theologian, Father Wojciech Giertych is today the official resident theologian in the papal household where Benedict XVI lives in retirement. Father Giertych's opinion matters, and it is that priests love the church in a characteristically "male way" when they show concern "about structures, about the buildings of the church, about the roof of the church which is leaking, about the bishops' conference." Although a Catholic woman may sincerely believe she is called to the priesthood, this subjective belief does not objectively indicate that she has a vocation. "Women don't need the priesthood because their mission is so beautiful in the church anyway." Why? Because they are better able than men to perceive the "proximity of God" and enter into a relationship with Him.[19]

Boston's presumably progressive Cardinal Seán O'Malley, who is considered close to Pope Francis, remains among those backing away from the notion of a female priesthood. Interviewed on the CBS-TV program *60 Minutes*, he made headlines all over the United States for saying that, were he to start a church, he would "love to have women priests. But Christ founded it, and what he has given us is something different."

But the women were not accepting this. In an open letter to O'Malley from the Women's Ordination Conference sent November 20, 2014, the sisters retorted that "thanks to the work of historians and theologians, including the Vatican's own Pontifical Biblical Commission in 1976 that concluded there is no theological basis to exclude women from the priesthood, we believe that Jesus did not ordain anyone, male or female, but actively sought out the companionship, conversation, and witness of women."

———

A website called www.womenpriests.org claims to be the largest academic website promoting women's ordination. "We are faithful Catholics who show why the exclusion of women from priesthood is wrong," it begins. Its academic advisers include ten theologians from universities and colleges in seven countries.

For some, the church has little choice but to cave in sooner or later. Former editor of the *Catholic Herald* Cristina Odone expressed the pragmatic view that "anyone who steps into a church can see that women make up the majority of the congregation." In Britain today, polls show that 60 percent of the male population does not believe in God, but two-thirds of the women say they do. This means that the pool of potential male priests continues to shrink rapidly, and not only in Britain; global polls show similar results.

"With the ever-surprising Pope Francis at the helm," she writes, "I suspect the Catholic Church has put this on the agenda. Maybe not today, not tomorrow, but soon the Catholic Church will realize that if they want the priesthood to continue, it has to throw its arms open to the one group that has stayed constant in its faith: women."[20]

Even in traditionally Catholic Ireland, attitudes have already changed. In a poll there of a thousand respondents, conducted by the respected survey organization Amaras, 77 percent said that the church should admit women to the priesthood.

In case the Vatican failed to get the message, on a bright spring day in March 2013, just as the conclave to elect a new pope to succeed Benedict XVI was under way, a group of women set off a flare of pink smoke on a hill overlooking the Vatican. In mimicking the smoke emerging twice daily (blackish for no pope elected yet, white to show one had been chosen), their point was to remind the all-male cardinals locked inside the Sistine Chapel of their conviction that women should be ordained.

The protest was organized by a number of groups including the Women's Ordination Conference, which is based in Washington, D.C. "The current old boys' club has left our Church reeling from scandal, abuse, sexism and oppression," conference director Erin Saiz Hanna told a Reuters reporter. "The people of the Church are desperate for a leader who will be open to dialogue and embrace the gifts of women's wisdom in every level of Church governance."[21] Most of the women with her were dressed in pink and wore ORDAIN WOMEN badges; one considered herself already ordained and wore the white vestment of a priest.

The pink smoke shooting up from Rome's Janiculum Hill followed on the heels of a pink smoke rally held in New Orleans the previous weekend and others in Washington, D.C.; Madison, Wisconsin; Chicago; San Francisco; and elsewhere. Participants included men as well as women. After each tiny pink smoke flare rose into the air, the demonstrators—in Washington they included one playing a guitar—prayed together and sang. The idea behind the demonstrations, which came to be called "Pink Smoke Rises," caught on in the United Kingdom and in Ireland as well.

The Women's Ordination Conference was first organized in 1975 and is the oldest such organization in the United States. Its chief aim is to allow women to be ordained, and it objects to their exclusion from the priesthood on the theological grounds that Christ had only men as his apostles. "It's unbelievable that there is no female voice in the hierarchy of such a massive institution," said Jeannette Mulherin, president of the conference. "The church is missing 50 percent of its voice. It's not inclusive or accountable."

A poll of U.S. Catholics suggested that a majority (59 percent) supported that position at the time of Pope Francis' election, according to the Catholic magazine *Sojourners*.

The adoption of pink smoke symbolizing women's claim to the priesthood was echoed in a documentary film called *Pink Smoke over the Vatican*, directed by Jules Hart and produced in 2011 by Eye Goddess Films of Carmel, California (Hart is its president). This documentary, with interviews with women ordained despite Vatican opposition, was voted Best Documentary at the Santa Fe Independent Film Festival and Best Faith-Based Film at the Action On Film International Film

Festival held in Monrovia, California. At the same festival, Hart, who had begun in cinema as a fashion model before studying film at UCLA, was named Best Female Filmmaker.

In the film, Father Roy Bourgeois, nominated for the Nobel Peace Prize in 2009, is among those interviewed by Hart. While in his twenties, Bourgeois, born in 1938 in Louisiana, had served in Vietnam as a naval officer for four years, and had been awarded a Purple Heart. On leaving the navy he was ordained a Maryknoll priest in 1972, and gradually became passionately opposed to U.S. foreign policy in Latin America. For his involvement in a nonviolent protest against the training of Latin American soldiers inside the U.S. Army base at Fort Benning, Georgia, he was sent to a U.S. federal prison for four years. Father Bourgeois subsequently became an advocate for women's religious rights, and following his participation in the ordination of a Catholic woman priest in 2008, he was ordered to recant or be excommunicated.

After a second canonical warning that he was expected to recant, he wrote a letter to the Maryknoll leadership on August 8, 2011, in which he spelled out his point of view:

> *I believe that our Church's teaching that excludes women from the priesthood defies both faith and reason and cannot stand up to scrutiny. This teaching has nothing to do with God, but with men, and is rooted in sexism. Sexism, like racism, is a sin. And no matter how hard we may try to justify discrimination against women, in the end, it is not the way of God, but of men who want to hold on to their power. As people of faith we believe in the primacy of conscience. Our conscience connects us to the Divine. Our conscience gives us a sense of right and wrong and urges us to do what is right, what is just.*
>
> *What you are asking me to do in your letter is not possible without betraying my conscience. In essence, you are telling me to lie and say I do not believe that God calls both men and women to the priesthood. This I cannot do, therefore I will not recant. I firmly believe*

*that the exclusion of women from the priesthood is a grave injustice
against women, against our Church, and against our God.*

On October 17, 2011, accompanied by a group of Catholic women
priests, Bourgeois came to Rome to try to deliver a petition to the pope.
Instead he was physically removed from the Vatican by its gendarmes,
and just one year later expelled ("canonically dismissed") from the
priesthood and from the Maryknoll Fathers and Brothers, even though
157 Catholic priests had signed a letter in support of his right to conscience without risk of sanctions.

Needless to say, he remains a popular figure on these issues—and
in December 2012 an editorial in the *National Catholic Reporter* came
out in staunch support of him and his campaign on behalf of women's
rights to ordination:

> *Bourgeois brings this issue to the real heart of the matter. He has said
> that no one can say who God can and cannot call to the priesthood,
> and to say that anatomy is somehow a barrier to God's ability to call
> one of God's own children forward places absurd limits on God's
> power. The majority of the faithful believe this.* [22]

Many believe that pink smoke is here to stay. In a recent demon-
stration in which young and older women, young men and male priests
participated, their homemade posters said:

• WE ARE CHURCH

• IN CHRIST THERE IS NO MALE OR FEMALE. WE ARE ONE.

• ORDAIN WOMEN

• PRIESTLY PEOPLE COME IN ALL GENDERS

• WOMEN DO PRIESTLY WORK. ORDAIN THEM.

And there are still other points of view, some subtle, some less so. For Dublin's powerful Archbishop Diarmuid Martin, under Pope Francis the church has shown itself to be more open about its failings on subjects like child abuse and a lack of compassion toward gays. Like the pope himself, Martin says that he favors women occupying a more prominent role in debates in the church. Already, he says, women carry out numerous pastoral tasks in Catholic churches, which include dispensing the Eucharist and handling administration where priests are stretched too thin across parishes.

But the archbishop hesitates about supporting women's ordination, saying that ordaining women is "not on the table at the moment." His hint at future change by using the words "at the moment" brought a protest from a grumpy Irish canon lawyer, who added the phrase "and they never will be."

———

To what extent is the pope listening? Does he see the pink smoke rising?

The question remains open. Although the pope has called for "a more incisive presence for women in the church," in the opinion of Robert McClory of the *National Catholic Reporter*, "I think most observers doubt that any serious scrutiny leading to resolution will occur during the pontificate of Pope Francis. He has indicated he does not wish to touch the hot buttons of Catholic doctrine."[22] Of these, says McClory, contraception is among the hottest; so, of course, is the question of women's ordination. Other experts explain that Pope Francis established as his priorities the failures of bishops behind the two almost overwhelming scandals he inherited upon his election, financial disarray, and clerical abuse of minors. For Francis, addressing these tough issues, as he has done, sufficed, even as he left cracks open for future debate.

If so, it means that the issue of women priests will remain in the background for the attention of his eventual successor. Still, the discussion is open, and Francis has not hidden it completely under the table.

4

Execrable Acts

It were better for him that a millstone were hanged about his neck, and he cast into the sea, than that he should offend one of these little ones.
—LUKE 17:2

The truth is the truth, and we must not hide it.
—POPE FRANCIS, NOVEMBER 25, 2014

More than a year passed before Pope Francis began to take action on the clerical sexual abuse scandals that had been festering within the Catholic Church for at least three decades. For years the Vatican had been in denial that serial acts of sexual abuse had been committed against children in many parts of the world by clerics of all ranks: cardinals, archbishops (including a papal nuncio, or ambassador), and bishops. And hundreds—if not thousands—of parish priests, lay workers, and even some nuns had been systematically abusing young boys and girls.

Pope Benedict had met in private with small groups of clerical abuse victims during several of his foreign visits—including one to the

United States in 2008—in order to apologize for the misdeeds of his clergy. But Pope Francis made no similar gesture during his first trip to Rio de Janeiro in July 2013.

In July 2014, Pope Francis invited to his home inside the Vatican six victims of priestly sexual abuse. To the two from Ireland, two from Germany, and two from the United Kingdom he made a heartfelt personal apology. "Before God and His people I express my sorrow for the sins and grave crimes of clerical sexual abuse committed against you," he said. "I humbly ask forgiveness."

Then, addressing the grave and longstanding accusations of official cover-up, he went on to say, "I beg your forgiveness, too, for the sins of omission on the part of church leaders who did not respond adequately to reports of abuse made by family members as well as by abuse victims themselves."

The apology could not have been more frank. He admitted that the church had been guilty of "complicity" in covering up what he called "despicable actions and grave sins." Members of the church should "weep before the execrable acts of abuse which have left life-long scars."

The pope invited the select six to join him for supper, morning mass, and breakfast. Then he spent an entire morning listening to their stories, one by one.

"It was pretty amazing," said Marie Kane, forty-three, a mother of two from Bray in County Wicklow in Ireland. "There were no time constraints on the meeting, and the only others in the room were Cardinal Seán O'Malley of Boston, who acted as translator, and Marie Collins [another Irish victim] who came to support me." The pope listened intently while Marie Kane recounted how she had been abused at the age of twelve by a cleric in the Dublin diocese. The priest was recycled by transfer to another parish in Ireland; he was not defrocked, she told the pope.

Then Kane courageously went on to attack the then–head of the church in Ireland. "Until people like Cardinal Sean Brady are gone, I will never believe that there is change in the church. Cover-ups are still happening. You have the power to make these changes."

That same month, Cardinal Brady tendered his resignation to Pope Francis, a month before his seventy-fifth birthday. By August 2014 his resignation had been formally accepted.

Marie Kane handed the pope three letters. One signed by Kane herself called upon the pope to sack bishops who mishandled or covered up cases of abuse, and pleaded for an end to compulsory priestly celibacy.

The other two letters were even more poignant. Written by her son and daughter, both letters told the pope how their mother's experiences had meant that they themselves had grown up without the benefits of Catholicism. The priest's crime had deeply harmed their mother's childhood, but had also compromised their own relationship to the church.

She later told RTE, the Irish national broadcaster, that she found Pope Francis "very, very humble. There was no standing on ceremony. No pomp. I felt very comfortable, relaxed. He seemed genuinely frustrated at what he was hearing. He listened and seemed genuine. There was a lot of empathy. There was no looking at watches. I was the one who ended it as I had said all I wanted to say."

This incident had taken place thirty-one years ago, in 1983. At that time priestly abuse was a dark secret, particularly in Ireland. The very idea was appalling. As a reporter I knew nothing of this until 1991, when I was awakened in the middle of the night by a telephone call from Halifax, Nova Scotia. An agitated local newspaper editor asked me for Vatican comment on reports in Canada of scandals concerning abuse of children by priests. The Canadian Catholic Church was in "total disarray," he said.

I explained to him that the Vatican did not function at night, but that I would check in the morning with its press officer. I did so, and was given the familiar Vatican formulaic reply in Italian: "Non risulta" (No evidence of this). The meaning was clear: we know nothing about this, and even if we did, we would have nothing to say to you.

The Vatican press officer may well have been better informed; the Canadian press had been fully reporting on that scandal for some time, and it also later transpired that systematic sexual abuse by clerics and lay workers had been known in Vatican circles for many years. From Canada came reports of decades of abuse of hundreds of children at the Mount Cashel Orphanage in St. John's in Newfoundland, which was run by the Irish Christian Brothers. That orphanage had been closed in 1990 and was later razed to the ground and sold to developers, to raise funds to compensate the victims. Between 1996 and 2004 the Newfoundland and Labrador government and the Canadian branch of the Christian Brothers of Ireland paid out some $27 million to compensate the victims of physical and sexual abuse at that orphanage.

The press spokesman with whom I spoke that morning in 1991 was not the only one to feign ignorance. In 1984, Pope John Paul II, now St. John Paul, received a forty-two-page detailed confidential report on a sex abuse and cover-up case in Lafayette, Louisiana.

Although this had already been going on for literally decades, the report, as is known only now, brought it directly to the attention of the pope.

That report was hand carried to Rome by a deeply concerned Cardinal John Krol of Philadelphia, known to be an intimate friend of the Polish pontiff; his nickname in Philadelphia was "Krol the Pole." The pope's sole response was to appoint Bishop A. J. Quinn of Cleveland, Ohio, to look into the matter. Bishop Quinn visited the town of Lafayette twice but failed to take any action, according to Father Thomas Doyle, speaking at the SNAP 25th anniversary convention in Chicago on August 2, 2014.[1] Father Doyle, a former Dominican priest, had worked in the office of the nuncio to Washington in the 1980s and, as such, had access to confidential reports, like that of the abuse scandal and cover-up in Lafayette in 1984. In 2004, Doyle was quietly removed from a subsequent post as air force chaplain in Germany following a clash with his archbishop over "pastoral issues."

By 2002, clerical sexual abuse scandals had nevertheless surfaced in the U.S. media, and as if all at once. It was later learned that even before this, the American Bishops Conference had discussed the question during their annual meetings, but in complete secrecy; a case in Milwaukee, which would later become notorious, was known in the early 1970s. But even as late as 2002, care for the victims was not yet a concern; the U.S. media showed outrage and sympathy for the victims, but for the bishops, what mattered was still solely damage limitation.

Back in 1993, Pope John Paul II had written a letter to the U.S. bishops exclaiming dramatically, in a biblical quotation, "Woe to the world because of scandals." The sense was to blame an irresponsible mass media for sensationalism; if so the remedy, said the pope, was that "America needs more prayer." He later declared that this was "fundamentally an American problem."

That same year the bishops formed a committee that issued a four-volume handbook of guidelines that, to the extent that they addressed the problem, had no appreciable effect upon it.

However, Doyle and his colleagues warned the bishops that abuse allegations could cost the Catholic Church $1 billion over ten years unless it took urgent action. By 2012, nearly two decades later, the church in fact had spent over $2.6 billion in civil suits. The payments included therapy costs for victims and lawyers' fees, according to the U.S. bishops conference.

John Paul was not entirely oblivious to the problem: in 1995, he had fired the head of the Roman Catholic Church in Austria, Cardinal Hans Hermann Groër, after allegations that Groër had molested students at an all-male Catholic high school. But this appeared an isolated case; and by the time the full scandals actually broke after 2002, Pope John Paul was seriously ill in Rome. Given his poor health, his aides may have chosen to keep the gravity of the damage to the church hidden from him. In fact, during the celebrations of John Paul's canonization in 2014, his former press secretary Joaquín Navarro-Valls candidly admitted at a Vatican news conference, "I do not think Pope John Paul understood the 'cancer' of clergy sexual abuse immediately. I don't think anyone did."

One reason why Pope John Paul may have missed the point was the lack of reliable statistics about the pedophile priest problem. From 2002 through 2012—the apex of media attention to the scandals—Bishop Charles Scicluna from Malta was serving as the church's chief investigator and prosecutor for serious crimes (*delicta graviora*, in churchspeak), with the official title of promoter of justice for the congregation of the doctrine of the faith. As such, pedophile priests were his primary concern.

How great was the problem? Pope Francis, in the course of an interview in July 2014 with Eugenio Scalfari, editor-in-chief of *La Repubblica* newspaper, said that priestly pedophilia was a "leprosy" within the church, but that, in his opinion, it involved worldwide no more than 2 percent. "That 2 percent includes priests and even bishops and cardinals," the pope acknowledged. He intended to "confront it with the severity it demands," he said.

Before this three-page interview appeared in print, however, Scalfari had admitted that during his interviews with the pope he had made no notes. As a result Vatican spin doctors argued that perhaps he had misquoted the pontiff. Father Federico Lombardi, the pope's chief spokesman, said that Pope Francis had never checked the accuracy of the interview.

In his own interview in July 2014 with that same Italian daily, watchdog Bishop Scicluna acknowledged that "in the Vatican we never made statistical studies, even though we had examined and made decisions over hundreds of cases." Such statistics as are available come normally only from developed countries. Information from Africa and Latin America is usually only sketchy.

Nevertheless, the U.S. bishops had commissioned their own report a full decade before this. The John Jay Report of 2004, covering the period from 1950 to 2002, showed that, out of 109,604 American Catholic priests, 4,392, or about 4 percent, had been accused of various crimes of sexual abuse against minors—that is, generally those under the age of eighteen. Of those accused, only 252 were convicted in a court of law. Given that this covered a half century, many of the accused had already died before they could be tried, but one hundred actually were sent to prison.

In Australia, the chief executive of the Truth, Justice and Healing Council, a national church committee, said that he believed the figures were historically higher than the pope's estimate. In the committee's view the Australian clergy had been deeply involved in schools and orphanages. The council has compiled a database of clergy abuse dating back to the 1940s. Its preliminary work suggests that the number of perpetrators is about 4 percent, the same figure estimated by the John Jay Report in the United States.

The efforts to develop statistical studies raise the question of exactly how priestly abuse is to be defined. Some psychologists distinguish between epheberasty and pederasty, between a sexual relationship involving priests and teenage seminarians, and the abuse of very young boys and girls. For the John Jay Report, sexual abuse "includes contacts or interactions between a child and an adult when the child is being used as an object of sexual gratification for the adult." One out of five was under age ten, said the report, and four victims were only one year old. Most were between seven and fifteen, with a peak at age twelve. Of the abusers, half were thirty-five years old or younger.

In fairness, at the time many believed that psychological counseling could and would resolve the problem. Priests were therefore given counseling, and then shuffled to a new parish—and new occasions of sin.

———

The epicenter of scandal in the United States was in the Boston diocese, which vaunts two million Catholics. In 2001, Cardinal Archbishop Bernard Law admitted that as long ago as 1984 a bishop had warned him that one of his priests, Rev. John Geoghan, was a child molester. As was a frequent church solution at that time, Law had Geoghan transferred to another parish despite the allegations.

Charges were brought against Geoghan for indecent assault and battery on a boy of ten. In January 2002, Cardinal Law made a formal apology to victims of abuse and later offered his resignation, which Pope John Paul II initially rejected. After Cardinal Law was subpoenaed by a grand jury investigating "possible criminal violations by church officials who supervised priests accused of sexually abusing children," fifty-eight priests signed a petition requesting Law's resignation. On December 13, 2002, he resigned—and was transferred by the Vatican to become the archpriest of the Basilica of St. Mary Major, one of Rome's most venerable ancient churches and a church particularly beloved by Pope Francis. Law was formally retired only in 2011.

In a crescendo of horror, other notorious cases came flooding into the Vatican, to land upon the desks of prosecutor Scicluna and his boss, Cardinal Ratzinger, who headed the Vatican's Congregation for the Doctrine of the Faith before his elevation to the papacy as Benedict XVI.

Among the most devastating was the case of Father Marcial Maciel, a Mexican who founded the Legion of Christ, a congregation of priests and seminarians, in 1941. The congregation extended into almost two dozen countries and recruited seventy thousand lay members. Maciel was a frequent visitor to the Vatican and a generous contributor to Vatican funds, arriving with fat envelopes of dollars. He enjoyed the favor of Pope John Paul II until press reports revealed that Maciel was abusing minors. The pope opened an investigation that revealed that, besides abusing children, Maciel also had two secret wives and had fathered at least three children, and perhaps more.

In formerly staunchly Catholic Ireland, a literally stunning report on sexual abuse issued in 2009 spoke of 14,500 child victims. One Irish priest admitted to sexually abusing more then one hundred children; another, that he had been abusing children for over twenty-five years.[2] The majority were between the ages of eleven and fourteen, but some of the child victims were as young as three.

Nuns too were shown to have been involved, and discredited for child abuse, but not only that: the film *The Magdalene Sisters* about the exploitation of unwed mothers forced to work as if slaves in a laundry set up for "fallen women" was shown in Irish cinemas in 2002. When I personally attended a showing in Dublin that year, the audience remained in dead silence for long minutes at the end of the film before slipping out, still silently.

Some within the church hierarchy in Ireland argued that media coverage was "excessive and disproportionate," but the shock was so great that attendance at mass slumped radically. Graffiti appeared on walls showing a priest chasing young children.

In Northern Ireland, some thirteen former children's homes run by the church became the subject of an official government inquiry. Individuals in their sixties and seventies who had refrained from speaking out for decades came forward to reveal horrific details of abuse. "I waited sixty-five years to speak out," said an individual known only as "10B," who testified that he had received regular beatings. In hopes of defending himself from sexual assault, he would urinate in his bed, he said.

"I was reared by the Sisters of the Congregation of Nazareth in Londonderry. It was the equivalent of being reared by the Taliban, such was their sadism, lack of empathy, fundamentalism, and their lack of dignity." After leaving the home, he tried to complain to a priest about this, but was told, "You must never speak about this.... You are the product of an evil and satanic relationship."

"That was the day I left the Catholic Church," he told the commission of inquiry.[3]

In Scotland, Cardinal Keith O'Brien, the newly retired head of the Roman Catholic Church there, was publicly outed in the London *Observer* by three priests and one former priest from the Archdiocese of St. Andrews and Edinburgh. In their article, the priests complained that O'Brien was "a sexual predator" who used his authority to compel the priests themselves into "coercive and abusive sexual relationships." This was not child abuse—it was a homosexual relationship—but it was still abusive. O'Brien admitted his guilt and resigned in February 2013, only one month before he was due in Rome to take part in the conclave that elected Pope Francis.

In the late 1990s, the Catholic Church in England and Wales faced a spate of cases of clerical sexual abuse. By comparison with what was happening elsewhere, Cardinal Cormac Murphy-O'Connor, archbishop of Westminster, took unusually decisive action. He commissioned Lord Nolan, a distinguished judge in the court of appeal in London who also chaired a parliamentary committee on standards in public life, to conduct a review of the measures taken by the church to prevent clerical sexual abuse of children. Lord Nolan, a devout Catholic himself, worked for a year to draw up guidelines, which church authorities then made mandatory in England and Wales.

By 2001, the church had also set up a national commission to protect children, which subsequently led to the defrocking of fifty-two priests over the following decade. Said Danny Sullivan, chairman of the National Catholic Safeguarding Commission (NCSC), "For eleven years now we have made it clear that if anyone comes forward with allegations, either current or from the past, we shall automatically refer [him] to the statutory authorities"—i.e., to the police. In 2010, no fewer than ninety-two clergymen were denounced. According to Sullivan, the rise in the figure at that time may have reflected the publicity surrounding the 2010 meeting of Pope Benedict with clerical sex abuse survivors during his visit to the United Kingdom.

Overall, between 2003 and 2012 there were 598 accusations of abuse reported by dioceses and religious congregations that were cooperating with the authorities in England and Wales. Peter Saunders, chief executive of the National Association for People Abused in Childhood, said that his association was pleased at the increase in the number of clerical abusers who had been defrocked. (Saunders was later chosen by Pope Francis to serve on his Vatican committee for the protection of minors.)

But Ann Lawrence, former chairperson of another organization, Minister and Clergy, Sex Abuse Survivors, disagreed. Said Lawrence: "These figures represent only the tip of the iceberg." Nothing within the Catholic Church system encourages people to come forward at a higher rate than the national average, she said. "There is evidence that it is probably harder to speak out if you are from a Catholic background."

Slightly more than 60 percent of Germans consider themselves Christians; of these, half are Catholics and the other half, Lutherans. In January 2013, a two-year-old nationwide investigation into clerical abuse in the German Catholic Church was dropped after the bishops' conference refused to make documents available, out of fear that information on clergy could enter the public domain. Their fears are not surprising: when the church set up a sexual abuse hotline in 2010, it received almost twenty-seven hundred calls in just three days.

An important factor here is that Germans pay a church tax between 8 percent and 9 percent in different states, but can legally avoid it by stating they belong to no church. In 2011, Catholic Church income from that tax was €4.9 billion ($5.5 billion) and accounted for 70 percent of church revenue. During the first half of 2014, there was a flight from the Catholic churches; in predominantly Catholic Bavaria, 14,800 left between January and June, four times the number who left the previous year, bringing a reduction in church income. The sex abuse scandals were among the main causes.

In Belgium, Monsignor Roger Vangheluwe, the bishop of Bruges, was obliged to resign in 2010 after acknowledging that he had sexually abused two of his own nephews, one of them only eleven years old at the time. Pope Benedict XVI accepted his resignation. He was not defrocked. His immediate superior was Cardinal Godfried Danneels, archbishop of Brussels from 1979 to 2010. During a police search for evidence, police found in Danneels' residence 450 secret church files containing reports of abuse. The files had been submitted to an internal church investigating commission.

The Catholic Church in the Netherlands was the object of an official government inquiry in 2011. Their report declared that between 1945 and 2010, "tens of thousands" of minors had been abused within church institutions, and identified some eight hundred clerics suspected of abuse.

Allegations of sex crimes committed by Catholic priests and members of religious orders began to surface in Australia in the 1990s. Exactly as they had in the United States and in Europe, victims' associations were formed and expressed concern at what they saw as the ongoing cover-up and the failure of bishops to prevent the transfer of culpable priests to other parishes where they had opportunities for further abuse. "It is widespread," said Kevin Carson, a police officer in Victoria. Carson also gave details of the suicides of at least forty individuals abused by Catholic clergy.[4] "The church has known about a shockingly high rate of suicides and premature deaths, but has chosen to remain silent."

His formal police report published in 2012 revealed that most of the victims were abused between the 1960s and late 1980s. "Many, many victims have met troubled lives—marriage breakups, abuse of alcohol and drugs and endless contact with police."

Helen Watson, whose son Peter was fifteen when he was sexually abused by a Catholic priest in Ararat, said the abuse sent her son on a "path of self-destruction" that ended when he took his life at age twenty-four. "The priest would take those young boys, give them alcohol and watch movies" before abusing them, she said.

As a result of this and other such reports, in January 2013 the Australian government set up a six-member Royal Commission into Institutional Responses to Child Abuse. Hearings were scheduled in every regional capital in the country.

Although 150 cases of clerical pedophilia were brought before courts in Italy in recent years, Italy has not emulated Australia, the United Kingdom, and the other countries that have created national investigatory bodies, as journalist Federico Tulli of the daily *Corriere della Sera* has pointed out. The weekly *L'Espresso* went so far as to publish a map with bright red dots showing the venues of the court cases, from Bressanone in the Northern Alps to Trapani on the remote corner of Sicily.

In 2012, the secretary of the Italian bishops' conference, Monsignor Mariano Crociata, nevertheless defended the church position in these mushy words: "You can't expect a bishop to become a public official, we cannot ask him to take the initiative" in denouncing cases of abuse of minors. A bishop is not hindered from so doing, but it is in contrast with church regulations, Monsignor Crociata went on to say, especially if the seal of confession is involved. The CEI itself acknowledged that between 2000 and 2011 there were 135 cases brought before Italian courts. Forty-three convictions resulted; twenty-one plea bargained; a dozen cases were dismissed and there were five acquittals.

The Italian website http://pretipedofili.it has published what it says is an incomplete list of known cases from 2000 onward, with one hundred names. Among the most recent are these three:

- Father Paolo Turturro from Palermo, Sicily, who became famous for his anti-Mafia activities, began serving a three-year prison sentence in November 2014 after a thirteen-year court inquiry. He has never been defrocked.

- Father Maks Suard, a Slovenian priest working in a parish in Trieste, near the border with Slovenia in northeast Italy, hanged himself in 2014 after he was accused of having abused a thirteen-year-old girl seventeen years previously. His bishop discovered the body.

- Sister Carmen Soledad Bazan Verde was a Peruvian nun who worked in an elementary school in Lucania in Southern Italy, and was sentenced by a lower court to eight years in prison for having abused very young children in her care. Before a full conviction, she was magically repatriated to Peru, renounced her vows, and left her order. Her return to Italy for further legal action does not appear likely.

Many Italian priests accused of sexual crimes obtain lenient sentences through plea bargaining. Many others dodge Italian justice because the Concordat (the 1929 legal treaty that governs relations between church and state in Italy) offers a loophole that is often invoked to protect Italian clergy from prying prosecutors.

Cases of clerical sexual abuse in the United States were particularly costly to the church there, not only in terms of credibility, but also in cash. Expensive litigation inflated the notoriety of the cases, and left fourteen dioceses and several religious orders bankrupt. Three of the dioceses declared bankruptcy after the election of Pope Francis. The

$2.6 billion paid in compensation impoverished the Catholic Church for years to come.

The legal tactics employed by the church to minimize liabilities have come under attack by canon lawyers as well as by victims' associations. There has been systematic minimization of assets "in bad faith," according to John Manly, a devoutly Catholic lawyer from Southern California who has been battling the Catholic Church for over a decade.

"I was raised Catholic, I went to Catholic military school, then a Catholic college for a year. I had a Jesuit spiritual director. I considered the priesthood," he told a national TV audience in 2013.[5] "In the last twelve years I have met and represented hundreds of people, from Alaska to New York, Delaware to Southern California. All tell the same story: that they were raped and/or abused in the most violent and egregious way possible as a child; and that when the church learned of it, they did nothing.

"When the church defends these cases, they don't defend it in a way that is consistent with their own theology and beliefs. All the values they say they believe in really go out the window."

Often assets worth billions of dollars are never declared by the church, he said in the same interview. "They claim they 'forgot' or it was an 'oversight,'" said Manly. "Even in the middle of a bankruptcy they [the church] will move money."

Indeed, Cardinal Timothy Dolan, who is now archbishop of New York and formerly of Milwaukee, attempted to protect local church funds in Milwaukee by shifting over $50 million of church funds into a so-called "Cemetery Account." The effect of his controversial transfer of funds made the money unavailable for the settling of victims' claims.

And there were victims, including in Milwaukee itself. One of the most heinous of the American cases regarded the late Father Lawrence C. Murphy, who has been accused of abusing two hundred boys in the St. John School for the Deaf, a Milwaukee residential home that housed children as young as five. Church documents obtained by the *New York Times* in 2010 showed that three successive archbishops in Wisconsin were informed that Father Murphy had sexually abused children between 1959 and 1974. The incidents were known to local law enforcement agencies, but doubts about the credibility of the accusers permitted the allegations to be overlooked and, in the end, canceled by the statute of limitations. When Rembert Weakland became archbishop of Milwaukee in 1977, Father Murphy was disallowed from saying mass, but did not retire as a priest until late 1993.

In Los Angeles, Rita Milla, who first told her story almost a quarter century ago, received five hundred thousand dollars in compensation for being allegedly raped over time by seven Roman Catholic priests while a teenager. "It was horrible because that was my whole identity," Milla, who sang in the church choir and hoped to become a nun, told the court. The physical advances began in the confessional, where the screen was broken. Later, when she asked church leaders for help, "I felt dismissed—as if God were hanging up the phone on me." When she became pregnant, a priest advised her to have an abortion, she said. Instead she chose to have the child.

Altogether in the year 2007, the Archdiocese of Los Angeles had to make a $660 million settlement for Milla and 507 other victims of abuse.

According to the U.S. Bishops Conference, between 1950 and 2012 nearly seventeen thousand individuals came forward to say that they had been abused by priests as children. Senior church officials say that the abuse crisis is now winding down: "The peak of the curve is not moving forward or broadening as time goes on," Al Notzon III told the bishops' conference in 2012. Notzon is the lay chairman who heads the National Review Board, a child abuse oversight commission created by the bishops.

Advocates of victims disagree. They say that it is too soon to be able to determine whether or not the crisis is subsiding because most victims do not report the incidents until they are adult or even elderly. Either way, hundreds of new allegations continue to pour in every year, according to Patrick Wall, a former priest who now acts as a victims' attorney.

———

During all these decades, what mattered for the church was its reputation and the protection of its bishops and priests. This provided the moral justification for smothering the complaints from the victims.

That there was a cover-up in the United States is made clear by Father Thomas Doyle, whose account is of particular importance because he had been privy to all the correspondence between the Vatican and Archbishop Pio Laghi, who was the papal ambassador to the United States. Recalling this in April 2014, Father Doyle specifically named Cardinals Bernard Law, and Roger Mahony of Los Angeles as part of the cover-up. He also heavily criticized Pope John Paul II for his repeated failure to take action.

Other than making nine recorded public statements, all of which were sufficiently nuanced as to be innocuous, and calling a meeting of the U.S. cardinals to tell them what everyone already knew, he did nothing positive. He promoted the careers of some bishops and cardinals who intentionally inflicted horrendous damage on victims and expended vast amounts of donated money to stonewall the process of justice.

John Paul, said Doyle, had completely ignored the pleas of thousands of victims. Many had written to the pontiff: "Victims and victims' groups bombarded the Vatican with letters and requested audiences." Not only were their requests ignored, but no reply of any kind was ever received, said Doyle.

"The sexual abuse scandal of our era has been the Catholic Church's worst nightmare, and it has been going on for thirty years. The spectrum of large numbers of priests, bishops and even cardinals sexually violat-

ing children, one of the vilest crimes imaginable, challenges the capacity
to grasp the enormity of such evil. Yet it not only happened, but it was
enabled by those who have professed to follow the Gospel and lead others on the same path."

As the victims' association had said, this was only the tip of the
iceberg, and statistics were finally making it clear.

In February 2013, just one month before the conclave, for the
Congregation for the Doctrine of the Faith (CDF), Monsignor Oliver
presented the first detailed statistical account ever made revealing the
number of priests who had been accused of sexual abuse. The year 2004
was particularly serious, with eight hundred cases being investigated.
From 2010 to 2013, the average was six hundred cases a year; the majority referred to acts of abuse committed decades previously, from 1965
to 1985.

At about the same time, again on the eve of the conclave, the U.S.
victims' advocacy association SNAP issued a list of a dozen American
cardinals who, they said, should be excluded from the election "out
of respect for the victims." These cardinals had failed to report to the
authorities those responsible "and had tried to justify the abusive priests
by willfully disregarding documentary evidence."

The Vatican could hardly ignore such an avalanche of accusations.
Seven months after Pope Benedict resigned in 2013, he made a rare public comment in a defensive letter written to a prominent Italian math-
ematician, Piergiorgio Odifreddi, a noted atheist, and published in *La
Repubblica* newspaper. In the letter, which Odifreddi said came "out of
the blue," the former pope denied that he had ever suppressed the investigation of pedophile priests. "I never tried to cover up these things," he
wrote. In fact, between 2011 and 2012, Pope Benedict ordered that four
hundred priests be defrocked; already he had dispatched four hundred.

In his letter to Odifreddi, Benedict also said, "That the power of evil
penetrated so far into the interior world of the faith is a suffering that

we must bear and at the same time must do everything to prevent its repetition." However, as he went on to say:

> *It is no reason for comfort to know that sociological research shows that the percentage of priests guilty of these crimes is no higher than in other professional categories. In any event, one must not stubbornly present this deviance as if it were a nastiness specific to Catholicism.*[6]

Not surprisingly, the flood of information about pedophile victims, and not only those who have suffered at the hands of priests, drew the attention of psychiatrists and social workers to consider and analyze possible causes. On January 14, 2013, the *Los Angeles Times* published a particularly well-researched synthesis of recent laboratory studies, written by prize-winning journalist Alan Zarembo, an investigative reporter who specializes in writing about medicine and science. The *Times* gave Zarembo this in-depth assignment because, as it was learned, the Los Angeles diocese had enacted one of the most extensive cover-ups, which had come fully to light only after the departure of Archbishop Roger Mahony in 2011 under a very dark cloud. That very month, in January 2013, Mahony's successor was obliged by court order to release the complete secret "and un-redacted" archdiocese archive on molesters. These documents then came into the public domain and provided the most detailed account ever made of clerical abuse and the cover-ups in the United States.

For the diocese, the embarrassment was the greater because the brand-new Los Angeles Cathedral of Our Lady of the Angels had created a special chapel devoted to pedophile victims. In it, a giant wooden cross, at least eight feet long, was plastered with the photographs of victims, including many young children. The hypocrisy of this chapel vis-à-vis the Mahony cover-up was all the more evident. As a result of all this, Catholics in downtown Los Angeles collected nearly ten thousand signatures requesting that Mahony, who was still a cardinal, be excluded from participation in the March 2013 conclave in the Vatican.

Ignoring the petition, Mahony refused, and took part in the conclave that elected Pope Francis.

From Zarembo's report:

> *The best estimates are that between 1 percent and 5 percent of men are pedophiles, meaning that they have a dominant attraction to prepubescent children.*
>
> *Not all pedophiles molest children. Nor are all child molesters pedophiles. Studies show that about half of all molesters are not sexually attracted to their victims. They often have personality disorders or violent streaks, and their victims are typically family members.*
>
> *By contrast, pedophiles tend to think of children as romantic partners and look beyond immediate relatives. They include chronic abusers familiar from the headlines—Catholic priests, coaches and generations of Boy Scout leaders.*

Others, Zarembo wrote, quoting Dr. Fred Berlin, a psychiatrist who heads the Johns Hopkins Sexual Behaviors Consultation Unit, are "good people who are struggling . . . tortured souls fighting like heck not to do this. We do virtually nothing in terms of reaching out to these folks. We drive it underground."

Some of today's researchers dismiss the oft-heard view that abusers were themselves victims as children, according to the Center of Mental Health and Addiction in Toronto. Instead the Toronto researchers believe that pedophilia has deep biological roots from birth that later show the involvement of neural responses in the brain.[7]

Other experts remind us that shame afflicts both victim and abuser, and this drives the problem into deepest secrecy. According to a psychiatrist working with convicted sex criminals in a U.S. prison, "They need careful psychological help—and they don't get it. And when they don't, they leave prison and begin again."

The *Los Angeles Times* points out that in Germany, seventeen hundred men responded to billboard advertisements that urged them to contact the Institute of Sexology and Sexual Medicine in Berlin. About half of those assessed admitted to having molested a child. A one-year program was set up to help them try to control their impulses. "The program could not be conducted in the U.S. and some other countries because clinicians and others are required by law to notify authorities if they suspect a child has been or could be harmed," according to Zarembo.[8]

In England the scandal about BBC comedian Jimmy Savile, whose child molestation was kept secret by the BBC itself for decades, unleashed a firestorm when the case became public knowledge in 2012. There were also attempts to understand the root causes. In its analysis, *The Guardian* made a distinction between actual pedophilia and attraction to adolescents: "Savile appears to have been primarily an ephebophile, defined as someone who has a similar preferential attraction to adolescents, though there have been claims one of his victims was aged eight."

Few agree about its causes: is pedophilia innate or acquired? Both Canadian and Harvard researchers formerly suggested that "pedophilia should probably be classified as a distinct sexual orientation, like heterosexuality or homosexuality," wrote *The Guardian* reporter Jon Henley.[9]

Not everyone agreed with that. Donald Findlater is director of research and development at the Lucy Faithfull Foundation, a charity dedicated to protecting children. "There may be some vulnerabilities that could be genetic, but normally there are some significant events in a person's life, a sexually abusive event, a bullying environment. . . . I believe it is learned, and can be unlearned," he told *The Guardian.*

Chris Wilson of Circles UK, which helps convicted offenders after their release from prison, also rejects the idea that pedophilia is a sexual orientation: "The roots of that desire for sex with a child lie in dysfunctional psychological issues to do with power, control, anger, emotional loneliness, isolation." [10]

Within the Catholic Church there may also be both other causes and particular systems of self-justification. The official church culture is that the church itself is inspired by God, and in some cases this conviction may serve to legitimize or justify the sacrifice of innocent victims. There is also the conviction that priests are different from laypeople. In turn, the laypeople, particularly adolescents of both sexes, may tend to be submissive when faced with a man or woman of God.

Within the church there were few good examples of dealing with such a difficult problem. Many a bishop, faced with the certainty of scandal on his watch, suggested a period of psychological counseling for the guilty priest, or had him transferred elsewhere on the assumption that, in this way, the priest would be removed from the individual who had attracted his attention. Most bishops themselves had more fear than knowledge of the problem, and literally no one to whom they could turn for advice.

An exception was Diarmuid Martin, who became the archbishop of Dublin in 2004. Martin, who had a distinguished career in Vatican diplomacy and was former Vatican representative at the United Nations in Geneva, is credited with having dealt effectively with the disastrous situation he found in his diocese. "The sexual abuse crisis in the church is not a chapter of past history," he said during a speech in Rome in 2014, but "can and still does take place."

———

This was the calamitous heritage awaiting Pope Francis.

Jorge Bergoglio ran Argentina's largest diocese, Buenos Aires, a megacity of thirteen million people, between 1992 and 2013, during a period when thousands of victims worldwide were stepping forward to report their abuse.

"In my diocese it never happened to me," he wrote in *On Heaven and Earth*, published originally in Spanish in 2010 and translated into English for the Image Division of Random House in 2013. The book, written in Argentina three years before his election as pope, is a wide-ranging collection of conversations with his close friend Argentine Rabbi Abraham Skorka.

"A bishop once phoned me to ask what to do in a situation like this. I told him to suspend the priest," Bergoglio added. Elsewhere in that book he stated that "the problem is not linked to celibacy. If a priest is a pedophile, he is a pedophile before he is a priest."[11]

Otherwise before becoming pope he showed little sign of recognizing the existence of clerical sexual abuse. According to the respected U.S.-based watchdog website www.bishop-accountability.org, the then-archbishop's claim of its "never" happening to him is "implausible." Their estimate, based on comparative figures in the United States and Europe, is that on his watch more than one hundred diocesan priests from Buenos Aires committed sexual crimes against children.

Whether or not this is guesswork, Bergoglio is known to have been personally involved in dealing with five specific cases. In all of these he declined to meet with victims. Even after Bergoglio was elected pope, the Argentine Bishops Conference has never issued a public statement on the question, according to www.bishop-accountability.org. Various Argentine bishops and religious superiors have sided publicly with convicted sex offenders, using threats and gag orders to silence victims. Priests who have been accused remain in their ministry; the Argentine bishops have no legal obligation to report to the police most incidents of child sexual abuse by priests and have argued in court that parents are to blame for their children's sexual assaults by priests.[12]

The problems were only in waiting. Pope Francis had been in office barely five months when he was faced with a particularly difficult situation. It involved the Vatican nuncio, or ambassador, to the Dominican Republic, Polish Archbishop Józef Wesolowski. In his midsixties, Wesolowski was filmed by a local TV crew in Santo Domingo cruising for boys in a notorious seafront pickup spot. Prosecutors in the Dominican Republic said they had convincing evidence that the prelate molested young men there, and he has also been accused of abuse in Poland.

Both Poland and Santo Domingo demanded his extradition, but he was already in Rome; instead of agreeing upon this, Wesolowski was belatedly put under house arrest in the Vatican. His trial before the Vatican's own criminal court on charges of sexual misconduct while he was ambassador of the Holy See began in July 2015. He faces separate charges of hiding child pornography in his computer while Vatican prosecutors decided how to deal with this embarrassing case.

Pope Francis is the first pope to introduce specific legislation allowing the Vatican to put accused priests on trial in its own court. Wesolowski, who had been ordained as a priest by Pope John Paul II, remains the highest-ranking Vatican official to be investigated for sex abuse, and risks up to ten years imprisonment.

Perhaps the worst known case of serial sexual abuse in Italy came to light in Verona in 2009, when a church-run school for the deaf was revealed as a hotbed of abuse. Eighty-seven former pupils accused twenty-four priests, brothers, and lay religious there. One former pupil claimed that he had been sodomized twenty years before this so many times that he came to feel "as if I were dead." Although the local bishop set up a commission of inquiry, no church action was taken. Fourteen of the accused priests are still alive; legal action had been considered, but the cases were dismissed on grounds that the statute of limitations had expired.

In January 2014, a group of former pupils wrote a letter to Pope Francis to ask him to intervene, but by year's end had received no reply.

At the general assembly of the Italian bishops' conference held in Assisi in 2014, their final communique stressed that accused priests must not "feel themselves abandoned to themselves." This suggests that the Italian bishops continue to give priority to their own rather than consider the needs of the victims, and that Pope Francis' message has not been fully grasped. In November 2013 the pope had denounced "the corrupt"—those who lived "double lives" and brought scandal to the church. In a colorful biblical reference, he quoted the words of Jesus about scandal: "It would be better for him if a millstone were put around his neck and he be thrown into the sea, than that he should scandalize one of these little ones." The double life of a Christian causes great harm, he concluded.

———

Following his election a full year passed before Pope Francis made his first public plea for forgiveness for the "evil" committed by priests who molested children, and in March 2014, Pope Francis finally set up a Pontifical Commission for the Protection of Minors, headed by Cardinal Seán O'Malley of Boston, who was also a member of the pontiff's kitchen cabinet. Among the commission's eight members were Marie Collins, an Irishwoman of sixty-seven, who had been abused by a prison chaplain at age thirteen while she was in the hospital in 1960. Father Paul McGennis had also taken lewd photographs of her.

For decades afterward, she has battled depression and was in and out of psychiatric hospitals. When she finally summoned the courage to report the abuse, her pastor told her it was her own fault. "I disintegrated into a thousand pieces. I did not speak to anyone for ten years," she has said.

In 1997 McGennis was removed from the priesthood. When civil authorities eventually prosecuted him, he was sentenced in two other cases of molesting children, and sent to prison.

In my own interview with Marie Collins in 2012, before Francis was elected, she was in Rome to speak at a symposium on clerical abuse held at the Gregorian University, the elite Jesuit-run pontifical academy. "I was surprised at the lack of knowledge that they [the Vatican] had—the effects on a life, that this can harm a person for a long time afterward. But having a real person in front of you telling a personal story does make a difference, I think.

"The church has not come to it easily, but it looks as if it may be moving forward. I have great hope that there will be no more silence, that the child will come first. The church moves slowly, and it is hard to trust them again after what we all have seen in the past."

As a sign of the new times, two other members of the commission created by Pope Francis were women: Baroness Sheila Hollins, former president of Britain's Royal College of Psychiatrists, and Hanna Suchocka, former Polish prime minister, justice minister, and experienced ambassador to the Holy See.

The following month the pope told members of the Paris-based International Catholic Child Bureau: "I feel compelled to take on personally all the evil that some priests—quite a few in number although obviously not compared to all the priests—to ask forgiveness personally for all the damage they have done."[13]

The damage was ever more out in the open, but efforts to sweep it under the carpet continued. In February 2014, the Vatican came under international pressure to take action over sex abuse allegations, this time from the United Nations, where it enjoys observer status. A UN human rights committee based in Geneva accused the Vatican of systematically adopting policies that allowed priests to rape and molest tens of thousands of children over decades. The UN demanded that the Vatican open its files on both pedophile priests and on those bishops who concealed the crimes.

Through its diplomatic mission to Geneva, the Vatican objected, arguing that although the Holy See was a signatory to the UN convention on the rights of the child, which it had ratified in 1990, it does not control either bishops or abusive priests. Archbishop Silvano Tomasi, the Vatican's UN representative in Geneva, declared on Vatican Radio that the UN report was "distorted, unfair and ideologically based." NGOs that favor gay marriage, he said, had probably influenced the UN committee in order to reinforce an "ideological" underpinning of the committee on the rights of the child.

The condemnations kept pouring in. A second United Nations torpedo arrived in May 2014, just three months later. The UN Committee against Torture demanded that the Holy See take "effective measures" to monitor individuals under its "effective control," and to desist from conduct that would violate the UN Convention against Torture. The long-standing argument, advanced under Benedict's secretary of state, Cardinal Tarcisio Bertone, was that the Holy See exercises control over only the one-square-mile territory of the Vatican State, and therefore cannot be held accountable for "the actions of Catholic priests and bishops throughout the world." The panel of ten experts rejected this argument.

To the Royal Commission investigating abuses in Australia, Cardinal George Pell of Australia had put forward a similar argument in response to criticism of Vatican policies. Testifying before the commission via a video link from the Vatican in August 2014, Pell surprisingly likened the Catholic Church's responsibility for child abuse to that of a trucking company for the behavior of its employees. "If a driver picks up some lady and then molests her, I don't think it is appropriate, because it is contrary to the policy [of the company] for the ownership, the leadership of that company, to be held responsible," Pell declared.

Publication of this testimony brought an irate response from Noelene Watson, head of the Australian Trucking Association. "There are more than 170,000 professional truck drivers in Australia," she said.

"They have families and children. Cardinal Pell's analogy is a deep insult
to every one of them."

———

Faced with this avalanche of criticism, information, and pleas for help,
Pope Francis gradually became more open and activist. That July he had
met with the six victims, and on that occasion had spoken frankly and
begged forgiveness on the part of the church.

Then, in September 2014, Pope Francis appointed Father Robert
W. Oliver from Boston as full-time secretary of the Vatican's own new
commission on the protection of victims of sex abuse. Oliver had served
for a year in the delicate role of promoter of justice (the senior Vatican
prosecutor in cases of priestly discipline) in the Congregation for the
Doctrine of the Faith. The new appointment added stature to the commission, which is to meet in the future at least once a year.

At the same time, the roots of the problem went so deep in the
U.S. that the pope was made to appear to stumble in selecting a new
promoter of justice. When Pope Francis appointed Jesuit Father Robert
J. Geisinger of Boston, a canon lawyer, to that sensitive and powerful
position, it was quickly reported that Geisinger himself had been one of
several Catholic officials who had permitted a notorious abuser priest
named Donald J. McGuire to remain in ministry years after the priest's
long history as a sexual predator was known.

McGuire was a globe-trotting Jesuit priest whose many influential supporters reportedly included Mother Teresa of Calcutta. He
befriended and traveled with young Catholics for decades, often sharing rooms with them. He was defrocked and in 2008 sentenced to
twenty-five years in prison for "interstate travel with a person under
age eighteen for the purpose of engaging in a sexual act." Two under-
age boys were involved. Documents obtained by the *Boston Globe* in
November 2014 showed that Geisinger had known about McGuire's

reputation many years previously, but had failed to notify police and had lagged in removing him from ministry. The Vatican put out a statement defending Pope Francis' choice, stressing Father Geisinger's "prosecution record, his commitment to justice and his concern for victims."

Cardinal Seán O'Malley of Boston, who chairs the pope's new Commission on Protecting Minors, told the CBS-TV program *60 Minutes* that "Francis is very committed to zero tolerance." Yet over two years passed before he accepted the resignation of the Kansas City bishop Robert William Finn, convicted by a U.S. federal court in 2012 for having failed to report suspected child abuse by one of his priests, a porno-loving Father Shawn Ratigan. The Vatican still seems obsessed by the need to protect clergy from what they consider unfair allegations, rather than compensating and caring for the victims.

In the wake of these events, Pope Francis set up yet another new panel. This committee is part of the Congregation for the Doctrine of the Faith, and has nine members charged with finding a way to reduce the huge backlog of clergy abuse cases awaiting a ruling by the Vatican.

That backlog was enlarged by the sudden explosion of yet another scandal, this time in traditionally Catholic Spain. Three Catholic priests and a lay teacher in a Catholic school were arrested in Granada in November 2014 on sexual abuse charges, but were subsequently released on bail. The scandal came to light in August 2014 when a twenty-four-year-old teacher from Granada wrote a five-page letter to Pope Francis in which he described how "several" local priests had sexually abused him when he was an altar boy. The alleged victim wrote that the priests had persuaded him to leave his family to go to live with them in a parish rectory, where he was repeatedly abused.

The self-described victim, identified only as "Daniel" for reasons of privacy, told Spanish media that he received a personal phone call from Pope Francis, who had apologized for the abuse and promised an investigation. After a police investigation uncovered a criminal network of pedophiles and laity from various parishes, the Catholic Church in Granada suspended ten priests and two laypeople. Emulating the pontiff, Francisco Javier Martínez, the archbishop of Granada, also made an unusual public apology, prostrating himself by lying down on the floor in front of the high altar of Granada's historic cathedral. With him prostrate on the floor were a score of other clergy.

During an improvised press conference on board the charter jet bringing Pope Francis back to the Vatican from a morning visit to the European Parliament in Strasburg, France, on November 25, 2014, a Spanish journalist asked the pope point-blank about this case, which was still making headlines in Spain. Pope Francis confirmed having received the letter from "Daniel," and said that he did in fact telephone the victim, whom he told to go to the bishop. The pope said that he had personally contacted the bishop over the case.

How had the pope felt when receiving the news? he was asked. "Con grande dolore, con grandissimo dolore" (With pain, with the greatest of pain).

"But the truth is the truth, and we must not hide it," he said firmly.

In June 2015 Pope Francis agreed to set up a new Vatican tribunal within the framework of the Congregation for the Doctrine of the Faith to investigate bishops accused of failing to protect children and vulnerable adults from sex abuse. Funding for premises and staff for the tribunal have been authorized and the results will be assessed after five years. This move was seen as one of the most forceful acts by the pontiff to date to tackle the church's legacy of abuse and cover-ups. Cynics however noted that ecclesiastical cover-ups are such a deep-rooted tradition inside the church that the effectiveness of such a tribunal remains to be tested.

———

Yet, the worrying case of the contested appointment in 2015 of a new bishop in a remote diocese in the south of Chile did raise doubts about just how much Pope Francis may be aware of continuing scandals. Bishop Juan Barros, accused of complicity in a notorious local case of clerical sexual abuse, had to be escorted by police from his cathedral at his installation ceremony when protesters dressed in black interrupted the ceremony. He had been closely associated with Father Fernando Karadima, a prominent Santiago priest found guilty by the Vatican in 2011 of abusing teenagers during two decades. Weeks of protest, candle-lit vigils outside the cathedral, and letters to Pope Francis all failed to convince the pontiff to reverse his decision.

"We are used to the blows by the Chilean Catholic hierarchy, but it's especially hurtful when the slap in the face comes from Pope Francis himself," said Juan Carlos Cruz, fifty-one, who claims he was abused by Father Karadima in the 1980s, in a telephone interview with the *New York Times*. "We hoped he was different."

Well, he clearly is different. But occasionally he stumbles. And that is why at the end of practically every meeting, public or private, he asks people to pray for him.

5

Family Matters

All happy families are alike; each unhappy family is unhappy in its own way.
            —LEO TOLSTOY, *ANNA KARENINA*

Think of the church as a family, unhappy in its own way. It was for this reason that not long after his election, Pope Francis decided to call a meeting of church leaders—a "synod"—on the topic of the family.

Initially a few critics considered this generic-sounding choice for a synod a cop-out: a soft solution that dodged the presumably still tougher issues dividing the church, such as pedophilia among priests. But these critics were wrong, for the subject matter of family life would ignite tough confrontations over the church's bans on artificial contraception, on divorced and remarried Catholics receiving communion, and on same-sex unions. However generic the theme, these fundamental, hot-button issues had caused Catholics to desert the pews in increasing numbers for decades.

Half a century before this, Pope John XXIII had called a ground-breaking Second Vatican Council, which had set the Roman Catholic Church on a new path for the twentieth century. Now Pope Francis arrived from Argentina to make a similarly significant imprint of his own upon the church-family of the twenty-first century. He had received the necessary mandate from both voting and nonvoting cardinals gathered in Rome in March 2013 during preliminary discussions in preparation for what would turn out to be a historic conclave.

At that meeting the cardinals had laid out a vision for reform following what many had come to see as the failed pontificate of Benedict XVI. After Pope Francis' election, in keeping with basic Jesuit management practice, he had been careful to bide his time before carrying out any radical pruning of the Vatican hierarchy; indeed, one of his first acts had been to confirm all existing heads of department in their current jobs in the Curia, the central government of the church. His own choices for appointments would come later, as we shall see.

The Second Vatican Council took place from 1962 through 1965, and in its early reforming stages both John Paul II and Benedict XVI had played significant roles. When introduced, the reforms had appeared draconian. The Roman Missal was rewritten, and the vernacular adopted in the mass. Priests were to face the congregation as they celebrated the mass rather than turn their backs upon the faithful. A friendlier attitude toward members of other religious faiths was demanded, in particular toward the Jews.

But with the passing of time many Catholics had become convinced that the spirit that inspired those reforms had become diluted. The reforms had never in fact been fully implemented. A ban on artificial contraception had been promulgated by Pope Paul VI in his 1968 encyclical *Humanae Vitae*, but in general Catholic couples ignored it, thus accentuating the watering down of the initial enthusiasm for the reforms promoted and promised by Vatican II just three years before.

Pope Francis' promise of radical reform was far more broad. A complete newcomer to Vatican politics, he chose to invent his own system of church government. He decided not to play the traditional role of the pope as monarch and sovereign of an independent state and absolute ruler of a medieval court. He ruled not through edicts, bans, and anathemas but rather by example. He chose not to call a third Vatican Council.

Instead he chose to act spontaneously, often surprising Vatican officials by his choices—for instance, his imaginative decision to reside not in the roomy papal penthouse atop the Apostolic Palace, but in a modest three-room suite inside the Vatican guesthouse. He dined at a common table with fellow clerics. He spoke in simple language that ordinary people could understand, and in his religious preaching he often referred to events in his own family life as a youth growing up in Argentina in the 1940s and 1950s.

Speaking to parishioners in one of Rome's working-class suburbs during a visit in December 2013, he recalled some of the odd jobs he had done before starting his studies for the priesthood. The young Jorge Bergoglio swept floors, ran tests in a chemistry lab, and even worked as a bouncer in a nightclub to earn some extra cash.

He personally contacted old friends and sought new ones, phoning for example Eugenio Scalfari, editor-in-chief of Italy's leading left wing daily newspaper, *La Repubblica*, whom he invited to drop by for a number of private chats that lasted hours and turned into lengthy published interviews. Scalfari is known as a nonbeliever.

One of Pope Francis' most dramatic exemplary—and even prophetic—acts was a flying visit to the Mediterranean island of Lampedusa, south of Sicily, to lay a tiny wreath in the waters in which hundreds of migrants had drowned. There he preached at a mass celebrated upon an altar made of a piece of a rickety boat that had overturned, drowning the migrants before they reached shore. Such exemplary actions had far-reaching effects: a group of Catholics then collected wood from another boat that had sunk off the Sicilian isle of Lampedusa and, from its wreckage, made an eleven-foot-long cross. They carried the heavy cross to Rome, where the pope kissed it and said, "Take it everywhere." And so they did, to Naples, Milan, Padua, and onward, until they hauled it all the way to the top of Mount Rosa, one of the highest mountains in the Alps.

During Pope Francis' visit to the Italian island of Lampedusa in July 2013, he had called for a "reawakening of consciences" to counter the "globalization of indifference" being shown to the migrants. Shortly afterward, a wealthy Italian American couple that now lives on the Mediterranean island of Malta—Regina Catrambone, born in Calabria, and her husband, Christopher, from New Orleans—were cruising in their private yacht when they were horrified to see a body floating by.

"We understood immediately that it was of one of the migrants who had drowned near here during the crossing from Africa," Regina told an Italian reporter. "My husband and I looked at each other, and decided that we could not remain indifferent and inactive in the face of such a tragedy. What inspired us was the appeal from Pope Francis." Using some $3.7 million of their own money, they founded an association they named Migrant Offshore Aid Station, and purchased a 131-foot rescue boat, the *Phoenix*, a converted fishing trawler.

"The fear in the eyes of the children on the boats—and there were newborn babies as well—changes you forever," said Regina. "We decided to use all our savings to contribute to saving the lives of human beings."

Eighteen months later family funds ran out, and operations had to be temporarily suspended while extra outside funding was sought. In the meantime, their rescue boat, with a crew of seventeen, had saved the lives of some three thousand migrants. On its last voyage in 2014, the *Phoenix* rescued 331 migrants from two different boats in distress. Hundreds more have already been saved during newly funded rescue operations in 2015.[1]

In November 2014, the Italian authorities ended their Mare Nostrum program, which had been designed to rescue migrants adrift in the Mediterranean. Some 150,000 migrants were brought to Italy under the scheme, but the monthly cost of €9.5 million (US$10.7 million) forced the Italian government to cease operations.

Save the Children called for the EU to restart Mare Nostrum "or another rescue system that has the mandate, the capacity and means to prevent other tragedies."

Mare Nostrum was replaced with a much smaller-scale frontier control operation code named Triton, which only operates a few miles off Europe's coast. Its job is to patrol Europe's borders and prevent illegal landings. Mare Nostrum patrols took Italian rescue ships up close to Libya's coast on their humanitarian mission.

With the deaths from drowning in the Mediterranean of at least two thousand migrants in the early part of 2015, the EU finally admitted the gravity of the crisis first highlighted by Pope Francis' visit to Lampedusa. EU leaders meeting in Brussels decided on a quota system whereby all twenty-eight EU countries would share the burden of providing food, shelter, medical treatment, and asylum for the ever-growing numbers of desperate and penniless Africans landing on Italian shores. Many EU leaders, including British Prime Minister David Cameron, seemed uncomfortable with such schemes, claiming that it actually encourages migrants to make the crossing. But Britain nevertheless sent a warship, HMS *Bulwark*, to join in the effort to save lives by beefing up Mediterranean patrols searching for boatloads of asylum seekers in distress.

———

In a first for the Vatican, Pope Francis appointed a kitchen cabinet of trusted cardinals from every continent to advise him on structural reforms in the Holy See, and on how to reach out more effectively than had his predecessors to his worldwide flock of 1.3 billion.

The first Synod of Bishops had been called by Paul VI in 1967 in the spirit of Vatican II. It was to be an experiment in collaboration between the center and the periphery. A long succession of more than twenty other synods followed every two or three years, but they were less than successful, as they tended to be hampered by rigid agendas and discussions tightly controlled by the cardinals of the Roman Curia. For Pope Francis, on the contrary, a synod was to be a sounding board of Catholic opinion, including beyond the massive walls of the Vatican.

In October 2013, he convoked what was officially termed an Extraordinary Synod, to begin the following year. It was to have three phases: first, a yearlong walkup to the synod of October 2014, to be followed by a year of discussion and analysis before a concluding synod in October 2015.

To attend it would be the 114 presidents of bishops' conferences from all over the world, plus all twenty-five heads of Vatican departments, thirteen heads of Eastern Catholic churches, sixteen "experts," and thirty-eight auditors. Among the latter was a solitary Irish nun named Sister Margaret Muldoon, a former superior general of the Sisters of the Holy Family. Thirteen married couples were also invited; together with Sister Margaret, these women were the only females at the synod. Nine foreign observers were invited, among them Archbishop Hilarion Alfeyeu, head of foreign relations of the Russian Orthodox Church in Moscow; an Anglican bishop, Paul Butler from Durham, England; and a Nigerian Baptist leader, Rev. Benebo Fubara-Manuel.

In announcing the full list of participants, Cardinal Lorenzo Baldisseri, secretary general of the synod, struggled to describe the new rules that Pope Francis was introducing in hopes of stimulating the sort of freewheeling discussion that had never before characterized a synod. "First we paint the picture," said Baldisseri, "then we add the frame." Mixing his metaphors, he went on to say that the new procedures would "provide the track along which the train of renewal proceeds. As we go ahead, the steps needed to change the rules will become evident."

Six months before the synod was to take place, Pope Francis began to reveal his own point of view on one of the contentious issues concerning the family. During one of the private homilies the pope delivers daily in the chapel at Santa Marta's guesthouse inside the Vatican, he declared that "the Church must accompany, not condemn those who experience the failure of their marriage."

Already Archbishop Pierre-Marie Carré of Montpellier in France had said publicly that many of the French faithful were calling upon the Catholic Church to emulate the Orthodox Church, which permits—after a period of penitence—divorced individuals to enter into a new union recognized by the church. This practice does not, according to Orthodox believers, put into question the indissolubility of marriage.

Opposition arose immediately from conservative Catholics, who assumed that the pope intended to use the synod as the launching pad for drastic changes in Catholic teaching. This opposition was particularly strong among leading cardinals in the Curia and with the churches of North America and Africa.

Pope Francis forged ahead nevertheless, setting up an eleven-member commission of Catholic theologians and lawyers to devise ways by which Catholics whose marriages had failed might find a legal loophole to enable them to remain loyal members of their church with a new partner. At present, an annulment, or so-called "Catholic divorce," is granted by local church tribunals only if it is proven that the marriage was invalid in the first place—for example, because one of the partners declined to have children. The annulment procedure is both costly and complex and requires two decisions, one by a lower tribunal and a second by an appeals tribunal. Pope Francis thus requested the commission to devise a way "to simplify the annulment procedure, making it more streamlined, while safeguarding the principle of the indissolubility of marriage."

In recent years about three thousand annulment cases have been referred annually from abroad to the Holy Roman Rota. The Rota is the highest level appeals court in Rome, located in the Palazzo della Cancelleria, a stupendous palace built for a Renaissance cardinal and now staffed by an international team of Vatican lawyers and bureaucrats. In 2011, there were 44,646 marriage annulments granted worldwide—just under half of them adjudicated in the United States. Only 2,515 were granted in Italy, with one quarter the population of the United States.

Although, as this suggests, there had long been a fast track for the particularly well connected and well-to-do, some of the dossiers coming to Rome for action dragged on for years. In 2012, definitive verdicts were handed down in 222 cases, although 1,020 annulment decisions were pending at year's end. Under Pope Francis the turnover time may be much reduced; he set up a review committee in 2014.

Aware that change was in the wind, Cardinal Raymond Burke, the archconservative American who at that time headed the Supreme Tribunal of the Apostolic Signatura, railed against any weakening of church doctrine on annulments. In a lecture at the Catholic University of America in Washington, D.C., six months before the synod was to begin, the sixty-six-year-old cardinal and former archbishop of St. Louis had declared, "It must be clear" that the annulment process "is not a mere matter of procedure but that the process is essentially connected with the doctrinal truth" of the church. Quoting from the Code of Canon Law, he added that "marriage . . . can be dissolved by no human power and by no cause, except death." Also citing John Paul II, Burke warned against that "false mercy, which is not concerned with the truth."

The word "mercy" had become a catchphrase in church-speak because, from the outset, Pope Francis has repeatedly extolled mercy as a prime Christian virtue. On the eve of the synod, when the pope addressed tens of thousands of believers massed in St. Peter's Square, Francis had highlighted that in modern society a breakdown in the family brings suffering. "The wounds have to be treated with mercy," said the pope. "The Church is a mother, not a customs office, coldly checking who stays within the rules."

Burke famously clung to ornate and outmoded ecclesiastical gear, including a type of red hat, the *galero*, that had been abandoned after Vatican II. On feast days he habitually wore in public an antiquated and elaborate flowing silk robe so long that its train, longer than any bridal train, needed two pages or altar boys to carry it. In November 2014, he was transferred by Pope Francis to a new post as patron of the Knights of Malta, one of the Catholic Church's oldest religious orders, originally set up at the time of the Crusades to provide hospital services for pilgrims visiting Jerusalem, today a worldwide charitable foundation. It was widely interpreted as a demotion.

Cardinal Burke's opposition to change was in net contrast with that of several other American dioceses. Cleveland, among others, had already shown approval of a new approach by canceling the four-hundred-dollar administrative fee exacted by the church tribunal to begin an annulment procedure. Similarly, on the eve of the synod in October 2014, Bishop Kevin C. Rhoades of Fort Wayne–South Bend similarly announced he was waiving the annulment administration fee.

A second tough issue facing the synod on the family was the status of those Catholics who had civil divorces, which are unrecognized by the church. If a couple has a civil divorce, and one partner remarries, he or she is officially denied communion because the church considers that person still married and hence living in sin.

That the prospect of change disturbed many was made public in mid-2014 when five die-hard conservative cardinals from the United States, Germany, Australia, and Italy produced a book in which they vehemently opposed any change in traditional teaching.[2] One of the authors was Cardinal George Pell of Australia, the pope's new finance czar. At the book launch at the Jesuit publisher's headquarters in Rome, Pell warned of the dangers that change might bring. He moreover explained that the pope's call for forgiveness and mercy—that term again—risked being misunderstood.

"The Christian vision of mercy is a central theme of marriage and sexuality," Pell said. In convoluted language he went on to say that, while mercy is "one of the most commendable aspects of our pluralistic societies," it is different from most forms of tolerance.[3]

In a foreword to a second book published shortly before the synod was to open, Cardinal Pell assailed those who urge greater tolerance of divorced persons who then contract a second civil marriage.[4] Said Pell: "The sooner the wounded, the lukewarm and the outsiders realize that substantial doctrinal and pastoral changes are impossible, the more the hostile disappointment (which must follow the reassertion of doctrine) will be anticipated and dissipated."

In short, do not expect change.

Elsewhere, Pell reiterated the church's traditional teaching of marriage as indissoluble: "It is no coincidence that, in the Judeo-Christian culture, monotheism and monogamy are associated," he declared. "Lifetime marriage is not just a burden. It is a gem. Church doctrine and pastoral practice cannot be in contradiction with each other. It is not possible to sustain the indissolubility of marriage while allowing the remarried to receive holy communion at the same time."

Again in convoluted church-speak, and again in an obvious attempt to squelch debate so as to preempt the possibility of change even before the synod opened, Pell also urged other conservatives to stand fast.

Both books were openly critical of the retired German Cardinal Walter Kasper, eighty-two, whom the pope was known to admire for defending those pressing for change within the church, particularly as regards the ban on divorced and remarried individuals receiving communion. The two camps had become openly hostile. Moreover, as Kasper declared, "When they attack me, their real target is *not* me, but rather the pope himself." And in another interview Kasper warned that what the opponents of change want at the synod is "ideological warfare."

Before retiring in 2010, Kasper had held important Vatican posts. In 1999, John Paul II had appointed him to head the Pontifical Council for Promoting Christian Unity, the Vatican's department in charge of relations with other Christian churches and with Judaism. He continued in this office under Pope Benedict, even though the two men had a long history of theological differences. In 1993, while still a diocesan bishop in Germany, Kasper and two other German bishops had instructed local priests that they might give communion to those divorced and remarried Catholics who were personally convinced that their first marriages were invalid, even without an official annulment. The then-Cardinal Ratzinger counterattacked, forcing the trio of bishops into an about-face.

In March 2013, only days after his election, Pope Francis had flung down a gauntlet by paying an enthusiastic tribute to Kasper. The pope praised the retired German cardinal's book, significantly entitled *Mercy: The Essence of the Gospel and the Key to Christian Life*. Kasper, stated the pope, is a "superb theologian," whose book has "done me so much good, so much good. Mercy changes the world—a little mercy makes the world less cold and more just." Mercy—that word again.

Cardinal Kasper lives in retirement in a comfortable Vatican-owned apartment a stone's throw from St. Peter's. He was Pope Benedict's neighbor during a quarter of a century. I called on him to try to find out how far he believes Pope Francis has the power to change the teachings of the church.

"In principle a pope cannot change the teaching of the church," Kasper replied. "You have to ask what is the real teaching of the church. There are many traditions which criticize the one tradition, or traditions in the plural.

"It is necessary to define the difference between the one binding tradition which cannot be changed, and those which can. The Second Vatican Council did this with religious freedom. There were teachings of popes in the nineteenth century that changed after a lot of discussion by the council.

"I think of celibacy for example. Celibacy is not teaching, it's a discipline. I don't think the present pope will change it totally, but it is not essential for the Catholic understanding of priesthood.

"We already reached agreement for example with the Anglicans who have married priests, and we could make that more generally available. Whether we would do this now is another question. We could do this with *viri probati* (married laymen). This is not excluded. Benedict did this with the Anglican married priests. It's not a binding teaching, its a discipline. It's the same with contraception. There's an obvious link between sexual intercourse and children. And then couples are free to decide how many children they want and what is responsible for them. It's also a question of the means of birth control. Personally I'm not convinced that this is a binding teaching.

"The point is that most Catholics don't care a hoot about it. Everyone ignores it. There's something wrong, a flaw somewhere! I think it's a question of the conscience of the couple. But I also think it is out of the question that the pope would change it officially.

"He will not make a priori decisions, he wants to listen. I think it's a new way of exercising his primacy. He will listen to the voice of the people, the *sensus fidelium*. He also wants to listen to the voice of the bishops. The bishops must have the courage to speak out openly. Most of the bishops are not accustomed to doing that. Say what they really think.

"Discussion is the only way to clarify a problem. He has clear ideas what he wants. He knows Catholic doctrine but he also knows human life. What it's about. The sufferings of people. He is a pastor, not an academic."

Is there widespread opposition within the Vatican?

"Of course there is opposition. It's a new way of exercising primacy. He wants to change the Curia. He changed it a lot already. The whole financial role has been taken away from the secretariat of state. It's no longer the same secretariat of state as it was before. During the reign of

Paul VI the secretary of state was the center, now the synod has become much more important. He wants to give much more importance to the synodality of the church."

Why did the synod not develop as it was conceived at the Second Vatican Council?

"The synods were not successful. It was a lot of work. It was boring. Every cardinal had just five minutes, and the speeches went on only from nine till 12 noon. Nobody made reference to the last or the next speaker. It was impossible.

"There was a crisis within the Curia. Vatileaks was a sign that it didn't function any longer. Most of the world's Catholics live in the southern hemisphere. At the beginning of the twentieth century, only 25 percent lived outside Europe. Now only 25 percent are in Europe.

"It was the intention of Vatican II to develop the synod, but I have the impression that Paul VI was afraid to give too much space to the bishops. And then in 1968 the church was on the defensive. Francis brings the agenda of the southern hemisphere to the center of the church.

"He is the first pope to come from a megacity, a metropolis. We do not have them in Europe. These are very pluralistic cities, people coming from everywhere, very rich and very poor side by side. I visited Buenos Aires four times. It's a very pluralistic society. Benedict came from a village in Bavaria. And John Paul's Krakow is an old city, but it's not a big city.

"Here in the Vatican they have a very narrow curial vision. A vision of centralization and of power. It will be a long process of learning. But we have reached a point of no return.

"There will be cardinals who want to go back, but I think they cannot be successful. After the death of John XXIII, they wanted to go back but it was impossible. I don't think that Francis has a detailed program. He wants to initiate a process and wants to see what will come out of it.

"He wants to propose, not to impose."

As the presynod debate gained momentum, the leading Jesuit magazine, *America*, also interviewed Kasper. When asked whether the cardinals shared the pope's fear that the whole moral construction of the church could collapse like a pack of cards, Kasper replied yes. The conservatives fear a domino effect, he said.

"If you change one point, all would collapse—that is their fear," he said, a fear linked to an ideological reading of the Gospel, "that it is like a penal code." But the Gospel is not a museum, he continued:

"It is a living reality. . . . A closed church is not a healthy church, and not inviting, when we discuss marriage and family, we have to listen to people who are living this reality. There is a *sensus fidelium* [sense of the faithful]. It cannot be decided only from above, by the church hierarchy, and especially you cannot quote old texts of the last century. You have to look at the situation today."

Asked if the new synod would be a replay of Vatican II, Kasper responded that there were indeed similarities: at Vatican II, he said, "Roman theologians . . . prepared all the texts. They expected the bishops to come and applaud, and in two or three weeks it would all be over. But it did not happen that way, and I think it won't happen this time."

At the same time, Kasper noted that the controversial books by Cardinal Pell and the other four conservative cardinals represented a genuine problem. "I don't remember such a situation, where, in such an organized way, five cardinals write a book like this. That is the way of politics, but should not be done in the church. . . . I don't think we should behave this way."

A rumor was meantime circulating that the books attacking the positions held by Kasper and the pope himself had irritated Pope Francis. When Cardinal Pell was asked about the rumor, he breezily dismissed it: "I see the pope every two weeks. I have never seen him irritated."

But even conservatives in the United States were not all in agreement with Cardinals Burke and Pell. Bishop Thomas J. Tobin of Rhode Island is known as anything but progressive; he had notoriously quarreled with Patrick J. Kennedy, a proabortion Rhode Island congressman. Bishop Tobin nevertheless wrote in a column for the *Providence Journal* in 2013 that:

> *My forty-one years as a priest and nearly twenty-two as a bishop have convinced me that the status quo [on the divorced and remarried] is unacceptable.*
>
> *We have got to do something for their spiritual well-being. We have a challenge here. We have at least to look at it and to talk about it. Otherwise, if we go through this long synod process for the next two years and end up right where we are now, it will be a failure. . . . I know I would much rather give Holy Communion to these long-suffering souls than to pseudo-Catholic politicians who parade up the aisle every Sunday for Holy Communion and then withdraw to their legislative chambers to deny the teachings of the church by championing same-sex marriage and abortion.*

Bishop Tobin then became the target of a barrage of hostile attacks on Facebook. Said one of these: "Where did you get your bishop's license—out of a Cracker Jack box?"

Despite the attacks on Kasper and, implicitly, on the pope himself, Francis continued to press forward. In a rap on the knuckles of those cardinals like Pell, and the bishops and priests who stress the inflexible rules of the church regarding sexuality, he warned against the temptation to "codify faith in rules and instructions, as did the scribes, the Pharisees and the doctors of law in the time of Jesus."

In the months before the synod, Pope Francis said repeatedly that he hoped for a freewheeling debate. He set the stage with a novel request in October 2013: that an opinion survey be taken among ordinary Catholics worldwide. The survey aim was to analyze the widening gap between Catholic teaching on sexuality and the actual behavior of Catholic families.

On this, in 2012, the U.S. Pew Research Center had conducted a survey showing that fewer than one out of five U.S. Catholics (19 percent) consider getting a divorce morally wrong. Almost half (45 percent) said that to get a divorce is not a moral issue, while one out of three (32 percent) called divorce "morally acceptable."[5] In February 2014 Pew followed up with another survey asking whether the Catholic Church should allow the use of artificial birth control. A massive 77 percent replied yes. Over half the respondents (56 percent) predicted that by midcentury this would become the norm.

On the part of the pope the Vatican survey was a historic gesture, for it allowed ordinary Catholics to have their say for the first time ever in the planning and agenda of a crucial Synod of Bishops. Perhaps surprisingly, an initial response from Catholics all over the world was criticism of the wording of the questions; outside North America and Europe the questions were described as obscure and Eurocentric. The critics also objected to the short window of time allowed for preparing their replies.

When they were returned, some of the results of that survey came as a shock to many in the Curia.

The broad picture from the German bishops' report, based on responses from twenty-seven dioceses and twenty church associations, was that, while German Catholics found the church family friendly, at the same time they considered the sexual morality of the church to be unrealistic. German dioceses reported that between 90 percent and 100 percent of couples seeking a Catholic wedding were already living together despite church teaching that sex outside marriage is sinful.

"The Church's offers of marriage, family and life counseling are highly appreciated within society, whilst the Church's theology on marriage and her sexual morality are virtually universally rejected."

On the question of the numerous divorced and remarried Catholics who still actively participate in their parishes, the bishops wrote that "divorce and remarrying frequently lead to a process of becoming distant from the church. Many no longer wish to be associated with an institution which they regard as unforgiving."

Most respondents totally rejected or simply ignored church teaching on contraception, and Catholics accepted civil partnerships for same-sex couples as a "matter of justice." Many complained they were "unable to follow the language and content of the theological statements."

In Switzerland, where almost twenty-four thousand responded, 80 percent of these Catholics told their bishops that marriage in church was still important, while 97 percent said they want their children to have a religious education. But nine out of ten (90 percent) also said they want the church to recognize and to bless divorced and remarried Catholics, and to allow them to take Holy Communion. They found church teaching both "discriminatory and lacking in charity." The Swiss attitude toward contraception was the same as in Germany: indifference. For many decades, they acknowledged, they had paid no heed to church teaching on that.

In the words of the report from the Swiss bishops, the church, by asking Catholics to follow behavioral rules uncritically and unconditionally, is going against its own interests in transmitting the essentials of the Gospel message. What they found surprising was the convergence of Catholic opinion among young and old, men and women, German, French, and Italian speakers.

In Japan, Catholics represent a highly educated social group with considerable influence. The Jesuit university in Tokyo is particularly prestigious, and Shinzō Abe, who was elected in 2008, is a fourth-generation Catholic and the first Catholic to become the prime minister of Japan.

From Japan came a fifteen-page report prepared by the bishops and released to the public. They told the Vatican bluntly that contemporary Japanese Catholics are:

> *Either indifferent to, or unaware of, church teaching on artificial contraception. Most Catholics in Japan have not heard of* Humanae Vitae; *and, if they have, they probably do not make it an important part of their lives. Social and cultural values as well as financial considerations are more important. There is a large gap between the Vatican and reality. Condom use is recommended in sex education classes in our schools.*

Attempts to convince Japanese Catholics to practice so-called "natural methods" of birth control, such as the Billings Method (which requires calculation of so-called safe days), have met with scant success. Even more pointedly, "For the most part the church in Japan is not obsessed with sexual matters." In their response to the Vatican inquiry the Japanese also discussed some of the unique challenges their country faces, such as a work ethic that allows little time for the needs of the family. A second crucial issue relates to the problems faced by many Japanese Catholics who are married to non-Catholics.

In situations where both parents work, many Japanese children return to an empty house. Family meals are rare. Consequently there are few opportunities for shared conversation. Each family member faces difficulties, but since there is no fellowship, each is lonely, and has little experience of loving or being loved.

The Japanese bishops also criticized the manner in which the Vatican questionnaire had been framed. In their view, it had been shaped within the mind-set of the Christian countries, in which the entire family is normally Christian. Japanese Catholics represent only 0.35 percent of their country's population, and about three-quarter of these marry non-Catholics. Said their report:

In Japan the overwhelming majority of marriages are mixed, and in this context the respondents asked what is the meaning of a Christian household and family. The number of people who do not marry is on the increase, as are single-parent families. Other particularly Japanese problems that had not even been imagined in the past are, according to the survey, the plight of the elderly and the aging, and the problems facing the children of older parents.

In the United States too, the survey results showed a disconnect between official church teaching and the beliefs and lifestyles of ordinary Catholics. Curiously, in a country that lives on its computers, only 72 out of 195 dioceses offered online access to the survey, which automatically limited its reach. In 2015, there was a similar disconnect.

Nevertheless fifteen progressive Catholic organizations conducted their own large national survey, which provided an opportunity for Catholics from everywhere in the United States to give feedback. From across the United States came 16,582 responses. Of these, 13 percent described themselves as members of a church reform movement, but over half (53 percent) said that they attend mass every week. This is particularly important because official figures show that average attendance at a weekly mass by U.S. Catholics is only 24 percent.[6]

On divorce and remarriage, three-quarters of divorced and remarried couples (75 percent) believe that their relationship is worthy of their receiving church sacraments, regardless of church recognition of their union. Simplification of annulment rules was urged by an overwhelming majority of 82 percent. Regarding same-sex relationships, a vast majority—73 percent—said that such couples are no less entitled to approach the sacraments of the church than are conventional married couples. In addition, 57 percent mentioned that in their state the law recognizes the equality of same-sex and traditional marriages.

Only 1 percent said that the teachings of *Humanae Vitae* were completely accepted, whereas 56 percent said they were not accepted at all; only 43 percent said they were accepted "in part."[7]

———

Fortified by these responses and, just in case any had missed the point, Pope Francis gave the conservatives further reason for concern in mid-September 2014, by celebrating a nuptial mass in St. Peter's Basilica for twenty couples from the Diocese of Rome. Held just two weeks before the opening of the synod, this was the first public papal celebration of a wedding since John Paul II had married eight couples during the Jubilee for the Families in the year 2000. Those whom Pope Francis invited included Catholic couples who had been openly living "in sin." The youngest was twenty-five, the oldest, fifty-six. Some already had children, some were actually divorced. Pope Francis kissed one of the brides in front of the cameras.

The couples were astonished when local parish priests advised them that they would not only be married in the church, but also in St. Peter's Basilica, and by the pope himself. One of the brides confided that she and her husband, whose previous marriage had been annulled, had already lived together for five years. "We had always wanted to get married in church and had felt deprived of the sacraments, but we also felt unworthy because of our age and personal background," she said. Her adult daughter attended the ceremony.

In his homily that day, Pope Francis called marriage not "some TV show," but real life in which families are "the bricks that build society." He returned to the theme of mercy, indicating his conviction that the church should forgive those who have sex outside marriage, or who fail to obey church teaching to the letter. "The love of Jesus can help whenever their love becomes lost, wounded or worn out."

The eighty-five-page document prepared for the beginning of debate was called the *Instrumentum Laboris* (Working Document).

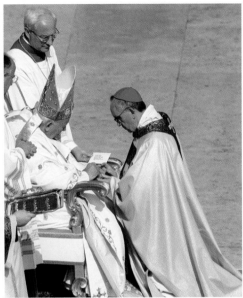

LEFT: Born in 1936, the son of northern Italian immigrants to Argentina, Jorge Mario Bergoglio, shown here as a twenty-eight-year-old seminarian, taught literature and psychology at the Colegio del Salvador in Buenos Aires. *(Escuela El Salvador)*

RIGHT: In a ceremony outside St. Peter's Basilica February 21, 2001, Archbishop Jorge Mario Bergoglio of Argentina kneels as an already ailing Pope John Paul II gives him his cardinal's ring of office. *(Grzegorz Galazka)*

Immediately after his election March 13, 2013, Pope Francis, flanked by cardinals from around the world, exits the Sistine Chapel while a cheering crowd of some 150,000 waits outside in the piazza. *(Osservatore Romano)*

Inside the papal summer palace at Castel Gandolfo, Pope Emeritus Benedict XVI (left) consigns to his successor, four days after Pope Francis' election, a large white box containing confidential documents. *(Osservatore Romano)*

Pope Francis kneels in confession inside St. Peter's Basilica in March 2015, after urging penitents to reconcile with the church and seek forgiveness. *(Grzegorz Galazka)*

ABOVE: A bustling Pope Francis on his way to a consistory, a worldwide assembly of cardinals, on February 12, 2015. *(Grzegorz Galazka)*

RIGHT: Pope Francis, shown here kissing the bride, performs wedding ceremonies for couples already cohabiting and with children, in an unusual break with church tradition. *(Grzegorz Galazka)*

On St. Valentine's Day, February 14, 2014, ten thousand engaged couples from all over the world gathered in St. Peter's Square at the invitation of Pope Francis, who advised them to learn how to say please, thank you, and sorry. *(Eric Vandeville)*

At a weekly general audience in January 2015, a juggler from Italy's Medrano Circus swaps green balls with the smiling pope, as a Swiss Guard stands stiffly by. *(Grzegorz Galazka)*

The Harlem Globetrotters basketball team, at an open-air general audience in St. Peter's Square May 6, 2015, offered the pontiff a team shirt bearing the number 90, for his 90 percent approval rating among U.S. Catholics. *(AP)*

Thousands dance the traditional Argentine tango in St. Peter's Square to celebrate the seventy-eighth birthday December 17, 2014, of Pope Francis, who admits having been a tango fan in his youth. *(Tony Gentile, Reuters)*

Inside their Vatican barracks, the Pontifical Swiss Guards, who have served as "Defenders of the Church's freedom" since 1506, try on their antique armor and tricolored uniforms, whose design dates from the Renaissance. *(Gerald Bruneau)*

The Vatican's own antiterror unit, staffed by former Italian Special Forces personnel, makes a rare appearance at a Gendarmerie parade inside Vatican City. *(David Willey)*

"Welcome, this is your house and everyone's house," Pope Francis told 150 homeless people he invited for a private tour of the Sistine Chapel and a meal. *(Osservatore Romano)*

RIGHT: The popularity of Pope Francis is on display around Vatican City, where refrigerator magnets are a hot-selling item in souvenir shops. *(Judith Harris)*

BELOW: In the Church of the Holy Sepulchre, Jerusalem, Pope Francis (left) and Orthodox Patriarch Bartholomew I pray together May 25, 2014, at the Stone of Unction, where tradition says the body of Jesus was prepared for burial. *(Andrew Medichini, Reuters)*

"Sister Internet" is what Vatican insiders call Franciscan nun Judith Zoebelein of New York, who created and managed the Vatican website www.vatican.va from its inception in 1995. *(Eric Vandeville)*

On May 25, 2014, Francis places the Lord's Prayer he has handwritten in Spanish into a crevice in Jerusalem's Western Wall on Temple Mount, the holiest Jewish prayer site. *(Grzegorz Galazka)*

A different wall: en route to celebrate mass in Manger Square in Bethlehem during his 2014 Holy Land pilgrimage, Pope Francis makes an unscheduled stop at the separation barrier dividing Israel from the Palestinian West Bank, minutes after begging both sides to end their conflict. *(Mheisen Amareen, Reuters)*

Seven million faithful, reportedly the largest gathering in history, flocked to Pope Francis' mass in Manila, ending his four-day visit in January 2015 to the staunchly Catholic Philippines. *(Paul Haring, Catholic News Service)*

Visiting the Philippines in January 2015, Pope Francis hugs former Manila street child Glyzelle Palomar, twelve, who burst into tears asking him, "Why does God allow such bad things to happen?" *(Paul Haring, Catholic News Service)*

After helping broker a historic thaw between the United States and Cuba (both countries the pontiff is to visit in September 2015), Pope Francis meets with Cuban president Raul Castro (left) in the Vatican May 10, 2015. *(Gregorio Borgia, Reuters)*

Before tens of thousands who spent hours fasting and praying for peace, Pope Francis led a vigil in St. Peter's Square on the night of September 7, 2013, and called for reconciliation in war-torn Syria. *(Eric Vandeville)*

As soon as it was disseminated, comments poured in from influential Catholics. Said the prestigious British Catholic weekly *The Tablet*, the document shows "a Church ill at ease with itself.... an institution for which marriage, sex and the family remain problematic, suffering a huge gap between theory and practice."[8] The document also showed that "the laity are solving the problem by themselves.... Many aspects of the Church's sexual morality are not understood today."

When the two-week synod actually began October 6, the heads of the Catholic bishops' conferences worldwide convened inside the modernistic Synod Hall. The hall is situated above the Paul VI Audience Hall, the main Vatican venue for general audiences. Near one side of St. Peter's Basilica, it was designed in 1971 by one of Italy's leading postwar architects, Pier Luigi Nervi.

Between that opening day and the closing session October 18, Pope Francis mingled frequently with delegates during coffee breaks but spoke out exactly twice. On the first day he said that the bishops were not to mince their words, nor to fear offending him, but to speak clearly and truthfully, and to listen with "humility."

Twenty-five synods had taken place since the first in 1967, but none had loomed like this. Vatican debating procedures had until now been extremely formal, the language restrained and redolent of church jargon, with long Bible quotations and citations from past and present papal documents. As if pleased at the controversial lead-up to the synod, Pope Francis called for a free, lively, and open debate. He made it clear that he not only had no fear of discussion and disagreement, but welcomed it.

"Do not get lost in discussing beautiful or clever ideas, or compete in seeing who is the more intelligent," he admonished the synod in what was once more a plea for kindness and mercy. Don't be greedy, he warned; to satisfy the greed for money and power, there exist "evil pastors" who may try to impose "intolerable burdens" on the shoulders of believers.

Behind his openness was, among other things, his experience at a synod on evangelization held in 2001. As he told a reporter for the Argentine newspaper *La Nación*, the then-Cardinal Jorge Borgoglio had been in charge of organizing and guiding the discussions. "I was the rapporteur of the 2001 synod, and there was a cardinal who told us what should be discussed and what should not. That will not happen now."[9]

At the end of a week of speeches behind closed doors, the synod issued a provisional position paper in which the church attitude toward homosexuality featured prominently. Homosexuals have "gifts and qualities to offer," it said, urging Catholics to accept gays and to recognize the positive aspects of same-sex couples. The church should find a "fraternal space" for homosexuals without compromising Catholic doctrine on the family, said the document.

German Cardinal Reinhard Marx, one of the nine members of the pope's kitchen cabinet on reforms, called this document "an honest representation of the way the debate had developed." For Marx, remarried Catholics who "acknowledge their failure should be able to apply for readmission to the sacraments after a period of penitence."

The international media immediately seized upon the new position as a major shift in the attitude of the Catholic Church toward gays. Already gay rights groups around the world had hailed the pope's use of the word "gay" for the first time in papal history, when he returned from his trip to Rio de Janeiro in July 2013. Now they hailed the position paper as a breakthrough.

Conservatives were appalled, and at least one informed Italian source reported that the progressive positions had actually been loudly booed. For the conservatives, the position paper represented a betrayal of church teaching. Its language had "sown confusion" among the faithful. The "liberals" within the committee that had prepared the text had railroaded the assembly, said Cardinal Raymond Burke, the senior American official within the Roman Curia. For Burke, the position paper did not reflect a consensus of the synod and for this reason should be changed. He called upon the pope to issue a clear statement defending traditional Christian marriage and the family.

For five days this first document, called a *relatio*, was keenly debated. In the end it was drastically revised and whittled down by a third. The three most controversial paragraphs, which dealt with homosexuality and allowing the divorced to take the sacraments, were weakened.

Paragraph 55 of the original *relatio* had urged "accepting and valuing the sexual orientation of gays and giving them a welcoming home." In its final version, the phrase "giving them a welcoming home" was revised and significantly watered down. The paragraph became more vague, repeating previous church statements that gays "should be welcomed with respect and sensitivity" and not suffer discrimination.

The originally proposed version had also held that the church should acknowledge that couples in same-sex relations offer each other "mutual aid and precious support in times of difficulty." This too was slashed from the final, enfeebled version.

In particularly stilted language, the final version stated that "some families experience having, within their interior, persons of homosexual orientation. The question was raised as to what pastoral attention would be opportune, when faced with this situation."

Referring to church teaching: "There is no foundation whatsoever to assimilate or to establish analogies, even remote, between homosexual unions and God's design for marriage and the family." To make this a shade less icy, a few cordial words were thrown in: "Men and women with homosexual tendencies should be received with respect and delicacy" and without "unfair discrimination."

In the published results of the vote, which Pope Francis had requested, 118 approved of this heavily revised paragraph (*placet*), while 62 did not (*non placet*). Some of those choosing *non placet* apparently declined approval because the wording had been too watered down.

In a few subsequent sentences, the synod scorched unidentified international organizations, which were accused of conditioning financial aid to poor countries upon their introduction of laws permitting same-sex marriage. This passed easily, with 159 approving and only 21 objecting.

Paragraph 53 addressed the issue of permitting the sacraments to divorced and remarried couples and to those partners living together. "Some of the fathers maintained that these could fruitfully seek spiritual communion," said the paragraph. But if so, others were asking why they could not receive the sacraments as well as "spiritual communion." However, a decision on this knotty question was officially postponed for further discussion in the light of the "theology of marriage."

On this the vote echoed that on homosexuality, with 112 *placet* and 64 *non placet*. Again one of the most controversial of the paragraphs indicated a split, two-thirds traditionalists versus one-third innovators (to simplify). But as the *Economist* had written on the eve of the synod, this specific question troubled liberal-minded Catholics, who were calling for "some easing" of the church's refusal to offer them Holy Communion. "The current situation causes distress to Catholics all over the world whose marriages have failed and who would like to be faithful adherents of the church."[10]

Most other questions were far less controversial. Paragraph 57, for instance, criticized the declining birth rate in wealthy countries and urged couples to have more children despite the economic cost. This passed easily, with 169 *placet* to 5 *non placet*.

In his concluding remarks at the synod—remarks that reportedly had been written (and revised a half dozen times) by an overworked Cardinal Gianfranco Ravasi—Pope Francis thus faced a formidable task. He was obliged to acknowledge at the very least that the debate had been heated, and that achieving consensus over the critical texts had been difficult.

Still, he was outspoken. He recognized that during the synod there had been "moments of desolation, tensions and temptations." What temptations? The first he warned against was what he called "hostile inflexibility":

That is, wanting to close oneself within the written word and not allowing one to be surprised by the God of surprises. From the time of Jesus Christ this is the temptation of the zealous, of the scrupulous, of the solicitous and of the so-called traditionalists of today, and also of the intellectuals.

Another temptation that Pope Francis warned against is the "destructive tendency of 'being good' [*buonismo*] in the name of a deceptive mercy that binds wounds without first treating and curing them—one that treats the symptoms, but not the root causes. This is the temptation of the 'do-gooders,' of the fearful and the so-called progressives and liberals."

Pope Francis, who has called the church a field hospital in an allusion to battle, concluded by pointing out that there was still a year for mulling over "the proposed ideas, and to find concrete solutions to so many difficulties and innumerable challenges that families must confront."

If he took the result as a defeat, he gave no hint of this, nor was he about to capitulate. He cannily ordered publication of the complete text of the sixty-two paragraphs together with the voting figures for each one. This enabled the immediate identification of the most controversial issues, which would be left for Catholics everywhere to debate in the twelve months before the synod of 2015 would convene.

At the end of these final remarks the entire assembly gave him a four-minute standing ovation. Whether or not they agreed with him, this acknowledged him as a unifying force; he was pope. As he had said in his closing words, "The synod has been held *cum Petro* and *sub Petro* [with Peter and under Peter], and the presence of the pope is the guarantee of it all." The bishops' first duty is to nourish their flock—to welcome them, he said.

But then he had corrected himself in what was, amazingly, a joke of sorts, for the word "welcome" was an inadvertent reference to the original position paper that argued for the church as a "welcoming home" for homosexuals. "Did I say welcome?" he asked. "I meant to say, go out and find them."

Most outsiders took the votes on the controversial issues as outright rebukes for Pope Francis. *Rorate Caeli*, a traditionalist Catholic blog, trumpeted, "For Francis, a resounding defeat." From the *Economist*: "Conservative Catholic bishops won the day when the final report of a meeting to discuss policy on families at the Vatican scrapped conciliatory language about gays and divorcées that had been included in earlier drafts."[11] From the Huffington Post came a scornful headline: "Catholic Bishops Scrap Welcome to Gays."

From the Philippines, the sole Asian country to vaunt a Catholic majority, Cardinal Luis Antonio Tagle of Manila criticized Western-dominated media reporting of the synod. Those attending the synod were being labeled in simplistic fashion as "progressive, conservative or traditionalist." Among the hundreds of international reporters gathered in Rome, Tagle said he had seen no Asian or African journalists. "Who will report on our concerns?" he asked. Only 3 percent of the world's Catholics live in Asia, but in the Philippines, with a hundred million population, because of its past as a former Spanish colony 80 percent are Catholic.

At the same time Tagle complained at the emphasis on divorce and homosexuality. Filipino families suffered a different form of separation, he said, because countless migrate from his country in order to earn a living and to support their families left at home. "Ours is not separation that says 'good riddance'—it is separation with pain," he said. "Our concerns are mixed marriages, domestic violence, pornography, poverty and the separation of families through migration."[12]

The Philippines is the only state in the world, apart from the Vatican, in which both divorce and abortion are outlawed. But there are signs that the position of the church there is softening. Speaking at the meeting of the Catholic bishops' conference held in Manila in 2013, Archbishop Socrates Villegas, conference president, said that a "change of tone" would be a fitting welcome for Pope Francis, who made his first visit there in 2015 and plans a second visit in 2016. "Perhaps we ought to reach out to more people by stretching our minds and lowering our fences, and listening without being judgmental or punitive," said Villegas on that occasion.

His words indicated a softening in local Catholic views there. In a major defeat for the Catholic Church, President Benigno Aquino III had signed a law requiring government health centers to hand out free condoms and birth control pills in 2012, despite the church's fifteen-year campaign against family planning laws. The law took effect in 2014 after the supreme court threw out an appeal by the church.

———

The synod was over, but the discussions were still beginning. In Rome in November 2014, Pope Francis told specialists of canon law at the Holy Roman Rota (the church's supreme tribunal in marital cases) that "the church has to dispense not only justice, but also charity over matrimonial situations. If these cases drag on too long, people get fed up and leave the church. I remember, for instance, the tribunal in Buenos Aires which deals with cases up to 240 kilometers [149 miles] from the Argentinian capital," he said. "Imagine simple people having to travel that distance to a court, and losing days of pay in order to get a decision as to whether their marriage was or was not valid."

He also said that he had had to deal with a public scandal in his native Argentina. It involved dodgy civil and canon lawyers who told their clients that with "'$10,000 I can fix everything, civil divorce proceedings and the church annulment too.' Please do not let this continue," he said. "This is not how the church should act."[13] In essence, he was suggesting that the process should be free.

Pope Francis showed little use for those cardinals who had opposed him during the two synod weeks. The American Cardinal Burke, in particular, had been an irritation. On November 8, Pope Francis transferred Burke from his position of power at the Segnatura Apostolica tribunal in the Vatican to a more or less honorary post as head of the Sovereign Order of the Knights of Malta. Among the reasons given in the press for the transfer was a harsh sentence attributed to the American cardinal: "The church is now rudderless."

In fairness, Burke accepted the demotion with apparent grace. Speaking to the Catholic news service *Aleteia*, he said, "Some of the media simply want to represent me as if I existed to oppose Pope Francis. This is wrong. I know that it is part of my serving [the church] to speak the truth, at a time when many people are confused." Just who was "confused" he did not say. What he did say was that in the church there are "truths that do not change and cannot be changed."

Burke was replaced by the newly promoted French Cardinal Dominique Mamberti, sixty-two, who from 2006 onward had been Pope Benedict's head of relations with states, the Vatican equivalent of foreign minister. Mamberti was in turn replaced by a British prelate, Monsignor Paul Gallagher, sixty, from Liverpool, former nunzio or papal ambassador in Australia with a long career in Vatican diplomacy behind him, having also served in Tanzania, Uruguay, the Philippines, the Council of Europe, Guatemala, and Burundi.

The retired Cardinal Kasper had the last word. "Francis is the pope of surprises," he said during a lecture at Catholic University of America in Washington in early November 2014. "He is not a liberal, but he is a radical in the original sense of the word, which refers to roots."

Among the biggest surprises has been the ease with which Pope Francis has taken to the new media. Although he admits that he prefers the traditional pen to the computer screen, and says he is not technologically gifted, he uses perhaps more effectively than any contemporary national leader the personal telephone call, tweets, and video messages. He is retweeted ten times more frequently than President Obama.

6

— ❧ —

@Pontifex

Dear friends, I am pleased to get in touch with you through Twitter. Thank you for your generous response. I bless all of you from my heart.
>   —POPE BENEDICT, IN HIS FIRST OFFICIAL
>   VATICAN TWEET FROM @PONTIFEX

"Wow! Is this true?! Pope Benedict XVI has started tweeting! Welcome Your Holiness! I am grateful for your blessing! Follow him!" was the twittery reaction of a titillated *@Joyful_Minoz* on reading the pontiff's, and the Vatican's, first-ever tweet December 12, 2012.

Other tweeters were less enchanted. Another that same day wrote, in response to Benedict, "For the first time in history, a man can communicate directly with some low-level press officer in the Vatican." Comedian Colm Tobin (not to be confused with the Irish novelist Colm Toibin), finding the pope's American English an occasion of jest, wrote to *@Pontifex* that "thou shalt not covet your neighbor's Twitter followers."

Tobin need not have bothered, for there was no need to covet: papal tweets were instantly trending. Following Benedict's departure, his successor, Francis, surged into the Twittersphere, sending several tweets weekly translated into nine different languages, even though he has admitted never having written in anything but longhand and never having gotten used to writing on a computer. During a video-conference described by the Vatican as a "Google Hangout" with a group of disabled children from around the world in February 2014, Pope Francis told a Spanish girl: "You want to know the truth? I'm a disaster with machines. I don't know how to work a computer. What a shame!"

All tweets are taken from the pope's own words in homilies, prayers, and addresses to the general audiences. Francis reviews each tweet personally while members of the social communications department tend to the translating and sending of tweets like this: "When one lives attached to money, it is impossible to be truly happy."

By June 2015, Francis' *@Pontifex* vaunted twenty-one million Twitter followers on nine different language accounts, including more than five million in English. More popular still were his tweets in Spanish, which attracted more than nine million, and another 1.4 million in Portuguese. Even his tweets in Latin attracted more than three hundred thousand Catholics.

Only President Obama had more "followers."

———

Despite such success, Pope Francis is notoriously more comfortable on the telephone than tweeting. He delights in picking up a phone to ring old friends, but also unknown individuals, especially if they have written him a poignant letter.

He also does occasional, more or less official business on the telephone. On March 15, 2013, at 10:15 in the morning only two days after his election, the new Jesuit pontiff attempted to call the Jesuit Father General at the order's motherhouse, located a few blocks away from the pontiff's new home inside Vatican City, at the St. Martha's Residence.

The young doorman who answered heard an anonymous voice say, "Phone call from the St. Martha's Residence." Then the doorman heard another speaker on the line, speaking in a "soft and serene" voice, according to Father Claudio Barriga, who recounted the incident via email to his fellow Jesuits worldwide.

"Buon giorno, sono il Papa Francesco," said the soft and serene voice in Italian. "Good morning, I'm Pope Francis. I'd like to speak with the Father General."

The doorman's first reaction was to say, "Sure, and I'm Napoleon," Father Barriga related. Instead the doorman said, curtly: "May I ask who's calling?"

Realizing that the doorman did not believe him, Francis said kindly, "Seriously, this is Pope Francis. And your name is . . . ?"

In another incident, Stefano Cabizza, a nineteen-year-old engineering student at the University of Padua, picked up the phone, saying, "Hi, who's this?" only to hear: "I'm Pope Francis, let's use the 'tu' [informal you] with each other." During August 2013, Cabizza had left a letter addressed to the pope at the papal summer residence (not used by Francis, who opened it to public visits). Recalling this with a sense of shock, Cabizza then heard the pope say, "Do you think the Apostles used the 'Lei' [formal you] with Jesus? Or called him 'your excellency'? They were friends then, just as you and I are now."

This widely reported incident was picked up by the authoritative northern Italian author and political commentator Beppe Severgnini (once a visiting professor at Middlebury College in Vermont). Severgnini obligingly published a list of helpful hints of what to do should *you* find yourself in that same position, with the pontiff on the other end of the line. "I mean, you're dousing the salad with olive oil. The phone rings, and you have to find the words to converse with the Vicar of Christ, no easy task," Severgnini wrote.[1]

Of course this Vicar of Christ is affable and witty. "So, being a little careful, you can have a good conversation—and by the way, Pope Bergoglio is probably the last person who still makes phone calls on a fixed line" (i.e., not a cell phone). Another hint: "Don't call him Frankie or Checco, just exclaim, 'Holiness,' and maybe ask him how the Argentine soccer team is doing." Don't fear being normal, Severgnini advises: "If he had wanted to be bored he'd have called a cabinet minister." And if you want to ask for a helping hand with a job or introduction or permit, forget it—he will just regret having made a phone call to Italy.

"Also, don't mention recent problems at the Vatican. They are not his fault."

Joking aside, the pontiff's telephone calls are no laughing matter, but they are effective, for they humanize the Vatican and project a warm personal quality. In speaking to one person, especially if suffering, Pope Francis appears to be speaking to all. As he has explained, it is a "service," and part of being a priest.

"When I was a priest in Buenos Aires it was simpler. Now it's not so easy to make a call, considering the number of people who write to me," he says. "But for me it is still a habit, a service. I feel it inside me . . . I am a priest. I like it."[2]

After Emilia Orlandi, 102, from near Bergamo, knitted a white scarf for the pope and mailed it to him, he phoned to thank her. When she eventually realized that it was Pope Francis calling, she said later, "He asked me to pray for the popes who were being made saints. I did—and I watched the canonizations on TV."

If a few of these calls seem kindly but slightly trivial, other papal telephone calls are deadly serious—literally. In August 2014 Pope Francis telephoned John and Diane Foley after their son, James Foley, a journalist, was beheaded by Islamic extremists after two years of captivity in northern Syria. This was the second time James had been captured; the first was in Libya. During that imprisonment in 2011, young Foley had written to Marquette University, from which he had graduated, saying that while in captivity he had begun to pray "what my mother and grandmother would have prayed," the rosary. In his own tweet after that tragic beheading the pope wrote: "Lord, with so much violence in Iraq, may we persevere in our prayer and generosity."

Rape victim Alejandra Pereyra, forty-four, of Argentina, also sent the pope a letter, and he telephoned to console her. "When I asked who was calling, I heard 'the pope' and was petrified. Hearing his voice made me feel as if I had been touched by the hand of God."

And on Christmas Eve 2014, the pontiff telephoned a group of Christian refugees huddled in a refugee camp at Ankawa, northern Iraq, who had been forced to flee from their homes by Muslim extremists. To the refugees the pope said, "You are like Jesus in the night, and I bless you and am close to you. I embrace all of you and wish you a holy Christmas."

One of the more startling telephone calls was to Diego Neria Lejarraga, whose local bishop in Plasencia, Spain, had helped forward to Francis a letter from Neria. Born female and raised devoutly Catholic, after his sex change operation in 2006, he found himself scorned in his local church, including by his parish priest. "I never lost faith, ever, but the other thing is the rejection," Neria told CNN.

Then, in what was presumably a first for a transgender individual, he received two telephone calls from Pope Francis with an invitation to his home in the Vatican. The meeting took place in the papal residence, the Santa Marta, on January 24, 2015.

With his telephone, the pope was literally kicking open the doors of churches to let outsiders in. In a homily in May 2013 so sensational that it was picked up by the Huffington Post, among many others, he explained why:

"The Lord created us in His image and likeness, and we are the image of the Lord, and He does good and all of us have this commandment at heart: do good and do not do evil. All of us."

'But, Father, this is not Catholic! He cannot do good.'

"Yes, he can. . . . The Lord has redeemed all of us, all of us, with the Blood of Christ: all of us, not just Catholics. Everyone!"

'Father, the atheists?'

"Even the atheists. Everyone! . . . We must meet one another doing good."

'But I don't believe, Father, I am an atheist!'

"But do good: we will meet one another there."[2]

———

For most of its two thousand years, the Catholic Church hasn't had a telephone at hand. Papal communications to the faithful began with a man on horseback delivering a papal bull (originally *bulla*, or seal), written first on papyrus, later on parchment.

The subjects of early papal bulls varied: a new law, a notarial act, an appointment, an excommunication. Since forgeries were not unknown, in the twelfth century a fairly crude lead seal showing the heads of the apostles Peter and Paul on one side and the pope's profile on the other was added for authentication. During the Renaissance, Benvenuto Cellini added artistry to the bull when he fashioned an elegant metal matrix in 1535 for use by the Farnese pontiff Paul III, Michelangelo's sponsor.

The first telephone was installed in the Vatican only in 1886. By that time Alexander Graham Bell's patented invention allowing conversations at a distance was a decade old, but Italy—unified for only sixteen years after having seized vast papal lands and properties—forbade use of the Vatican phone system outside its one square mile of remaining territory in Rome. Although the cardinals and their underlings were not allowed to phone outside the diminished Vatican state, Italian spies diligently listened to their conversations. This was how, during World War I, Italian intelligence snoopers gleaned news of a papal peace proposal in that tremendous August of 1917.

Italy kept the Vatican phone lines limited to house calls until, following the advent of Fascism, Benito Mussolini signed the Lateran Pacts with Pope Pius XI's secretary of state, Cardinal Pietro Gasparri, in 1929. The bargain was useful to both sides: the pontiff could at last set foot on Italian soil; Mussolini gained respectability; and the Curia and cardinals could phone their relatives in Rome.

Naturally if the pontiff made a phone call from his rigorously white and often elaborately elegant telephone, there would be a recipient inside the august halls of the Vatican. Hearing the voice of the pope on the line, the recipient was expected to sink down upon his knees to hear the message. Those old white telephones are now on view in a showcase at the Vatican telephone exchange staffed around the clock by devoted nuns.

It was another great leap forward when, after six years of planning, Guglielmo Marconi set up the first Vatican Radio station, then as now run by the Jesuit order. For its inauguration February 12, 1931, reporters and cameramen from the U.S. Paramount News had arrived by ship, bringing hand-powered cameras that for the first time in cinema history had a live soundtrack attached to the film footage (today the inauguration footage is among the treasures in the Vatican video archives).[3] Outside in Rome itself and even in faraway Turin, crowds gathered around loudspeakers to hear the pontiff speak. In London, thirty-five hundred Catholics stood waiting for hours in Westminster Cathedral in order to hear the pontiff, according to the London *News Chronicle*.

As the pope entered the Vatican Gardens, where the new Radio Transmission Station was erected, celebratory trumpets sounded. Marconi was already there waiting. Through earphones he had been preparing for the broadcast on two ten-kilowatt shortwave frequencies for listeners waiting as far away as New York, Melbourne, and Quebec. At last Marconi spoke into the microphone.

"I have the highest honor of announcing that in only a matter of seconds the supreme pontiff, Pope Pius XI, will inaugurate the Radio Station of the Vatican City State," a proud Marconi announced. "The electric radio waves will transport to all the world his words of peace and blessing."

Like Benedict's first tweet, Pius XI's first radio message was in Latin. Written by the pontiff himself, it began with the words "Omni creaturae [All creatures] . . ."The response was extraordinary. From New York, an editorial in the *Herald* gushed that "few events in the history of the world can compare with the profound impact the Head of the Holy Roman See made during his address directed to the entire planet . . . and such a thing could not have been foreseen by any preceding Pope. This is a miracle of science, and no less a miracle of faith."

By the eve of World War II, Vatican Radio had become far more international and was broadcasting over ten frequencies. In his radio message August 24, 1939, just one week before war broke out, Pope Pius XII warned listeners that "the danger is imminent, but there is still time. Nothing is lost with peace. All can be lost with war."

It was the peace that was lost, and Pius XII was then accused of being too close to both Mussolini and Nazi Germany and, as a result, secretly reluctant in his wartime broadcasts (by then in four languages) to criticize either. He certainly bowed to German pressure over Poland, but the larger reality was complex. Harold H. Tittmann was a U.S. diplomat who happened to be Protestant and actually lived inside the officially neutral Vatican City throughout the war. His office, and that of his British counterpart, Sir D'Arcy Osborne, minister to the Holy See, were located in the same building, which was later refurbished as the Vatican's guesthouse, the Casa Santa Marta, now Pope Francis' home. In his book *Inside the Vatican of Pius XII: The Memoir of an American Diplomat During World War II*, Tittmann writes that during wartime he had in fact asked the pope why he had not formally denounced Hitler on Vatican Radio. Tittmann relates his protest to the pontiff, and the pope's reply:

> *"Your broadcasts are too vague; they are open to many interpretations. We need something more explicit." The Pope then explained: "Well, I am sorry, I cannot do it and here are the reasons: first, there are over forty million German-speaking Catholics. If I should denounce the Nazis by name as you desire and Germany should lose the war, Germans everywhere would feel that I had contributed to the defeat, not only of the Nazis, but of Germany herself; for the German population not to be able to make the distinction between the Nazis and the Fatherland would only be human in the confusion and distress of defeat. I cannot afford to risk alienating so many of the faithful. One of my predecessors, Pope Benedict XV in the First World War, through an unfortunate public statement of the type you now wish me to make, did just this and the interests of the Church in Germany suffered as a result."*

On Christmas in 1942, Pius XII spoke on Vatican Radio against the persecution of "hundreds of thousands" of Jews and Gypsies who, "through no fault of their own, sometimes only because of their nationality or race, have been consigned to death or slow extermination."

Given its status as an independent state, the Vatican had already become a wartime radio news source for the Allies about both Fascist Italy and Nazi Germany. Vatican Radio also broadcast some non-Italian-censored news about the war and, reportedly, elements of pro-Allied propaganda as well. Not surprisingly, Vatican Radio news broadcasts were then banned in Germany along with other foreign newscasts. At that point Vatican Radio was also broadcasting with some coded messages, which the Allies (and not only they) tried to break.

In his recent book, *1943 Bombe sul Vaticano* (*1943 Bombs on the Vati-*

can), published by the Vatican in 2010, Italian author Augusto Ferrara reports that the Vatican was bombed on November 5, 1943, by Italian Fascists who believed that Vatican Radio was the main target for having broadcast "important information to the Allied Forces through its frequencies." The plane, a Savoia Marchetti flown out of Viterbo, seventy miles north of Rome, dropped four bombs in the Vatican Gardens, close to the Vatican Radio building, though without killing anyone. Initially the Allies had been blamed for the bombing.

The postwar period brought the expansion of Vatican Radio into eighteen languages and the creation in 1948 of a new department within the Roman Curia: the Pontificium Consilium de Communicationibus Socialibus (Pontifical Council for Social Communications). Needing more space for its shortwave radio broadcasting worldwide than the Gardens afforded, the Holy See acquired a 988-acre stretch of land at Santa Maria di Galeria nine miles north of Rome, which received extraterritorial status from the Italian Republic in 1952.

In 1957, Pius XII was still pontiff when, becoming ever more involved with the media, he issued an encyclical, or letter, called *Pastoral Instruction of the Means of Social Communication*. This was followed in 1971 by another media encyclical issued by Paul VI, declaring that "The Church sees these media as 'gifts of God' which, in accordance with his providential design, unite men in brotherhood and so help them to cooperate with his plan for salvation."

The worldwide importance of the media to the church in Rome was further bolstered when John Paul II created a new TV center in 1983. To store the film and cassettes, Vatican archivists built a library of both publicly and privately recorded video, containing twenty thousand items. The plan now is to digitize this unique archive.

Along with the heightened attention to the media came a host of new problems. Beginning with John Paul II, the popes had become a brand, marketed commercially by both the Vatican and private businessmen. For sale with the face of the current pope are solid gold coins, postage stamps, necklaces, bracelets, rosaries, refrigerator magnets, and phone cards. The latter are a special favorite of collectors; one available on eBay in 2015 was priced at over forty dollars, and a series of forty-three, around four hundred dollars.

———

The popularity of Pope Francis radically expanded the marketing efforts on the part of both the Vatican and private entrepreneurs. As one PR company put it in its own business terms, its scandals of finance and pedophile priests were making the Catholic Church a "damaged brand." The advent of Francis with his communication skills is restoring the quality of the brand and helping with "audience building," says media expert Clay Ziegler. His evidence: a Google search of "Pope Francis" churned up 656 million results after he had been installed only a few weeks.[4]

As London's *Daily Mail* put it, "After years of negative press, the Catholic Church is basking in the 'Francis Effect,' which has been credited with a 20 percent rise in congregations in Britain, and similar boosts around the world."[5]

"Pope Francis is a success as a brand," Bruno Ballardini, marketing expert, told journalist Vladimiro Polchi in an interview for the Italian weekly *Il Venerdi*.[6] Ballardini is the author of *Leader come Francesco, Perché il Papa è un genio del marketing* (*Leading like Francis: Why the Pope Is a Marketing Genius*). Asked what is the financial value of Pope Francis as a brand, Ballardini replied that the value of a Facebook fan was estimated at $150 or more, "and in October 2014 the pope had 2,638,010 Facebook fans."

Is it paradoxical that the pope of the poor is an object of aggressive merchandising? Yes, says Ballardini, but merchandising is communication, not commerce. "The real problem is that in the past the Church applied a marketing strategy without realizing it, but today it relishes this, creating its own agencies." Without care, there is always the risk of reducing the value of the brand, and hence the product—that is, of church doctrine, he concludes.

But this is not the whole story. "In his communications Pope Francis acts on various levels, beginning with image," Stefano Ronchetti, another Italian marketing expert, said in an interview.[7] Among the first objects that define Pope Francis' image is the pectoral cross he wears, made of iron, not of gold. Then there are the ordinary shoes he wears, having rejected the traditional red silk papal slippers worn by Benedict and earlier popes.

Pope Francis is also communicating a message when he rides in an ordinary service car rather than a limousine, carries his own briefcase onto the plane when he travels, hugs the disabled and disfigured, washes and kisses the feet of prisoners, and removes his shoes to enter a mosque. "This tells the viewer that, 'why, he is like me,'" says Ronchetti. "Especially in this period when most people have financial difficulties the listener identifies his personal struggles with the spiritual quest of the pope. It makes one better able to accept one's own problems."

Pope Francis' use of language in a highly personal, informal manner is another element encouraging ordinary people to identify with him. Whole books and academic papers have been written on the words he uses. Speaking in his native Spanish, he occasionally adopts local Buenos Aires slang to get his meaning across more vividly. Lunfardo is a lower-class dialect that originated in the Argentinian capital in the late nineteenth and early twentieth centuries. From Lunfardo the pontiff has borrowed the word *balconear*, whose literal meaning is to "watch life from the window or the balcony"—that is, to remain a spectator rather than participant. As used by Pope Francis, it means to fail to dive into Christian life.

People listening to him in St. Peter's Square for the first time after his election responded immediately to his informal manner of speaking. This makes him popular, but can boomerang. Shortly after the massacre of *Charlie Hebdo* cartoonists by Islamic extremists in Paris on January 7, 2015, a French journalist aboard the papal flight from Sri Lanka to the Philippines asked Francis his opinion of freedom of expression, referring to the cartoons mocking the Prophet Mohammed. The pope's cautious reply was that "there is a limit. Every religion has its dignity. . . . In freedom of expression there are limits."

The influential Polly Toynbee of the *Guardian* was only one of the many challenging the pope's words. For her, the flurry of scandal over Oxford University Press' stopping its children's writers from referring to pigs or pork for fear of risking Middle East sales—or the Harper Collins atlases for export that mysteriously omit Israel for the same reason—was akin, and showed just how easily freedom slips away unless scurrilous outriders like *Charlie Hebdo* can keep mocking church and mosque.[8]

Pope Francis then compared the *Charlie Hebdo* cartoons with an offense to one's mother, and ventured that, should someone "say a curse word against my mother, he can expect a punch." Although many might secretly agree, commentators were shocked at the pope's use of the word "punch," for it appeared to justify the use of violence. Toynbee, for one, proclaimed: "Verbal provocation is never an excuse for violence—that's the wife-beater's defence. Is he [Pope Francis] saying we must respect any old cult: followers of Black Sabbath, Odin, Scientology, astrology? Or is it the size of a faith that earns it the right to gag mockery?"

As if in defiance of those (mostly Anglo-Saxons) who had assailed his use of the word "punch," one week later Pope Francis intentionally used the word "kick" while speaking to the press on the return flight from his visit to the Philippines January 19, 2015. While seeking funds for the poor of the Argentine slums, the pontiff related, two government flunkies in Buenos Aires had offered him four hundred thousand dollars, on condition he return half in a kickback. "At that moment I thought about what I would do—either I insult them and give them a kick where the sun doesn't shine [in the butt] or I play the fool."

In the end "I decided to play the fool," said the pontiff, "and told them that I had no bank account."

Others of Pope Francis' homey and improvised comments can take him into dangerous territory. At a general audience at the Vatican February 4, 2015, the pope, meaning to encourage fathers to be involved in family doings, spoke approvingly of a certain father who had confided that "sometimes I have to spank [*picchiare*] my children a bit—but never on the face, so as not to upset them too much." Adding his own observation to this, the pope commented, his face serious, "How beautiful! He [the father] shows a sense of dignity. He has to give a punishment, he does it properly, and goes forward."

An American Catholic therapist, Dr. Gregory Popcak, reported receiving many emails of protest over Pope Francis' support for spanking as a suitable punishment for naughty children. Although Popcak referred the objectors to the full context of the pontiff's remark and his intent, the view of the American Psychological Association is that "physical discipline is increasingly being viewed as a violation of children's human rights," and that research shows that "spanking and other forms of physical discipline can pose serious risks to children."

Pope Francis also communicates by material gesture. In St. Peter's Square one day he had Vatican employees hand out to pilgrims twenty thousand tiny packets resembling a box of aspirins. Marked MISERICORDINA, each packet contained a rosary, an image of a merciful Christ, and a little sheet of instructions for prayer. In this way the pontiff communicated the idea that prayer is a spiritual medicine. Needless to say, his giving away the boxes of Misericordina was broadcast on Vatican Radio as well as reported in the official daily newspaper *L'Osservatore Romano* and in VIS, the official Vatican news agency. The news was then repeated worldwide. Later the little boxes were advertised for sale online.

Other gifts from Pope Francis have also made worldwide headlines (which is not why he did it, of course). For his seventy-eighth birthday Francis gave the homeless bunking down regularly in the street near St. Peter's four hundred sleeping bags. And in March 2014 he surprised pilgrims attending his weekly audience by first asking the crowd how many read the Bible every day, then told them, "It is good to have a little Bible that you carry with you in your pocket or in your bag. Always carry a Bible with you, even on the bus." Volunteers then distributed hundreds of nicely printed, pocket-sized copies of the New Testament, 5½ by 3¾ inches, with the pope's signature on page one.

In private-sector marketing, one Italian publisher invented a lavishly illustrated newsweekly entirely dedicated to Pope Francis, with a first edition of half a million copies. Another launched an all-cartoon magazine about Francis, "so as to bring little children close to the pope through simple words and charming drawings." French publisher Hachette issued fifty collectable rosaries of Pope Francis, sold in weekly installments at around eleven dollars each. In the cinema, prominent Italian directors Liliana Cavani and Daniele Luchetti are each preparing movies about him.

And there is tourism. Visitors from Argentina rose by 40 percent during the first months of the papacy and by 20 percent from all Latin America, to the delight of Roman hotelkeepers and restaurateurs. "For them, Pope Francis is already a saint," concluded Polchi.

———

When the pope is not speaking for himself, there is the 150-year-old Vatican daily *L'Osservatore Romano*. Founded in 1861 under Pope Pius IX, its publishing plant had to be moved from downtown Rome into the Vatican City to save it from marauding Fascist thugs in 1929, after its editorials had criticized Benito Mussolini. Today, under editor-in-chief Giovanni Maria Vian, its six weekly editions remain influential despite its fairly modest daily circulation of only fifteen thousand.

The pope also has a busy press office and an official spokesman. The first one I came to know personally as a correspondent in Rome was Professor Federico Alessandrini. He was a soft-spoken lay journalist and a staff member of *L'Osservatore Romano,* who was appointed chief Vatican spokesman by Paul VI in 1970. He was no spin doctor—on the contrary, he made himself relatively inaccessible to us in the working press even though he had set up the very first press room for reporters covering the Vatican during the years of Fascism.

Alessandrini was replaced by Pope Paul VI in 1976 by Father Romeo Panciroli, who continued the tight-lipped Vatican public relations tradition to the point that we of the media called him "Padre Non Mi Risulta" (Father I Have No News on That). We fifty or so Vaticanists would gather regularly to hear him, which is to say not to hear him, in the big press room off Via della Conciliazione, only a few steps from St. Peter's, in a building dating from the Holy or Jubilee Year declared by the Vatican in 1950.

Father Panciroli left the spokesman job in 1984 for a new post in Vatican diplomacy, serving in Liberia and Iran. He died at age eighty-two in 2006.

His successor as head of the Holy See press office was a multilingual Spaniard, Joaquín Navarro-Valls. Now in his late seventies, Navarro-Valls had been trained as a medical doctor, including at Harvard University, before working toward an advanced degree in psychology. At the same time he took a degree in journalism. I got to know him when he joined the traveling Vatican press as Vatican correspondent for the mass circulation Spanish daily *ABC.* He also happened to be a high-flying member of the Opus Dei, a controversial right-wing Catholic institution founded in Spain in 1928 by Father Josemaría Escrivá, later made a saint by John Paul II.

As a member of the Vatican press corps, I traveled regularly with Pope John Paul II, who made extensive visits abroad. The pontiff himself was communicative; I was once startled when, seated half-asleep with my shoes off on a papal trip, John Paul came to sit down beside me. Combined with John Paul's gregarious, outgoing nature, the importance of the media and of his chief spokesman's role expanded enormously; Navarro-Valls was the first professional journalist hired for that position. Unlike Alessandrini in the fifties, Navarro-Valls was most definitely a spin doctor, and by 1984 had become the public face of John Paul, for whom he worked for twenty-two years.

Navarro-Valls had wit and charm. Like Pope Francis, Navarro-Valls had enjoyed dancing the tango as a youth, he confided in an interview in 2005 with the Italian magazine *L'Espresso* entitled, "The Holy See to the Rhythm of the Tango: The Pope's Spokesman in His Own Words." The two were obviously close friends, and frequently shared meals.

Navvaro-Valls' expertise as a physician became important in communicating to the world press the declining health of Pope John Paul, who suffered from Parkinson's disease. Their close emotional relationship became ever more apparent as the end drew near for John Paul, and the final press conferences Navarro-Valls gave as the pontiff lay dying were deeply moving. Later Navarro-Valls said that John Paul had been "one of the smartest popes in history."

Succeeding John Paul, Pope Benedict chose as his spokesman a Jesuit priest, Father Federico Lombardi, the head of Vatican Radio. With degrees in mathematics and theology, Father Lombardi maintained a low-key style. His press experience had been limited to working for the Jesuit magazine *La Civiltà Cattolica*. Taking up his new post he said dismissively, "I don't think my role is to explain the pope's thinking or to explain the things that he already says in his extraordinarily clear and rich way."

He found instead that he had to do some explaining. During Benedict's visit to Israel in May 2009 (which I covered for the BBC), the Israeli press accused Benedict of having been a member of the Hitler

Youth. At a briefing Father Lombardi vigorously denied this, only to be obliged to retract it later. The pope had himself admitted this, in an extended interview with German writer Peter Seewald in his book *Salt of the Earth*. As this shows, the job of papal spokesman demands not only charm, tact, and language skills, but also an encyclopedic knowledge of the papacy and of world geopolitics.

While traveling on the plane for a score of papal trips in the course of a decade, Father Lombardi would brief us journalists, but he was clearly not always well informed about the pontiff's thinking; he and the pope did not have that personal friendship shared by Pope John Paul and Navarro-Valls. Frequently Father Lombardi would appear stymied for responses to the questions of prying Vatican correspondents and had to admit that he didn't know the answer.

Nevertheless, upon the election of Pope Francis, the first Jesuit pope, the role of Father Lombardi, also a member of the Jesuit order, suddenly expanded. Both he and Francis are outgoing, but clearly he has less direct access to Pope Francis than did Navarro-Valls with Pope John Paul; their contacts are normally through the Secretariat of State. He has been kept extraordinarily busy with a crescendo of short papal visits around the world, and with an ever more numerous international press corps accredited permanently to the Holy See, even as he continues to direct Vatican Radio. He is personable and rather gentle.

Among his aides, the congenial American layman Greg Burke, fifty-five, stands tall. A former journalist with *Time* magazine and for a time a Fox TV News correspondent, Burke was hired in June 2012 as senior communications adviser inside the Vatican Secretariat of State. Like Navarro-Valls, Burke is also a member of Opus Dei. "Francis' marketing mastermind," as the *Daily Mail* dubbed him, Burke has worked steadily behind the scenes to help shape the image of Pope Francis.

In a BBC interview Burke stressed that the pontiff's short excursion to Lampedusa to celebrate a requiem mass for hundreds of drowned migrants was, like the day of prayer he had called for peace in Syria, Francis' own idea. "We just helped with the media," said Burke, admitting at the same time, "We never quite know what he will be doing next!"

A corollary of all this are rising expectations, which, if they fail to be realized, could bring disappointment.

————

Even as the Vatican's attentions to the media expanded, so did its problems. By 1999 the electromagnetic emissions from Vatican Radio's forest of thirty transmitters, soaring above the huge stretch of Vatican-owned land north of Rome, had become, in some cases, twice that permitted by Italian law, according to tests by the regional Civil Protection agency. When two investigations were conducted by the Lazio Region with backing from the University of Florence, they showed an unduly high incidence of leukemia in the surrounding area, and legal actions against Vatican Radio were begun.

Local residents sued, and the case went before the Court of Appeal, which ruled that the emissions indeed exceeded "all special laws in the matter." A Rome prosecutor had declared that "regarding the potential link of cause between exposure to non-ionizing radiations and the cases of leukemia in the area under investigation, [we] hold that the weight of evidence is in favor of the existence of that link."[9]

But there were no consequences. First, before coming to court a priest being sued had died. Then the cardinal in charge of the Rome Vatican Radio office slipped off the hook because the statute of limitations had expired. And at any rate the area had extraterritoriality, meaning that Italian law was not applicable.

Still, the Vatican began backing away, if only gradually, and if only because it had taken a beating in the Italian press. In June 2012, the official Vatican spokesman Father Federico Lombardi, who had also been director general of Vatican Radio since 2005, announced that short- and medium-wave broadcasts would cease in "most of" Europe and North America, there being less need thanks in large measure to Internet transmissions, which can be rebroadcast on local Catholic radio stations around the world.

However, the Vatican's shortwave broadcasts continue to South America, Africa, and Asia.

Perhaps the biggest media problem of all was the scandal that came to be nicknamed "Vatileaks." Its importance cannot be understated, for it was in good measure responsible for the resignation of Pope Benedict and hence for the election of Pope Francis.

Paolo Gabriele, a forty-six-year-old married layman with three children, was Pope Benedict's personal valet and butler in the papal penthouse apartment on the top floor of the Apostolic Palace. A fervent Catholic, in the morning he laid out the pope's clothes before attending the pope's private mass. At mealtimes he served at table. When Benedict rode in the Popemobile, Gabriele sat in the front seat next to the chauffeur.

These occupations left him with long hours of tedium. To give the butler something to do, Benedict's personal secretary and fellow German, the much younger Monsignor Georg Gänswein, had an extra desk and a computer set up in the secretaries' office next to Pope Benedict's study.

There, for seven years, Gabriele whiled away the time downloading and printing documents that interested him. From chatter overheard while he served at table, he also developed a few notions of his own, becoming convinced that there was something rotten in the state of the Vatican. Peeking into the pope's desk proved to him that this was indeed the case, and so Gabriele quietly borrowed documents, which he photocopied. Some of the papal correspondence revealed instances of kickbacks, bribes, money laundering, and nepotism. He also became convinced that within the Apostolic Palace itself a poisonous atmosphere had festered for years.

Taking with him these photocopies and the printouts from what he had downloaded, Gabriele became a packrat, gradually filling, floor to ceiling, a giant cupboard inside his Vatican apartment. But his knowing this, his possessing the documents, was not enough. Ever more convinced that what they revealed should be broadcast for the benefit of the church, he slipped a set of the incriminating documents to an Italian priest described by Gabriele as his "spiritual adviser." The priest, whose name has never been revealed, told the butler to confess what he had done to the pope, and burned the copies given him by Gabriele.

Instead Gabriele passed a second copy of the documents to Italian investigative journalist Gianluigi Nuzzi, who began leaking bits and pieces of them in early 2012. In May, Nuzzi's book *His Holiness: The Secret Papers of Benedict XVI* was published. In it were facsimile copies of particularly damaging documents. Letters signed by, among others, Carlo Maria Viganò, former Vatican administrator to the pope, spoke of abuses brought to their attention by underlings.

Three senior cardinals launched an investigation, which produced a seven-hundred-page report. Initially Gabriele denied responsibility, but in May 2012 he was confronted by the pontiff's private secretary, Monsignor Gänswein, and admitted responsibility. Then Vatican police found the towering pile of documents in his home. Claudio Sciarpelletti, an Italian computer technician who worked in the Vatican's Secretariat of State (its political as well as diplomatic directorate), was accused of aiding and abetting Gabriele in the leaking of the documents.

Gabriele told investigators that he believed Pope Benedict had not been correctly informed of the dastardly goings-on inside the Vatican, and that publication of the documents would deliver a "salutary shock" that would set the Vatican back upon the path of righteousness. Gabriele said he was doing this as "the agent of the Holy Spirit."

Another version of his motives exists: some suspect that Gabriele had collected the documents for self-protection in case he tangled with his boss, Gänswein. Vouchsafing this theory, *Guardian* reporter Andrew Brown opined in a world-weary tone, "Almost anything is more credible than the idea of a secret network of reformers in the Vatican, bravely conspiring to leak all its secrets to the outside world."[10]

Uninterested in his motives, Vatican gendarmes seized Gabriele and put him into a holding cell, advising him that he risked a four-year sentence in an Italian prison, the Vatican having no appropriate long-term jail. Sciarpelletti risked a one-year imprisonment.

Gabriele was convicted of "aggravated theft" of the documents and sentenced to eighteen months in prison. But as Christmas 2012 approached and Gabriele had been in the Vatican prison seven months, the Holy See, which is to say Pope Benedict, formally pardoned him in order to give him and his family "the possibility of resuming their lives peacefully." The author of the Vatileaks was released, and not only that: he was given a new job and a new place to live, no longer inside Vatican City, but near the Bambino Gesù Children's Hospital.

For some observers, the pardon effectively acknowledged that the butler had indeed acted in what he believed were the best interests of the church.

Most important, the trio of cardinals delivered their report December 17; the pardon to Gabriele came five days later; and an obviously exhausted pontiff resigned for reasons of health February 11, just seven weeks after his pardon of Gabriele.

———

Pope Francis, who had initially planned to travel as little as possible, in an about-face visited Brazil, Jordan, the Palestinian territories, Israel, South Korea, Albania, France, Turkey, Sri Lanka, the Philippines, Bosnia, Ecuador, Bolivia, and Paraguay during the first two and a half years of his pontificate. Of all these pastoral visits, his four-day tour to the

Philippines beginning January 15, 2015, was the most media hip. In the week before he arrived and during his visit, the 3.3 million tweets about it broke Twitter records in the Philippines, according to Smart Communications, the country's cell phone and Internet platform. The most retweeted was in Tagalog: "Ang Pilipinas ay patunay ng kabataan at kasiglahan ng Simbahan" (The Philippines is witness to the youth and vitality of the Church).

Miguel R. Camus, journalist with the Philippine *Daily Inquirer,* reported afterward that the pontiff had enjoyed a "rockstar turnout," and his influence had been "just as powerful in social media, a space the world leader has used to effectively spread the teachings of the Roman Catholic Church."[11]

This tour de force was no improvisation. Before the visit Smart Communications had teamed up with Twitter to provide free Twitter access for the duration of the papal visit. This allowed Filipinos to "participate in the social media conversation" by sending greetings to the hashtag *#DearPopeFrancis,* Camus reported. Simultaneously the pontiff's own Twitter account *@Pontifex* grew by over 365,000 new followers.

Today his twenty-one million followers place Pope Francis second in popularity on Twitter among world leaders; only Barack Obama, with over thirty-nine million, has more, while the next world leader down the list, Indian Prime Minister Narendra Modi, has only one-third of the pope's.

Other religions also tweet, of course. Several Christian evangelical leaders enjoy large Twitter audiences, whose many thousands of retweets multiply the visibility of their messages many times over. In one case an evangelical preacher had the same number of retweets as did pop singer Katy Perry, with 64.5 million Twitter followers.

Where religion and politics merge, Twitter matters. During the papal visit to the Philippines, *#jesuischarlie* surged to a top world Twitter spot, only to be followed January 17 by the Muslim hashtag *#we_love _prophet_mohamad.* "Social media have opened up the opportunity for young Muslims to engage with their faith and their co-religionists," a UAE-based journalist, Shelina Zahra Janmohamed, said in an interview with the Saudi-owned *Al Arabiya*. As she also pointed out, "The most successful are not necessarily the most influential."

The New York–based global communications and public relations firm Burson-Marsteller has a website, twiplomacy.com, which makes an annual global study of the use of Twitter by heads of state and government and ministers of foreign affairs. Influence comes with retweets, their study of 2014 showed, and here Pope Francis is in the lead, with eight times the retweets of President Obama:

> *Despite the [U.S. President's] account's massive following, the @BarackObama tweets are on average only retweeted 1,442 times. By this standard, Pope Francis @Pontifex is by far the most influential tweep with more than 10,000 retweets for every tweet he sends on his Spanish account, and over 6,000 retweets on his English account.*

Why? Official spokesman Father Lombardi explains that Pope Francis' words are "ideal for Twitter and can be translated easily into concise and inspirational points for reflection." The pope's preaching is ideal for tweets because his words are dense in meaning, and his phrases are "very efficient," repeated again and again until embedded in the memories of the faithful.

Father Antonio Spadaro, director of the Jesuit magazine *La Civiltà Cattolica*, explains the popularity of the papal tweets in this way: "Pope Francis is well aware of the importance of communication and of being in the street with men and women today. In the pontiff's "digital paths,"

> *you cannot evangelise if no direct relationship is created. The Pope loves contact. He is used to physical contact, but does not neglect the digital contact that is so important in today's world. Today's religious messages cannot simply be transmitted; they must be shared.*[12]

Until the arrival of Father Spadaro, editors of that rather sober Jesuit magazine appeared remote, but he is both open and spontaneous, sending out hundreds of tweets with photographs he himself took while traveling prior to the pope's visit to Sri Lanka and the Philippines. Father Spadaro also took a "lovely" photo of the smiling pope, which he put on his own Facebook page. "Within a short space of time it was shared 1,600 times. In the hectic life we live there is a need for something acute and intelligent that can break the daily routine and plant a seed for thought and meditation," wrote Spadaro.

Another of the pope's off-the-cuff remarks made aboard the plane from the Philippines on January 19, 2015—that Catholics should not feel compelled to breed "like rabbits"—had fur flying, even though he quickly added, "Excuse the expression." Relatively small numbers of U.S. and European Catholics still respect the Catholic doctrine forbidding artificial birth control; a Gallup Poll of 2012 showed that only 8 percent of the American Catholics surveyed said they consider birth control "morally wrong." Still, the informal comment reportedly shocked and offended parents with large families who respect church teaching.

Here Twitter played a role, with tweets suddenly awash with mocking photos of rabbits. From one reproachful tweet: "Rabbit breeders tell Pope Francis: 'Rabbits do not have a rampant sex drive.'" From Rome, *Telegraph* correspondent Nick Squires reported that Erwin Leowsky, president of the German Association of Rabbit Breeders, called the pope's allusion to rabbit fecundity "stupid."[13] Contrary to popular opinion, Leowsky said, rabbits do not have a rampant sex drive, and the pope "should really think harder about giving up expressions like that and allow people to use contraception instead. I think it would be much more appropriate than saying such stupid things."

Squires' rabbit article was shared 931 times, retweeted 140 times, and put onto 701 Facebook slots. Tweets followed: "German rabbit breeders criticize pope's sex comments . . . ha!!!" Another said simply: "German rabbit breeders 1, Pope 0."

In the end Pope Francis said he regretted the remark that had created such controversy. This too was tweeted, naturally: "Surprise, pope rows back."

As this suggests, however much the Vatican takes pride in the popularity of papal tweets, the pontiff's openness and ease with words, combined with the open nature of the medium, brings its own problems. In an example, on January 29, 2015, Pope Francis tweeted this, in Latin: "Si reapse amamus, id non facimus flocci quod alii nobis dolorem inferunt. Siquidem amor gaudet bonum facere." (True love does not pay attention to the evil it suffers. It rejoices in doing good.) Within hours it had attracted one hundred comments including a few in Latin, as well as in Chinese and Korean. One, from Dat Boi Kino in the Philippines, was ecstatic: "@Pontifex I love you."

But because of the use of the word *amamus*, "love," other twitterers made angry denunciations of the pedophile clergy whom Pope Francis has worked to eradicate. "@Pontifex You should win 'Stupid tweet of the day' for this mind numbing crud." From other outraged critics came equally harsh judgments: "@Pontifex Are you trying to say all those raped kids were given 'true love'?" and "@Pontifex The rape victims of your criminal institution must not have received true love because they suffered evil at the hands of evil."

Defenders of the pope then chimed in to the Twitter brawl. "No one's arguing with their belief, and they are not privileged to insult or say anything bad to the Pope just because" (here the writer ran out of his 140 spaces and continued in a second tweet) "they don't believe that GOD exists."

Another papal tweet, devoted to the International Holocaust Remembrance Day at Auschwitz January 27, 2015, ignited yet another Twitter quarrel. The pope wrote, "Auschwitz cries out with the pain of immense suffering and pleads for a future of respect, peace and encounter among peoples." This drew both enthusiastic responses, such as that eleven thousand Jews in Rome had been saved during World War II (the writer presumably meant by the Vatican), but also criticism: "11,000 Jews versus 6 million murdered, while Pope Pacelli [Pius XII] blessed the Nazi armies? WHAT ARE YOU SAYING?"

The occasional nasty argument on Twitter is sometimes laced with snide off-color remarks as well, and Vatican cardinals became understandably concerned. In May 2014 Archbishop Claudio Maria Celli, who heads the Vatican Pontifical Council for Social Communications, acknowledged in a speech in New York that offensive Twitter responses were creating a "crisis" in the Vatican.[14] For this very reason Pope Francis does not have his own Facebook account, he said, although the Vatican maintains an equivalent on its website www.news.va. In New York, Celli also revealed that the Vatican spends many hours removing objectionable material including obscene comments. However, he added, "educational" debates are left in place.

Vatican Insider, a section of the important Turin daily La Stampa, explained more. "The Vatican assigned a team of IT technicians to look into ways in which to prevent offensive or inappropriate messages and other such material from being posted on the Pope's page, but they concluded it was not possible."

All of these forms of communication, from telephone to Twitter through Vatican Radio, TV, and the rest, have been under review by a newly appointed committee chaired by Britain's Lord Patten of Barnes, seventy, composed of eleven media experts from Europe, the United States, Latin America, Asia, and various Vatican offices. Chris Patten, as he is known familiarly, has a uniquely rich background. The last British governor of Hong Kong, he is cochairman of the board of trustees of the International Crisis Group and chancellor of both Newcastle and Oxford universities. He served for five years as one of two U.K. delegates to the European Commission, and from 2011 through 2014 chaired the BBC Trust, the broadcasting corporation's governing body, until ill health forced him to resign. He is also an author of six books; his most recent is *What Next? Surviving the Twenty-First Century*.

Chris Patten also was responsible for the highly successful organization of Benedict's visit to England and Scotland in 2010.

Patten worked with Cardinal Pell, the Vatican's financial czar who has made cost-cutting a priority. Pell is among those promoting greater use of the new social media technologies and their integration with traditional media. By Pell's estimate, only about 10 percent of the world's Catholics are currently reached by the traditional Vatican media, including Vatican Radio and the daily *L'Osservatore Romano*, which also runs a weekly, and its foreign-language editions.

The Patten committee's goal is to advise Pope Francis on how to enhance the number of Catholics reached by the Vatican PR machine, and to reduce costs. Reviewing the Vatican media budget, Patten has admitted that some areas "are a little more opaque than one might like," as he told Vatican Radio reporter Philippa Hitchens in an interview September 24, 2014.

"I think what strikes us all, as Catholics particularly strongly, is how His Holiness is such an extraordinary communicator himself," said Patten. "It makes us realize how much the rest of us have to do—to use a sporting phrase—to up our game!" But media technology is changing rapidly, and "the young receive information in a different way. . . . It doesn't mean they're not informed, it means they get informed in different ways." We must consider how Vatican media needs to keep up with these technological changes, Patten said.

Asked about radio listeners, he replied, "We all know how important shortwave radio still is in communication with some of the poorest groups around the world, particularly in Africa and Asia. . . . We want to make sure that the Vatican's resources, which aren't limitless, are spent as effectively as possible."

Lord Patten's first experience working as a Vatican adviser and insider did not turn out as a particularly happy or effective one however, as we shall see in my final chapter.

Working with Patten was his committee's secretary, Monsignor Paul Tighe, a Dublin priest appointed by Pope Benedict as secretary of the Pontifical Council for Social Communications in 2007. For Tighe, with his long experience first in Dublin as diocesan director of public affairs and then in Vatican communications, cultural challenges matter more than the technical constraints of the new technologies.

"Our work is advocacy," Tighe explains. "It is to promote globally the importance of communications in the life of the church, and not only in the church."[15] As for Twitter, "We wanted to be sure that the pope's presence in social media would be authentic." The church must be present effectively "in a world that is wired differently, where the conversations are changing." Though understanding little about technology, Pope Francis saw that Twitter is "a way to engage with people, and also to show bishops and priests around the world the importance of the social media," says Tighe.

———

To this end the pope app was created in mid-2013. "We realized how much material was becoming available, but not necessarily attractively packaged. So we developed a website that aggregated the content and made it more visual. We realized we needed an app—we knew that middle-aged people are not reading long texts on a small device, and that images and live streaming are important. It became like the mother ship." The mobile app, put out by the Italian news agency ANSA, is called papa-francesconewsapp.com.

"But even more important than the content is the sense of connection. People feel that in their pocket they have something that connects them to the Vatican," says Monsignor Tighe.

"It is about information, but also about the relationship."

7

Saving the Sistine

In the room the women come and go
Talking of Michelangelo.
—T. S. ELIOT, "THE LOVE SONG OF J. ALFRED PRUFROCK"

Like it or not, Pope Francis has had to come to terms with the fact that he is now the personal custodian of one of the world's most important art collections. As many millions of people crowd into the Vatican Museums and shuffle through the Sistine Chapel every year as those who come to pray in St. Peter's, or to attend religious functions at the Vatican. Francis' first attempt to combine his care for the poor and the marginalized with this custodianship took place just over two years after his election. He invited 150 homeless people living on the streets of Rome to spend an afternoon admiring Michelangelo's *Last Judgment* fresco and his huge ceiling painting of the story of the Creation in the Sistine Chapel. He surprised them by turning up in person and told them: "You are welcome! This is everyone's house and your house. The doors are always open for all."

Not quite true, although once a month the Vatican Museums do throw open their doors to the public for free.

In the Vatican, as people come and go, they not only talk of Michelangelo, they see his works all around them. First they see the imposing façade of St. Peter's Basilica and its cupola. Later they spend twenty precious minutes inside the Sistine Chapel. Finally they stand in awe in front of his sculpture of the dead Christ in the arms of his mother, the *Pieta*.

But not everyone lives Michelangelo in the same way. As an article in *L'Osservatore Romano* pointed out back in 2011, "There is a widespread opinion of long standing that the Vatican is where very important art and cultural treasures are conserved, but that it is no longer a place of lively cultural achievement. There is only erudition, with scant life and little intellectual passion." The election of Joseph Ratzinger as Pope Benedict XVI was an important sign of change, the author went on to say, as was his appointing art historian Antonio Paolucci director of the Vatican Museums.[1]

Fine—but what of Pope Francis? What are his interests in the visual arts? Father Federico Lombardi, official papal spokesman, once said: "He is a great fan of literature"—which seems a tactful way of saying that the visual arts are not among Pope Francis' keen personal interests, Michelangelo notwithstanding.

Yet Father Antonio Spadaro, editor of the leading Italian Jesuit magazine *La Civiltà Cattolica* (*Catholic Civilization*) managed to tease out of Pope Francis revealing insights into his personal cultural and artistic interests during a marathon series of interviews in his lodgings at the Casa Santa Marta during August 2013, while most people who work inside the Vatican were away on their summer holidays.[2]

Surprisingly it is not Michelangelo Buonarotti, sculptor, painter, architect, and poet of the High Renaissance, but Michelangelo Caravaggio, one of Rome's most admired and robust Baroque artists, a street brawler frequently in trouble with the papal police, with whom Pope Francis says he has perhaps the closest artistic affinity.

On his visits to Rome from Argentina—when he used to stay at a residence for clergy in the Via della Scrofa in the heart of the historic center, not far from the house where Caravaggio used to lodge and had his studio—the then-Archbishop Jorge Bergoglio used to sneak inside the nearby French church of Saint Louis to gaze on one of Michelangelo Caravaggio's most famous paintings, *The Calling of Saint Matthew*. The dramatically lit painting, which can be seen in a side chapel to the left of the main altar, was finished in 1600 and shows Jesus pointing his finger toward his future Apostle, picking him out from a group of Romans dressed in the fashionable doublets and hose of those times, all gathered around a tavern table.

"That finger of Jesus, pointing at Matthew. That's me. I feel like him. Like Matthew. It's the gesture of Matthew that strikes me: he holds on to his money [Matthew was a tax collector] as if to say, 'No, not me! No, this money is mine!' Here, this is me, a sinner on whom the Lord has turned his gaze. And this is what I said when they asked me if I would accept my election as pontiff."

A year passed before we of the press were informed that the pope is also a "devoted fan" of the paintings of the Jewish artist Marc Chagall, and in particular of his *White Crucifixion*, painted in 1938 in France as a reaction to the Kristallnacht, the concerted attacks on German synagogues and Jewish-owned stores and buildings by the Nazis, the prelude to the Holocaust. In the painting, now in the collection of the Chicago Art Institute, Christ on the Cross is depicted wearing as a loincloth the *tallit*, or Jewish prayer shawl.[3]

In early 2014, Pope Francis was preparing his visit to Jerusalem when representatives of the American Jewish Committee called on him in Rome and presented him with the catalog of an exhibit of paintings by Chagall, just then on view at the Jewish Museum in New York.

"We showed him page 105 ... where a print of *White Crucifixion* is included because of its relevance to the exhibit," Rabbi Noam E. Marans, director of interreligious and intergroup relations for the American Jewish Committee, told a reporter from Religion News Service. "Pope Francis was moved by our recognition of his emotional connection to the painting, and responded with a joyous smile."

It is typical of Pope Francis to be identified with, and to respond with deep emotion to, a painting whose focus is a link between Judaism and Christianity.

Rome is the unique custodian of the historic Christian heritage, and Pope Francis is responsible for the conservation of Christian Rome, including its centuries of art and architecture.

It was his predecessor Pope John Paul II who created in 1982 a charitable foundation that has raised millions of dollars from wealthy North American and European philanthropists to help pay for the maintenance and restoration of some of the Vatican's most precious art treasures. Over a thousand members of Patrons of the Arts in the Vatican Museums pay an annual family subscription of twelve hundred dollars for the privilege of lifetime free entry to the museums and a regular series of private viewings inside the Vatican including a week-long session of receptions—and even an occasional meeting with Pope Francis himself. In October 2013, he thanked them at a private audience for their "outstanding contribution" to the restoration of paintings, sarcophagi, and even Egyptian mummies preserved in the Vatican's art collections. Contributions from the Washington, D.C., chapter of the Patrons of the Arts paid for the purchase of a latest generation optical fiber ArtLight II laser, which enables restorers to use noninvasive techniques to analyze the best methods of bringing fragile or damaged artworks back to life.

The Catholic Church's patronage of the arts dates back to at least Pope Callixtus I (219–222), responsible for the initial construction of the subsequently reworked church of Santa Maria in Trastevere; in the twelfth century another pontiff commissioned a fine mosaic showing the Coronation of the Virgin for that church.

In the most elemental way, Pope Francis is both the custodian and today's court of last resort for decisions about maintaining the super-abundance of these extraordinary treasures of Christian art and architecture created over the centuries in Rome, the former papal states, and beyond.

Many of these treasures date from the grand era of papal patronage during the Renaissance and the Baroque eras. But they begin far earlier with the historical vestiges, and there are many, of the earliest years of Christianity, and especially with what is buried in the underworld of today's bustling Rome. An example: among the sixty known ancient catacombs where Christians (and others) were buried in Rome is one only recently discovered beneath a Fiat automobile dealership. Its restoration, overseen by the Vatican, required five years of work and financing. Such new discoveries continue, and not only in Rome; in February 2014, extensive catacombs (owned by the Vatican) and dating from the fourth century AD were discovered at Carini in Sicily.[4]

While holding final responsibility for overseeing conservation of the ancient Christian heritage, the pope must also foster the new in the sacred arts and architecture in Rome. In so doing Pope Francis is not alone, of course. These tasks, which include construction of new churches in Rome, are delegated to three Vatican offices: the Pontifical Council for Culture, the Pontifical Commission for the Cultural Heritage of the Church, and the Pontifical Commission for Sacred Archaeology. Since 2007, all three have been headed by Cardinal Gianfranco Ravasi.

Ravasi's career and role in the church are fairly unique. He is the Vatican's minister of culture, as well as an intellectual powerhouse—congenial, affable, brilliant. And he was also a leading Italian candidate for the papacy prior to the election in which Francis was chosen.

Cardinal Ravasi can be as outspoken as he is charming. In his view, preaching in churches has become so formulaic and boring that it risks becoming "irrelevant" to congregations accustomed to the excitement and immediacy of television and the Internet. Reflecting this view, the Vatican has produced a booklet on how to preach sermons that are short and punchy.

As Ravasi told a conference in Rome, Twitter is an effective way to spread the word of God.[5] Elsewhere he has said, "I want to affirm, as an a priori, the compatibility of the theory of evolution with the message of the Bible and the theology of the Church." Neither Charles Darwin nor his *The Origin of Species* had ever been condemned by the church, he pointed out.

Gianfranco Ravasi was born in 1942 in Merate, near Lecco in Northern Italy. His father was an anti-Fascist tax official who served Fascist Italy as a soldier in World War II and reportedly deserted; his mother was a schoolteacher. Renouncing his original plan to become a teacher of classic languages, young Ravasi entered the priesthood in 1966 at age twenty-four. He subsequently studied at both the Pontifical Gregorian University and the Pontifical Biblical Institute, and spent summers working with archaeologists in the Middle East. Pope Benedict XVI created him cardinal in 2010, and that same year he was proclaimed cardinal deacon of the fourth-century Basilica of San Giorgio in Velabro, near the Circus Maximus in Rome. (The church was damaged by a bomb planted there by the Corleone mob of the Sicilian Mafia on July 27, 1993.)

It has been Cardinal Ravasi's stated goal to draw the Vatican into cultural modernity. "My aim," he said in an interview, "is to try to reconstruct what was essentially a divorce between art and faith." As art trends gradually turned away from the figurative toward the abstract, many people, priests included, failed to keep up with changing tastes, he added. "Today our problem is to get ordinary people to welcome this type of art. We need to help them understand that art is part of the spirit."

To this end he lobbied successfully to have the Vatican present at the fifty-fifth and fifty-sixth Venice Biennale Art Exhibitions in 2013 and again in 2015. The two, Biennale and Vatican, had a long and uneasy history, however. When the first Biennale was held in 1895, a painting by Giacomo Grosso of Turin scandalized the Vatican because it depicted five naked women swooning over a coffin in which lay the body of Don Giovanni, the fictional libertine and seducer immortalized by Mozart. Because the painting was seen as legitimizing a life of moral turpitude, the Patriarch of Venice—later Pope Pius X—assailed the work as immoral and demanded it be censored (it was not, and later won a prize). Another factor that had led to a weakening of ties between artists and the church was the unification of Italy in 1870, which reduced Vatican possessions from a large swath across the center of the peninsula to only 110 acres in the middle of Rome.

Paolo Baratta, president of that Biennale, introduced the Vatican exhibition at a press preview. "Today," Baratta said, "Cardinal Ravasi is convinced that art and faith, as in the centuries of the great patrons of the arts, must continue to produce masterpieces."[6]

Ravasi and curator Micol Forti were careful not to put on view works that would represent traditional Catholic themes like crucifixes and paintings of the Virgin and Child. Instead their chosen theme was a representation in three parts of the first eleven chapters of Genesis, in what was also a modern homage to Michelangelo's five-centuries-old Sistine Chapel ceiling. "None of these works is liturgical art, and we did not ask the artists their religion. I doubt that anyone asked Leonardo da Vinci about his faith," said curator Forti.

It worked: though attacked by a few irate bloggers, and also criticized by some as "bland," the Vatican pavilion literally stole the show from the other eighty-eight countries with exhibitions at the Biennale at the opening June 1, 2013.

Working with and answering to Cardinal Ravasi is the second most important figure in the Vatican arts world, Antonio Paolucci, born in Rimini in 1939. The former director of the Florentine museums, he was appointed director of the Vatican Museums in 2007 by Pope Benedict XVI. It is no accident that they are called "museums" rather than "museum": within the apostolic palace are six separate museums: the traditional picture gallery, the Pinacoteca Vaticana, the Gregorian-Etruscan Museum, the Ethnographic Missionary Museum, the Gregorian-Egyptian Museum, the Chiaramonti Museum, and the Vatican Historical Museum.

Altogether they are extraordinarily popular. Immediately before the election of Pope Francis, the Vatican Museums and St. Peter's Basilica had over four million visitors each year. The figures continue to rise: the popularity of Pope Francis has meant that both were visited by 5.5 million people in 2012, and 6 million in 2014.

Among Paolucci's first acts was to organize prebooking for tickets to the Vatican Museums in order to speed up the entry process and to shorten the lines already snaking far down the street every morning at 8:30 A.M.

Paolucci's concerns are no less important than Ravasi's and his curriculum is exceptional. For decades Paolucci was a superintendent of various Italian museums owned and managed by Italy's Ministry of Culture. Pope Francis renewed his Vatican contract for a further three years.

Whereas Paolucci's experience in heritage management is vast (he was himself Italy's minister of culture in 1995–1996), his vision appears conservative in comparison with that of Cardinal Ravasi. The official Catholic daily, *L'Osservatore Romano*, describes him in this way: "Paolucci's particular quality is that he does not limit himself to an aesthetic vision of the masterpieces conserved [in the Vatican Museums], but sees them in their historic and living dimension."[7] For example, Paolucci finds even some of the newer churches in Rome designed by celebrated architects unattractive, "museum spaces which do not invite to prayer."

Paolucci is endlessly busy. Even after a yearlong illness, he returned to his office, where he still carries on valiantly and industriously. Perhaps not surprisingly, he can sound grumpy. He makes no secret of disliking the ornamental lighting of the cupola of St. Peter's Basilica and of the Castel Sant'Angelo, the ancient Roman mausoleum and later refuge of popes. "Men and women should rediscover the beauty of darkness," he complained to Italian journalist Vittorio Zincone in an interview. "Museums are no longer linked to the concept of culture and knowledge. A museum visit now comes into the category of 'leisure' time activities."[8]

Indeed for many this is true. But the Vatican is not only about its museums as a venue for leisure time, and this duality makes the work of the custodians of its art treasures particularly complex.

That work begins with welcoming the faithful as well as the tourists at St. Peter's Basilica. Every day separate queues form of pilgrims waiting to pass through Vatican security in order to enter the basilica, and of tourists intent on visiting the Sistine Chapel.

For the visitors interested in the arts, the greatest single drawing card is the work inside the Vatican by Michelangelo Buonarotti. He was the principal architect of the façade of the basilica and of the original plan for the cupola, and the artist whose masterpieces in sculpture and paint lie within the basilica and two of its chapels.

Michelangelo worked on and off in Rome from 1496 through the end of his life in 1564. In 1497, the year after his arrival from Florence, he began two years of work on what would be one of his most famous sculptures, the *Pietà*, carved from marble from Carrara on commission for a French cardinal in Rome. In the sculpture, a young and tender Mary holds the dead and limp body of Jesus in her arms.

This was the sculpture inside the basilica that was attacked on

May 21, 1972, by a mentally disturbed, unemployed Austro-Hungarian geologist named Laszlo Toth. With a hammer Toth smashed part of her nose, which had to be replaced with a section of the marble removed from her back.

On May 21, 2013, the Vatican Museums under Paolucci held a special daylong seminar on the statue and on its restoration, which had become controversial. Nazzareno Gabrielli, the last surviving member of the team that restored the statue, told conference participants of the restorers' "anxiety and perplexities" as they experimented to find the best ways to repair the statue.[9]

"It is a good thing the hammer blows were vertical," a fellow restorer said in a documentary shown at the conference. "If the blows had been horizontal they would have torn off the entire head of Mary."

For two years Toth was confined to a Roman mental hospital, then deported to Australia, where it is believed he died in September 2012.

————

Another masterpiece by Michelangelo is invisible to almost everyone outside Pope Francis' inner circle. The Pauline Chapel, or Cappella Paolina, is the pope's personal chapel, inside the Apostolic Palace of the Vatican City. Built by Antonio da Sangallo the Younger between 1538 and 1540, it is named after Paul III, the Farnese family pope who had been Michelangelo's benefactor for years, and who commissioned the aging Michelangelo to create two huge paintings for the side walls of the chapel in 1538. The first was *The Conversion of Saul* and then, on the right side of the chapel, *The Crucifixion of St. Peter*, the last painting Michelangelo ever executed.

Paul III did not live to see its completion, for he died in November 1549, three months before Michelangelo finished the work.

And therein lies a tale. Unlike the Sistine Chapel, visitors are not normally admitted to the Pauline Chapel, but photographs show clearly, in the second and more shocking of the two frescoes, St. Peter crucified upside down. Large black nails bind him to the cross. He is naked save for a wispy wrapping over his intimate parts. But the martyr's entire aspect appears vividly alive; and, instead of raising his eyes to Heaven for solace, the white-bearded Peter—a mirror image of the Saint Peter in the *Last Judgment*—twists his head to glare furiously and directly into that large chapel in which, as Michelangelo well knew, a new pontiff would shortly be elected to succeed the late Paul III.

In June 2009, a $4.6 million, seven-year-long restoration of the chapel was complete, down to new LED lighting, and Vatican Museums director Antonio Paolucci made a formal presentation of it to the patrons who had donated the money for its conservation. "The Pauline Chapel is a religious place reserved for the Pope and for the pontifical family," he said. "In a certain sense, even more than the Sistine Chapel, the Pauline Chapel is the place most identified with the Catholic Church."

However, Paolucci went on to say, Michelangelo had worked on the two side walls off and on for ten years. "By then he was seventy years old and in poor health. He was exhausted from the immense fatigue of painting *The Last Judgment*. He was worried about his designs for the cupola of St. Peter's. And his world was disappearing around him: in 1547, the poet Vittoria Colonna died, and then 'his' pope Paul III also died."

As a result, in Paolucci's view, Michelangelo's twin frescoes reveal an artist suffering from "a vast sadness and profound pessimism."[10]

Quoting Paolucci, the official Vatican daily, *L'Osservatore Romano*, added this:

> *The restoration of the Pauline Chapel is directly linked to its function as the Pope's private chapel, where the Holiest Sacrament is preserved. Michelangelo, by then aged, had painted Saint Peter offering*

himself as a martyr. He turns his deep and thoughtful eyes towards
the face of the pontiff who enters as if to tell him, "you are Peter, and
the Cross is your destiny."[11]

Are those eyes, as they gaze toward a future pontiff, thoughtful?
And was there in Michelangelo's attitude only sorrow and pessimism,
as Paolucci has said?

Not everyone agrees with this interpretation. Italian art historian
Antonio Forcellino, a conservator and the author of biographies of both
Raphael and Michelangelo, points out that in the fresco of St. Peter
crucified, the nails affixing Peter to the cross were added after Michelangelo died, and completely ignored the philosophy behind Michelangelo's vision, which was that Peter had willingly placed himself upon the
cross. Michelangelo painted the crucifixion without Peter nailed to the
cross because they were not needed.

"This was the first conceptual work of art in history, and in it Michelangelo was saying that only faith, not the nails, can sustain Peter. That
faith is interiorized, and the fresco is a sort of manifesto of a heretical
spirituality," said Forcellino.[12]

Perhaps the fresco did not begin that way, but it certainly became
heretical. During Michelangelo's years of work in the chapel, he belonged
to a group known as the Spirituali, whose leader within the church was
the eminent English cardinal Reginald Pole, the last archbishop of
Canterbury before England broke definitively with Rome under King
Henry VIII. For thirty years the Spirituali, who included Michelangelo's close friend the poet Vittoria Colonna, had worked to reform the
church from within. They promoted reconciliation with the Protestant
Reformation and the "evangelical" followers of Martin Luther; some
authorities believe that Paul III, who had commissioned Michelangelo
to paint the twin frescoes in the chapel in the first place, was in sympathy with the Spirituali. The movement failed by a hair. When Paul III
died in November 1549, Cardinal Pole was a front-runner to succeed

him, but on February 7, at the end of ten weeks of bitter fighting within the conclave, Pole lost by exactly one vote.

Instead the conclave elected Cardinal Giovanni del Monte, who took the name of Julius III (1487–1555). Del Monte, born in Rome, reigned as pope for five years. During that time he reinforced the Inquisition, and his papacy was deeply mired in personal scandal involving a penniless youth of seventeen whom he had his brother adopt. The *Catholic Encyclopedia* offers this tactful if candid description of their relationship:

> *The great blemish in his pontificate was nepotism. Shortly after his accession he bestowed the purple on his unworthy favorite Innocenzo del Monte, a youth of seventeen whom he had picked up on the streets of Parma some years previously, and who had been adopted by the pope's brother, Balduino. This act gave rise to some very disagreeable rumors concerning the pope's relation to Innocenzo.*[13]

"Bestowed the purple"—that is, the sixty-something Pope Julius III made his one-time teenage lover a cardinal, with all the perks this implies. By the way, after Julius' death, Cardinal Innocenzo murdered two men and was accused of raping two women.

After Michelangelo died, the two huge frescoes of the Pauline Chapel—the last paintings he ever made—were snubbed by his contemporaries, who compared them negatively with his earlier work on the ceiling and far wall of the Sistine Chapel. "They were considered the shoddy work of an old man," according to biographer Forcellino, who says that in his painting of Saint Peter, Michelangelo had been openly provocative. "He was being censored, as is clear from the fact that in 1549 the Vatican declined to pay him to finish the frescoes in the chapel. They were completed by other artists in 1572, twenty-two years later."[14]

Like the painted nails, the wrapping over the saint's genitals was an addition from that later tidying up of Michelangelo's work. "In Greek classical sculpture an unadorned figure was a reference to the status of the depicted person or deity: athletes and gods could be identified by their adornment or lack of it," according to Dr. Anna Tahinci, the author of *Removing the Fig Leaf*.[15]

What is significant here, however, is that during the seven-year restoration of the Pauline Chapel, completed only in 2009, or two years after Paolucci's appointment as head of the Vatican Museums, the restorers had chosen not to remove either the belated additions of nails or the mini loin cloth. Neither had been in Michelangelo's original work, but no complaint seems to have come from the Vatican cultural czars, and they are still there, the nails looking like "cockroaches," as one outraged art historian put it because the critics missed the point entirely—that the saint had given himself up willingly to God, not because he had been forced to the cross.

Today's cardinals still meet in the Pauline Chapel to pray before entering the Sistine Chapel to begin the proceedings for election of a new pope. And this is also the chapel where, immediately after his election, Pope Francis withdrew to pray alone for a few minutes before appearing before the crowds gathered to welcome him for the first time in St. Peter's Square.

Of all Paolucci's responsibilities, none looms larger than the Sistine Chapel, which he has called the spiritual heart of the Roman Catholic Church worldwide, because within its august walls popes are elected. Five hundred years old in 2012, the Sistine Chapel is also the chief calling card for the Vatican Museums—a "transcendent work of genius," to quote from the *Smithsonian* magazine—for it houses what most art historians consider the two greatest single works of art produced in the Western world. It is one of those places that foreigners of all faiths and all nations expect to see when they come to visit Rome; for many, it is why they visit Rome, and reason enough.

Michelangelo was thirty-four years old when he began painting the ceiling with scenes from the Book of Genesis. After four years of solitary, painful labor, an exhausted Michelangelo set down his paint-brushes, and the finally complete Sistine Chapel was formally blessed and inaugurated by Pope Julius II with a mass on November 1, 1512.

The unveiling of the ceiling came as a shocking surprise for the papal court, for, as art historians tell us, the pope and cardinals had been expecting to see the likes of a flock of flying angels. Instead they saw what seemed acres of human flesh, and this came to them as a not altogether agreeable experience.

Michelangelo began painting the *Last Judgment* on the wall behind the chapel altar in 1536, a quarter of a century after the ceiling. Four years later, when he was sixty-six, that too was complete. In its host of figures—four hundred of them—covering forty by forty-five feet of painted surface was a sturdy St. Peter gripping two huge keys; the face and beard are those Michelangelo would repeat in the Pauline Chapel, but the saint is gazing directly at the Christ figure, and not yet glaring at the cardinals.

In Michelangelo's time many within the church considered the *Last Judgment* fresco obscene because it too had many stark naked figures. Biagio da Cesena, who was the papal master of ceremonies, called the scene "very disgraceful . . . a work not for the chapel of a Pope, but for the public baths or a tavern." Some translate public baths as "brothel." Here is Vasari's account, from *Le Vite*:

> *When Michelangelo had completed about three quarters of the work, Pope Paul went to see it, and Messer Biagio da Cesena, the master of the ceremonies, was with him, and when he was asked what he thought of it, he answered that he thought it not right to have so many naked figures in the Pope's chapel. This displeased Michelan-gelo, and to revenge himself, as soon as he was departed, he painted*

him in the character of Minos with a great serpent twisted round his legs. Nor did Messer Biagio's entreaties either to the Pope or to Michelangelo himself, avail to persuade him to take it away.

"Round his legs"—well, around his private parts, and not entirely, in fact, for the serpent twisting around the body is plainly, openly biting Cesena's genitals. As if this were not enough, this high official of the Curia, whose face was uniquely recognizable as a portrait, is shown as Minos, hell's demonic judge of sinners, and is given the ears of a foolish donkey. Supposedly the pope jokingly replied to Cesena's appeals for it to be removed that the figure showing Cesena was in hell, and because the pontiff had no jurisdiction there, donkey ears and coiled serpent could remain.

Michelangelo died on February 17, 1564. That same year the Council of Trent decreed that the purpose of religious art was visual and theological clarity—that is to say, to teach the illiterate. Nudity was formally disapproved for religious paintings and sculptures. It was all the worse that Michelangelo's Christ in the *Last Judgment* had been inspired by pagan depictions of Apollo, and some saw a Venus behind his Mary. The result was that many of the painted nudes of the *Last Judgment* were given modesty drapes by Daniele da Volterra. One of Michelangelo's pupils and a caregiver at the end of his life, Daniele for his role in overpainting his late master was later given the dismissive nickname Braghettone, or the britches-maker, *braghetti* being a somewhat crude word for pants.

The overpainting was part of the church's new didactic approach—an element of the official church propaganda that Michelangelo had rejected while he was alive. The Counter-Reformation was in full sway, and that same year the *Index Librorum Prohibitorum* (Index of Prohibited Books) was officially proclaimed.

———

Almost from the beginning, the chapel paintings presented a serious practical as well as moral problem: candle smoke. In 1543, only two years after Michelangelo completed painting the ceiling, it had to be cleaned. Pope Paul III himself appointed an official chapel cleaner, whose yearly duty was to use bread crumbs and fine linen cloths to wipe away the deposited grime. Later, some artists overpainted figures so as to heighten the contrasts.

By 1980, the Sistine Chapel paintings had been dulled by further centuries of greasy candle smoke, and a full-scale restoration of Michelangelo's ceiling paintings began, bankrolled by a Japanese television network in exchange for exclusive rights to document the work. Among other things, those old overlays were removed.

When it was completed in 1994, after fourteen years of work, a number of influential art critics argued furiously that the frescoes had been seriously damaged by overly zealous restorers who eliminated their nuances and added vulgarly bright colors.

Vatican officials went on the defensive, arguing that these were Michelangelo's true colors, previously unseen because dimmed by the centuries of accumulated grime. They also argued that the many retouchings of Michelangelo's paintings over centuries had falsely emphasized the chiaroscuro.

Fabrizio Mancinelli, curator and codirector, with Gianluigi Colalucci, of the restoration, claimed in 1986 that the restoration "had brought to light (and will continue to bring to light) a totally new artist, a colorist quite different in character from the unnaturally somber character who has in the past fascinated generations of historians, connoisseurs and fellow artists." [16]

To this a group of angry American art historians and artists responded with a petition of protest, in which they complained that the restored colors were unlike those that Michelangelo had habitually used. In particular, the late Prof. James Beck of Columbia University protested that an entire layer of glue covering the surface of the paint-

ing had been heedlessly scraped away by the restorers. Beck, who died
in 2007, aged seventy-seven, was an Italian Renaissance specialist and
cofounder with Michael Daley of ArtWatch International. Their position was that this glue layer had been intentionally applied by Michelangelo as a topping for the frescos, in order to enhance their sculptural
effect with a final layer of subtle shading.[17] And indeed comparative
photographs demonstrate the elimination of significant details and
nuances. The drastic overcleaning, moreover, also exposed the entire
surface to modern pollution, he said.[18]

In October 2013, Paolucci was asked about future restorations. His
reply was that he hoped never to see another one because they are "so
traumatic" to the works of art. "There won't be any more restorations,"
he said—at least not on his watch.

But maintenance continues, he added. Indeed it does; as the manager of the Sistine Chapel today, he faces other maintenance problems
that are both complex and immediate. The first and foremost is how to
avoid the slow but inevitable destruction of the 2,730 square yards of
wall and ceiling paintings that are being sacrificed to their very popularity. The Vatican's creation of a free-of-charge 3-D virtual visit in 2012
had been intended to reduce the presence of tourists but, if anything,
made a real visit all the more enticing. The elevation of Pope Francis contributed further to attracting ever larger numbers of visitors to
Rome and the Vatican, by at least 10 percent.

These visitors must cram themselves into a severely limited space. The
chapel floor covers just 5,896 square feet. In order to keep the daily flow
of almost 17,600 moving along at the rate of almost two thousand every
hour, the faithful and the tourists are allowed entry at twenty-minute
intervals, and are actively discouraged from remaining longer than that.
During a quick gawk at the ceiling and *Last Judgment*, they are constantly
hushed by Vatican custodians and urged to keep moving, as indeed they
must at the risk of being trampled by the next group of arrivals who have
snaked their way through seemingly endless access corridors.

The twenty minutes allow just time enough for a selfie, to show you have been inside a place sacred to art and religion. The custodians are not to blame; the chapel is small, and the visitors are many.

But in the meantime, the damage is done. The Sistine Chapel managers know well that the people pressure translates into massive pollution from breath, but also from dust, sweat, perfumes and deodorants, the soles of shoes, the stench of cigar and cigarette clinging to clothes, and the textile fibers exuded from clothing.

For this reason, in December 2011, a pollution detector was installed to measure temperature, humidity, and chemical and air currents using thirty-six suspended and fourteen other detectors fitted on the walls of the chapel. The sensor data obtained was then compared with the number of visitors at any one time, counted via thermal cameras fitted on the doors. (If its results have been released, we have not seen them.)

The sensors were expected to be a first step before deciding upon improved air-conditioning, to the extent that this is possible. Less than a year after their installation, Pietro Citati, an influential Italian writer and literary critic, wrote after a visit that the chapel risks an "unimaginable disaster." On entering the chapel he was met by a "horrendous wall of human breath," he wrote in the daily *Corriere della Sera*.

In June 2014, three years after the sensors were placed in the chapel, the Vatican formally announced that work would be completed by the end of that year on installing new air-conditioning—a "landmark system," the Vatican and its manufacturer described it, for heating, ventilating, and air-conditioning (HVAC) specifically designed to protect the chapel masterpieces from deterioration. The new system was designed to have twice the efficiency and three times the capacity of the previous system, Vatican Radio predicted, adding: "The custom-engineered solution uses energy-saving technologies, as well as methods of minimizing noise and limiting air motion around the frescoes."

"The Sistine Chapel in Rome now has a new air-conditioning and illumination systems that will permit the number of visitors to

be tripled," crowed an Italian website called Aria, under the headline
"Celestial Air for the Sistine Chapel."[19]

The system's manufacturer, Carrier, a subsidiary of United Technologies Corp. (UTC), is the same company that installed the air-
conditioning system immediately after the restoration of the early
1990s. The new system was installed at year-end. "We are confident that
Carrier's HVAC system will enable us to realize our goal of ensuring the
preservation of Michelangelo's masterpieces in the Sistine Chapel while
allowing visitors to continue to behold the frescoes for years to come,"
said Paolucci.

To behold the frescoes is the point, but to do so in this day and age
and at all seasons and hours is a challenge, especially during those dark
evenings when well-heeled visitors pay $250 or so for the privilege of
seeing the Vatican highlights in private after 6 P.M. in what one promoter described as "without the daytime crowds or summer heat . . . in a
quiet, stress-free environment." A type of illumination never envisioned
by Michelangelo has become de rigueur, and so artificial lighting is now
required, and this presented yet another knotty problem.

In the late 1980s, a new lighting system was installed. The best
available in its time, it utilized halogen lamps emitting 90 percent heat
but only 10 percent light.

On Paolucci's watch in late 2014, these outdated lights were
replaced by seven thousand new cold LED lights following an open-
ended European Union competition. Long used in traffic lights and
other outdoor illumination, LED lighting is increasingly popular in
art galleries and museums; London's National Gallery began installing
LED lighting in 2011.

German manufacturer OSRAM Licht AG won the bid, and
throughout 2013 the company's Munich laboratory worked together
with Vatican technicians in Rome to study and analyze the project's
visual qualities and possible conservation risks. The lights, which can be

dimmed, were applied to existing overhead beams and hence are invisible to the viewer from below. Lighting is indirect, with no glare. LED lights contain none of the damaging ultraviolet rays of sunlight, said an OSRAM spokesman in an interview.

The new system cost around $2.6 million, paid not by the Vatican, but by the European Union together with five international commercial sponsors. Running costs will be reduced by at least 60 percent, says OSRAM, in part due to reduced lightbulb packaging and to lower CO_2 emissions.

Speaking at a conference at the Smithsonian Museum in Washington, D.C., Joseph Padfield, senior scientific officer of the National Gallery, pointed out that while all visible light is potentially damaging to artifacts, lighting is necessary in order to view them. That said, a problem is that LED lights must be specifically designed for color; they do not give off ultraviolet rays, and give more light than ordinary lightbulbs, but do not cast sunlight-type light. They are color-toned in three colors, which are adjusted as they fix upon every given, variously colored surface so as to exalt that color, which is why such a large number of lights are needed. Some critics have suggested the result for the Sistine Chapel might turn out to be a gaudy, "nightclub look."

Fortunately, when the new lighting was switched on in October 2014, the effect was stunningly beautiful. It is a daunting thought that not even Michelangelo had ever seen his paintings illuminated so perfectly.

In theory, another practical conservation step could be to limit the number of visitors, but until recently Paolucci has opposed this on religious grounds, given the chapel's importance in the history of the Catholic Church and to the faithful. He has admitted that he is at least thinking about the problem and has acknowledged that should the new air-conditioning system prove ineffective, "I'll be forced to impose a limited number of visitors, but that would be a painful solution."[20]

Painful in various ways: the money involved is considerable. The Vatican Museums are among the most visited and profitable in the world, and in 2012 had an income of $113 million through ticket sales, plus almost as much again through merchandising. The Sistine Chapel can also be rented for occasional corporate events.

As Italian reporter Andrea Bevilacqua has pointed out, it is not easy for the Vatican to say no to the mass purchase of tickets to visit the Vatican museums, since many go solely to visit the Sistine Chapel and enter and exit rapidly. In the United Kingdom the *Guardian* quickly picked up this story and commented acidly that even if the Vatican needs "funding for its various activities," it is preferable to eliminate such "monstrosities" as the overcrowding of the Sistine Chapel.

In places of religious and artistic pilgrimages elsewhere, limitations upon the number of visitors have been successfully applied. The administrators of the Chapel of the Scrovegni in Padua, whose masterpiece fresco cycle was painted by Giotto between 1303 and 1305, faced a similar problem. Ever since its restoration was completed a decade ago, the number of visitors permitted there has been limited. Tickets when paid by credit card must be purchased through a call center at least twenty-four hours before a visit; if by bank transfer, three days in advance. Tickets must then be picked up at least one hour before the time assigned for entry.

At one point Paolucci considered construction of a high-tech replica of the Sistine Chapel where visitors could linger to study the complex paintings. In an interview with journalist Judith Harris for *ARTnews* some years back, he mentioned that it could be built on an old tennis court close to the museums. Successful replicas are now becoming common where precious ancient sites are involved, including the painted Upper Paleolithic Altamira cave near Santander in Spain, built in 2001 to acclaim, and the replica, built in 2013, of King Tutankhamun's tomb in Egypt, which faced the same array of pollution problems as the Sistine Chapel.

From earliest Christian times a patrimony of the arts and architecture, and the upkeep of the acquired church possessions, went hand in hand with politics. A thousand years later, politics continued to affect the church, including its heritage possessions. By the time of Italian independence (the *Risorgimento*) the Papal States—also known as the "Republic of Saint Peter"—stretched some sixteen thousand square miles across central Italy, from Lazio to eastern Emilia-Romagna.

Unification of Italy in 1870 shrank that Republic of Saint Peter to just two-tenths of a square mile. "Monasteries and Catholic schools [were] suppressed, convents disbanded," writes Robert P. Lockwood in his history of Pius IX, who was pontiff from 1846 to 1878, all particularly difficult years for the church.[21] Under the terms of a law passed in 1873, the new state had the right to seize ecclesiastical properties, including seminaries like Rome's prestigious Collegio Romano, which was then converted into a state school. Within the newly miniaturized Vatican state, entirely encircled by Rome, Pius became a virtual prisoner by his refusal to set foot on Italian soil.

That situation of hostility was definitively resolved, and the then-pontiff Pius IX finally freed, only after Cardinal Pietro Gasparri and Benito Mussolini signed the Lateran Pacts of 1929. By the terms of their Article 30, Vatican ownership of its patrimony and properties, like the Palazzo della Cancelleria in Rome, was once again guaranteed.

One article in the 1929 Concordat granted the church custody of all the catacombs in Rome along with the crucial obligation for "keeping, maintaining and conserving them." The church also received the right to conduct future excavations in Italian territory; the corollary was that when and if new catacombs were found, the Vatican would have the obligation to keep, maintain, and conserve these too.[22] And indeed new catacombs were and continue to be found, including important ones in Sicily, with consequent financial responsibilities. At the same time Italian politics also brought disaster for the church. When Mussolini's Fascism drew Italy into war on the wrong side, the church shared in the ensuing tragedy. In 1943 Rome's medieval Papal Basilica of Saint Lawrence Outside the Walls (San Lorenzo fuori le Mura), which had been constructed atop an oratory built by the first Christian Emperor Constantine, suffered serious bomb damage that included the destruction of several of the precious frescoes on its facade. In early 1944 Allied planes dropped fourteen hundred tons of bombs onto the Abbey of Montecassino, which had been founded by Saint Benedict in the year 528 on the foundations of a temple to Apollo, and then enlarged in the eleventh century. By the time the Allied advance through Italy drove German troops away, the Abbey lay in ruins. Eighty miles south of Rome, it was entirely, expensively rebuilt at the end of the war.

Catacombs and monasteries are only a part of the physical heritage of the church still guaranteed by the Concordat, and not only in Rome, but in the rest of Italy and even beyond. Long lists of the Vatican-owned properties—buildings used by the church like the Cancelleria in downtown Rome, but also buildings that bring in rental income—exist.

Where are they? No one knows. Writing for the respected Italian weekly *Il Mondo*, investigative reporter Sandro Orlando affirmed that church properties have "dodged every census in the almost eighty years passed since the Concordat was signed in 1929."[23] In 1985, when Parliament was debating a bill that would provide funds for churches in Italy (presumably for their upkeep as well as construction of new ones), a Radical Party deputy named Francesco Rutelli read out an "interminable list" of buildings owned by the no less interminable ecclesiastical organizations in Rome. Thanks to the Christian Democratic Party in power from 1947 onward, said Rutelli, the Italian state was already providing the church in Italy with "trillions of lire" solely for maintenance of the churches of Rome.

Ironically, Rutelli himself would later become mayor of Rome, and would, in the Jubilee Year 2000, successfully expand the earthly belongings of the church in Rome. As mayor, he promoted public contributions for restorations of chapels and church buildings, plus construction of new hospices for the expected arrival of pilgrims and even public parking lots.

By Orlando's estimate, the church in Rome owns 400 institutes for nuns, 300 parishes (churches), 250 Catholic schools, 90 religious institutes, 65 medical facilities, 50 missions, 43 high schools, 30 monasteries, 20 old-age homes, 20 seminaries, 18 hospitals, 16 convents, 13 oratories, 10 confraternities, 6 hospices, almost 2,000 religious organizations inside Rome, and properties of some 20,000 pieces of land and buildings; one fourth of Rome belongs to the Curia.[24]

More properties were being added. With the approach of the Jubilee Year in 2000, the activist Cardinal Camillo Ruini, vicar general of the Diocese of Rome from 1991 to 2008, launched a campaign to build fifty new churches in the towns that had mushroomed on the outskirts of Rome after the 1950s. These are not garden suburbs, but bleak conurbations, with ten-story buildings jammed together higgledy-piggledy. Ruini's goal was to upgrade the poor architectural quality of that neglected Roman periphery or *periferia*, as Pope Francis would call it.

The Italian Bishops Conference (CEI) held an international competition. The world-famous Richard Meier won the contract to build the Church of God the Merciful Father (Dio Padre Misericordioso) in Tor Tre Teste outside Rome. Meier gave the church three gigantic white, slightly curved concrete sails, like a trio of stone sheets hung out to dry. Attached to the church proper, these sails overhang the church's tall, Spartan, all-glass entrance, which resembles a Times Square hotel entryway, and separate it from the densely populated high-rises of its neighborhood context. (Meier's controversial work on Rome's publicly owned Ara Pacis Museum followed in 2005.)

Of Ruini's fifty desired new churches for these suburbs, forty-five have been completed. The very fact of so many new churches in the often bleak Roman outskirts has been celebrated by many in Rome as a step forward because they provide an otherwise absent focal point for community life as well as worship.

Cardinal Ravasi does not look so kindly upon them, however. During a lecture at Rome University La Sapienza in 2011, Ravasi dismissed the new churches as "congress hall spaces, akin to sports palaces. They are vulgar and ugly places." [25]

Two years later, speaking at the launch of a book illustrating these new Roman churches, Vatican Museums director Antonio Paolucci took the microphone to say that he too was less than impressed by them. "I cannot help pointing out, having examined this new book more than once, how much confusion there is under the Roman skies because of these new churches. How can one not be concerned? Churches? Parishes? At best we are looking at a museum space—the sort of place which does not invite either prayer or meditation." [26]

Paolucci argued that Rome's new modernist churches fail to have the "visible tabernacles, the cupolas, icons and images of the life of the Church which help the parish priests teach the catechism. Even the Russian Orthodox churches fully carry out these tasks of formation and catechism teaching."

A later speaker, Professor Marco Petreschi of Rome University, rebutted the cardinal's critique firmly if politely. Petreschi is the architect who designed the great altar, gigantic cross, and huge stage expressly requested by Pope John Paul II for the celebration of the first World Youth Day in Rome in 1986. Also for the year 2000 Petreschi created the modernist Church of Saint Thomas the Apostle, located twelve miles outside Rome at Lunghezza. It was dedicated in 2013 to Mother Teresa of Calcutta, and became the forty-fifth completed since Cardinal Ruini's project began.

Said Petreschi: "It is clear that the professor [Paolucci] is accustomed to historical analyses of the churches designed by the great architects of the past. But it is too easy to analyze historical [building] complexes which had the benefit of ample financing." Today's architects, he pointed out, work on drastically limited budgets. "And if in the *periferia* there are forty-five new churches, it is an authentic miracle, aside from aesthetic and architectural judgments."

When Pope Francis made his first local parish visit as bishop of Rome, he chose the new parish of Prima Porta that has recently grown up around one of these rather stark new churches completed in 2010 in the outer northern suburbs of the capital. Previously, Sunday mass had to be celebrated there in the garage of an apartment block.

———

Probably the least known of Pope Francis' responsibilities for preservation of the Catholic cultural heritage is his role as overseer of the Vatican's literally unique collection of ethnological artifacts, sent to Rome by missionaries from all over the world. The first arrivals came in 1692 from Oceania, China, Australia, and the Americas.

When Pope Pius XI called a Holy Year for 1925, an anthropologist priest named Father Wilhelm Schmidt (1868–1954) appealed to Catholic missions worldwide for artifacts to be displayed at the Universal Missionary Exhibition. Schmidt was the founder of *Anthropos*, a journal that reported field research in ethnography conducted by missionaries, especially in New Guinea and Togo, and the goal for the Holy Year was to illustrate the reach of the church beyond Europe.

Missionaries working as far afield as the Easter Islands, South America, and the Congo responded. The one hundred thousand artifacts that arrived from Native American tribes, and from Hindu, Buddhist, and Islamic religious cultures, were displayed in twenty-four pavilions erected within the Vatican Gardens, and were seen by one million people.

Today these objects form the core of the Vatican's collection, housed in the Ethnological Missionary Museum within the Vatican Museums complex. The oldest single item in the collection is a chipped stone tool made two million years ago.

"When people think of the Vatican Museums collections, they often forget that over half of what we have is not European," said Jesuit Father Nicola Mapelli, the Ethnological Museum's director, in an interview. "The missionaries were the links between the church in Rome and aboriginal peoples."

Many are of particularly delicate materials, from ostrich plumes to woven straw, leather, wood, crocodile, and glass beads. To protect this heritage, the Vatican also created a Diagnostic Laboratory for Conservation and Restoration, which today stands in the forefront in worldwide studies of conservation of cultural artifacts outside the European standard, which is largely based upon classical and Renaissance antiquities.

At the closing of the Exhibition of 1925, Pius XI predicted that "the Missionary Museum [will remain] like a school, like a book that is always open." In fact, the diagnostic laboratory, in which fifteen restorers work, is actively involved in the exchange of conservation experiences worldwide, and to consideration of how preservation of an ethnographic heritage can promote local cultural identities, including marginal cultures, while also enhancing cultural exchange. To this end, in 2014 the Vatican published a handbook, "Ethics and Practice of Conservation," on ethnographic heritage policies.

An example of how the Vatican today reaches out to other cultures is its contribution to restoration of panels depicting the life of Buddha and his reincarnations on the monumental Borobudur compound, built in Java, Indonesia, in the ninth century AD. Weather and the interaction of iron rods and cement had taken its toll upon a series of carved stone panels illustrating the life of Buddha, and details were lost. Fortunately, the Ethnological Museum had both plaster and cement casts of the panels, on which details lost on the originals were visible, and two diagnostic laboratory restorers went to Borobudur to help in their conservation.

From its Ethnological Museum, the Vatican loaned precious copies of ancient pages from the Koran, for a temporary exhibition in 2014 at the Sharjah Museum of Islamic Civilization in the United Arab Emirates. For that exhibit, "We selected our most beautiful objects so that we might know each other," said Father Mapelli. "We not only want to work on preservation of an object; we want to give life to it and to connect with the populations who created the objects. What is important to us is to have a connection with people."

In the 1920s, a missionary was given a mask from the Yaghan indigenous people in Tierra del Fuego in Chile. "To learn more, we went there, and managed to locate the 90-year-old daughter of the Yaghan who had offered the mask to the missionary. The daughter wove a basket for us," said Mapelli. That basket is now in the Ethnological Museum collection, next to the mask.

Vatican technicians have also become coveted partners with other museums. They share their cutting-edge knowledge of how to use lasers for restoration of ancient objects with other museums, such as the Egyptian Museum of Turin. A laser was also used for restoration of the Scala Santa at the Chapel of San Lorenzo in Rome.

Another Vatican partnership with the world of high tech is a project of one of the oldest libraries in the world, the Vatican Library, to digitize its unique collection of eighty thousand manuscripts and make them available to scholars worldwide. Under a four-year program begun in 2014, the Japanese NTT Data Corporation has sent a team of technicians to work with Vatican staff on digitizing a first selection of about three thousand manuscripts. Scanning of books illuminated with gold and silver requires special equipment and the project could drag on for decades. So far the Japanese company has invested $20 million. The

Vatican Virgil, one of the earliest manuscripts of works by the Roman poet dating from the fourth century AD, should be online by 2018.

Pope Francis made an unusual choice for the artist who would paint his first official portrait. Shen Jiawei, sixty-seven, was born in Shanghai and became famous as an official propaganda artist for the Chinese Communist regime. His painting *Standing Guard for Our Great Motherland* of 1974 shows a trio of rosy-cheeked soldiers from the People's Army peering into a frozen landscape. Madame Mao Zedong herself selected this painting as a propaganda tool and the painting was reproduced millions of times. Tiring of Communist life, Shen Jiawei emigrated to Australia in 1989, where he began an international career as portrait artist. In 2002 he had painted Pope John Paul II together with Mikhail Gorbachev inside the Sistine Chapel.

From Rome's historic underground, where worshippers of Apollo and Isis lie buried side by side with the earliest Christians, to the endangered Sistine Chapel, to the new redbrick suburban churches built on a shoestring, to a Yaghan mask from Tierra del Fuego at the southern tip of South America and to the conservation of one of the world's most valuable collections of ancient manuscripts and printed books: this is today's complex, fascinating Roman Catholic Church heritage of the arts and architecture, which it is the task of Pope Francis to maintain. Francis, in his personal crusade on behalf of the world's poor, has shown no inclination so far to divest his church of its artistic riches and sell off some of its priceless art treasures, as some feared he might do when they first learned of his election as head of the Catholic Church.

8

The Pope of the Periphery

You all know that the duty of the Conclave was to give Rome a
bishop. It seems that my brother cardinals have gone almost to
the ends of the earth to get him.
—POPE FRANCIS, ON HIS ELECTION MARCH 13, 2013

Like other pontiffs, Francis, who was elected on a rainy night in
March 2013, began his papacy by speaking from the great balcony
on the façade of St. Peter's Basilica. To the sea of enthusiastic followers
huddled under umbrellas in the piazza below, he said that to find him,
the cardinal electors had traveled "almost to the ends of the earth."

During the first two years of his papacy, Pope Francis showed that
the opposite was also true: that as pontiff, Francis was reaching out,
metaphorically as well as physically, to the far shores of the earth, much
farther than his 265 predecessor popes. Of these, 217 had been born in
Italy, and the rest no farther from Rome than Europe and North Africa.

To begin with, Jorge Bergoglio displayed no intemperate haste in
returning to his native country to bask in reflected glory as leader of

the universal church. Pope John Paul II returned to his native Poland no fewer than nine times between his first return visit to Warsaw and Krakow in 1979 and his last trip home in 2002. Clocking an astonishing 104 journeys outside Italy, Pope John Paul traveled farther and more widely than all previous popes combined.

Pope Francis has been a more restrained traveler. His trips abroad have so far all been of short duration, very carefully focused and finely calibrated. His first return trip to Argentina is not planned until July 2016.

As archbishop of Buenos Aires, the only intercontinental trips he made were to the Vatican. He traveled economy class, without a secretary, and he left his cell phone at home.

Prior to his election he had never looked forward to his business trips to Rome to attend synods or other official Vatican meetings. He used to tell friends, in all seriousness, "It's bad for my faith!"—a reference to the often toxic atmosphere he had already detected inside the Roman Curia. He was also reluctant to be asked to stay on as archbishop in Buenos Aires after age seventy-five. (Under canon law all diocesan bishops are required to submit their resignation to the pope upon reaching that age.) He had already booked his place in a retirement home in Buenos Aires when he suddenly found himself launched at seventy-six into a new career as spiritual leader of the world's 1.3 billion Catholics.

Even when visiting Italy, he rarely left Rome, apart from an occasional quick side trip to greet his distant relatives in Piedmont. The first pope in history to take the name Francis had also never been to Assisi, the Umbrian birthplace of his namesake, until his one-day trip there in October 2013.

As bishop, Bergoglio did not travel much. He was a street pastor "with the odor of sheep," as he once said, and this is what he always urged his priests to be. He did not have itchy feet, nor was he ever an "airport bishop."

He used to refer to his diocese as "la mi esposa" (my wife), alluding to the matrimonial bond between the bishop and that bit of church entrusted to him. Given this bond, he was unwilling to stay away from his "wife" too long.

Until his visit to Washington, New York, and Philadelphia was planned for September 2015, the first pope from the Americas had never set foot in the United States. Of all the popes the church has had over the past eighty years, the only other church leader who had not visited North America before or during his pontificate was Angelo Roncalli, the future Pope John XXIII. All the rest did, even before becoming the successors to St. Peter: Cardinals Eugenio Pacelli, Giovanni Battista Montini, Karol Wojtyla, and Joseph Ratzinger. Pacelli, the future Pius XII, was the first Vatican secretary of state to go on a pastoral or diplomatic mission to the United States, and in 1934 was invited to Buenos Aires (Bergoglio wasn't born yet) as pontifical delegate to the World Eucharistic Congress. In 1936, he went to the United States to meet President Roosevelt.

In 1951, Giovanni Battista Montini, the future Paul VI, traveled to the United States and Canada, when the Cold War was in full swing. He went to America again in 1960 and visited Brazil that same year. Then in 1962, the year before he was elected pope, he visited Africa for the first time.

Before he became a globe-trotter pope, Karol Wojtyla went on many international trips while he was archbishop of Krakow. In 1976 he spent three weeks in the United States, where he was invited to tea at the White House by Gerald Ford.

As this shows, these popes had a strong diplomatic background. By contrast, before his election Francis had spent little time outside Latin America save for brief periods in Ireland and Germany.

Bergoglio's decision to limit his travels to essential, focused journeys is not a sign of cultural provincialism or a preconceived closure to

the Western world. It is the conscious expression of a precise pastoral
choice: to root oneself in one's diocese, to be close to the faithful, to live
a lifestyle devoid of luxury and the superfluous, and to emulate as closely
as possible a lifestyle akin to that of Christ himself.

An exception was Bergoglio's keen desire to visit the Holy Land. In
1973, when he had been provincial father of the Jesuits in Argentina for
only a few months, he accepted an invitation from the Israeli government. Lodging in the legendary American Colony hotel in Jerusalem's
Arab quarter in early October, he strolled through the Old City and
prayed at the Church of the Holy Sepulchre. Just then the Yom Kippur
War broke out, virtually ending Bergoglio's pilgrimage. For security reasons Bergoglio had to remain closeted in the hotel, although he did man-
age to see both Bethlehem and Ein Karem, a village filled with churches
near Jerusalem, reputed to be the birthplace of John the Baptist.[1]

As pope, Francis continues to limit his travels to the essential. He
tries to keep his journeys as short as possible, so he is not away from
Rome for too long; during his first official pilgrimage to the Holy Land
as pope in May 2014 he spent only three days and two nights there.
Again, he spent just four days, plus one day of travel, when he flew to
South Korea in August 2014.

In his appointments Francis also continues to reach toward "the ends
of the earth." The influence of popes upon the long-term development
of the church is necessarily slow; change comes through a pontiff's
appointments of bishops and members of the electoral college of cardinals. Vacancies to the electoral college occur upon death or obligatory
retirement at eighty. Pope John Paul's pontificate—among the longest in
history—allowed him time to ensure posthumously that those in command of the church at a senior level both at Rome and abroad would
continue, even for decades, to reflect his conservative politics.

Their number is fixed, but in theory nothing prevents Pope Francis' changing the rules to expand their number beyond the traditional 120 to 130. He has already imposed a radically different geographical spread. Some within the Vatican were shocked when they found that nine of the batch of nineteen new cardinals he appointed in 2013 had come not from dioceses in the wealthier and more powerful countries, as had been customary, but from such relatively remote and less privileged places as Burkina Faso, Haiti, and Ivory Coast.

The following year, 2014, Francis appointed twenty more cardinals. Of these, more than half were from distant shores like Vietnam, Ethiopia, Myanmar, Mozambique, the Cape Verde islands in the mid-Atlantic, and the very remote and tiny Pacific island of Tonga. Just three were Italians, and only one a native speaker of English, from New Zealand. Although five were over eighty, and hence could not vote in a future conclave, Francis' preferences for a larger global reach plainly altered the composition of the conclave that will choose his successor. The process is inevitably slow, but he has already paved the way for another possible outsider to succeed him.

"Change in the Catholic Church happens over centuries," Mark Mullaney, president of the Boston lay group Voice of the Faithful, said in an interview with the *Boston Globe* in early 2014, "but just in the year since Pope Francis' election, that change has been a lot faster than we thought. It's a throwback to John XXIII. All of a sudden a breath of fresh air came into the church. We can have discussions where discussions were not allowed before."[2]

Francis, a pope in a hurry, has also bypassed the traditional power structure inside the Roman Curia by creating a permanent advisory group of senior cardinals representing the worldwide church. This "kitchen cabinet," weighted in favor of the developing world, functions as a parallel to the Curia, and indeed one of its goals is to develop plans for reform of the sluggish Curia, as well as to advise the pope on foreign policy. What is known to insiders as the "C-9" (for Council of Nine) meets regularly every few months. But as their recent meetings have shown, here too change has been excruciatingly slow to come, as the kitchen cabinet was seriously bogged down in early 2015 over setting up its own rules and regulations.

Pope Francis' foreign visits to places like the Palestinian West Bank, Sri Lanka, Albania, and Bosnia similarly reflect his efforts to extend the reach of the Catholic Church beyond traditional horizons.

At the same time, he is also vividly aware that globalization creates its own problems. In a book that he cowrote while still archbishop of Buenos Aires with his Argentinian rabbi friend, Abraham Skorka, he wrote:

> *If we think of globalization as a uniform billiard ball, the rich virtues of each culture is lost. True globalization, which we have to defend, is like a polyhedron, in which everyone fits, but each one keeps their particular characteristics, which, at the same time, enrich the others.*[3]

In elementary geometry, the multifaceted polyhedron is a three-dimensional solid whose surface has flat faces, straight edges, and sharp corners or vertices. Distances from its center therefore vary, making its unity awkward; in its essence, a polyhedron is a solid but lacks the harmony and proportions of a sphere. Despite this it holds together. And this is one of Pope Francis' favorite images.

Even as the foreign policy of the church under Francis reflects the pontiff's priority commitment to the marginalized, the Vatican also plays a key role on the broader international stage, as is exemplified by the pontiff's scheduled address to the U.S. Congress September 24, 2015. He is the first pope to address a joint session of Congress, and his appearance in Washington literally marks an American milestone. Of the 535 members, 164 are Catholic, and half of these are Republicans (again, according to the Pew Research Center).

While in the U.S., Francis is also slated to attend the United Nations summit on Sustainable Development Goals and will be the third pope to address the General Assembly. The first was Paul VI, half a century ago; John Paul made two visits in 1979 and 1995, and Pope Benedict spoke at the UN in 2008.

Like these predecessors, Francis addresses the United Nations because he is head of a sovereign state, the Holy See, which as such enjoys a series of legal prerogatives. As a state, the Holy See, which is to say the Vatican, enjoys official observer status at the United Nations, and is represented at international congresses on such varied questions as migration, organ transplants, autism, and the environment. In November 2014, Francis addressed the United Nations Food and Agriculture Organization (FAO) meeting in Rome on nutrition, and in February 2015, the Vatican hosted an international conference against human trafficking.

Despite the pope having no military, and despite the Holy See having a physical territory that is barely one square mile in size, Francis is an influential world political leader, with a diplomatic corps accredited to 174 countries under the direction of Secretary of State Cardinal Pietro Parolin, an Italian born near Vicenza. Seventy-eight countries maintain permanent diplomatic missions in Rome accredited to the Vatican, many because the Vatican influences opinion worldwide, but also because with its network of far-flung churches and parishes, it is an excellent listening post, able to call upon the opinions and observations of fifty-one hundred bishops and over four hundred thousand priests in 180 countries.

The Vatican's peculiar dual role as political entity as distinct from the church as a whole was challenged in 1994 when it made common cause with Muslim nations and several Latin American countries at an

International Congress on Population and Development held in Cairo. At the conference I observed how they worked together to water down the decisions being made there on reproductive issues. Since the conference twenty years ago, women's organizations and the more liberal states within the UN have accused the Vatican of being obstructive and reactionary. Some reproductive rights campaigners sought to have the Vatican's diplomatic status removed on grounds that it was solely a religious organization, but they failed.

However, the UN has an ongoing program of regional conferences to review its twenty-year action program and lay the basis for a renewed plan of action by the international community, and to draft new development goals. "This might prove to be an acid test of Pope Francis' 'poor Church for the poor,'" said the British Catholic weekly *The Tablet*. As permanent observer to the UN, the Holy See plays a "pivotal role" around such issues as contraception and abortion. The newer UN documents reflect conflict: attitudes to sexuality have grown more liberal, but religious conservatives—evangelicals, Catholics, and Muslims—continue to join forces in what is an "informal lobbying voice" at the UN on behalf of the American Christian right, again to quote *The Tablet*.[4]

During one of his typically whirlwind visits, Pope Francis addressed the twenty-eight-member European Parliament on November 25, 2014. He was the first pope to speak there since John Paul II in 1988, when there were only a dozen member nations. During his three hours and fifty minutes in Strasbourg, Francis criticized the EU for, among other things, its treatment of migrants, and assailed an aging, "haggard" Europe, whose "rather selfish lifestyle" made the continent resemble "a grandmother, old and sterile." (This latter phrase irritated many a grandmother, incidentally.) Although he was applauded thirteen times and given a standing ovation, EU Commission President Jean-Claude Juncker and Martin Schulz, president of the European Parliament, appeared less than pleased by this rap on the knuckles.

Just three days after his election, the new pope was speaking to journalists when he suddenly thrust aside his prepared remarks to exclaim,
"How I would like a poor church, a church for the poor!" In the first two
years of his papacy this has been a constant, synthesized in his recent
remark that the words of the New Testament "are to be spoken in poverty. Salvation is not a theology of prosperity."

At home, Francis appointed a Polish priest, Archbishop Konrad
Krajewski, to be his personal "almoner" to dole out small charity offer-
ings because the pope himself could not wander about St. Peter's Square
to do so himself. There was a precedent: as archbishop of Buenos Aires,
the then-Cardinal Bergoglio would wander at night incognito to break
bread and converse with the homeless. Krajewski said the pope told him
to sell his desk so as not to sit idly, but to tend to the needs of the poor
on the streets of Rome and even to "hug" them.

As this indicates, Pope Francis projects his philosophy of defending
the less affluent and less powerful nations upon the poor everywhere,
including around the corner in the Vatican; in a homespun and well-
publicized effort to illustrate the church's renewed commitment to the
have-nots, he had three hundred umbrellas and four hundred clean and
cozy sleeping bags handed out to the homeless in St. Peter's Square on
a cold and rainy day in February 2015.

Francis did not invent church social doctrine. In 1891, during the
first industrial revolution, Pope Leo XIII addressed the problems of
the exploited working class, its "misery and wretchedness," in *Rerum
Novarum*, an encyclical on the rights and duties of capital and labor. In
1962, Pope John XXIII issued another groundbreaking social encyclical, *Mater et Magistra*, which spoke of the "earthly interests of the poor."
This was followed by John Paul II's *Centesimus Annus* of 1991, a centen-
nial homage to *Rerum Novarum*.

Pope Francis' *Evangelii Gaudium*, considered one of his most important documents, represents a continuum of these. In this Apostolic exhortation (a form of papal writing considered only slightly less authoritative than an encyclical letter) he spelled out in detail in November 2013 his social commitment to the poor. Its essence is that the heart of the Christian moral message is love for one another, which includes an obligation to help the poor and work for social justice.

Not everyone received this message with enthusiasm. In the United States, some Catholic conservatives claimed that his rejection of "the idolatry of wealth" and his calling for more regulation of financial markets is essentially Marxist. Pope Francis was also accused of "pauperism" to the point that he felt obliged to issue a response in an interview with the Italian daily *La Stampa*, reprinted in a collection of his writings called *The Economy Kills*.[5] "If I had simply repeated some passages of sermons by the early church fathers in the second and third centuries on how we should treat the poor, I might be accused of giving a Marxist sermon," he rebutted. "This concern for the poor is within church tradition.

"It is not an invention of Communism, not something to be construed into an ideology," he added, in a clear reference to the liberation theology that had left its mark on Latin American Catholicism. "I recognize that globalization has helped many people to exit poverty, but it has also condemned many others to die from hunger."

This reaching out to the marginal world, which he calls "the periphery"—to the distant and poorer nations and to the poor everywhere—also extends outside the faith, to those who do not share the pontiff's religious views. In an interview October 1, 2013, with the ninety-year-old Eugenio Scalfari, who is the atheist editor-in-chief of the Italian daily *La Repubblica*, Pope Francis said: "I believe in God, not in a Catholic God: there is no Catholic God. There is God, and I believe in his incarnation Jesus Christ, teacher and pastor. But God—Abba the Father—is the light and the Creator. Are we so very distant?"

The interview, one of a series with Scalfari, caused a sensation in Italy. The pope's question, "Are we so very distant?" intimates that an atheist may yet be welcome in the Kingdom of Heaven. Some inside the Vatican hemmed and hawed at this, and it was eventually pointed out that no recording existed of the pontiff's exact words since Scalfari had subsequently admitted that theirs had been merely a "cordial conversation to exchange views." As if intending to placate Vatican conservatives, Father Federico Lombardi, the pontiff's official spokesman, downplayed the conversation quoted by Scalfari (and others in the same series of interviews, like the one where the pope allegedly acknowledged the existence of "thousands" of pedophile priests) because it had "all been from Scalfari's memory."

————

The scandal of pedophile priests and the cover-up efforts was only one of the Vatican problems inherited by Pope Francis. The financial disarray in the Vatican bank was another that would challenge any world leader. As if the dramas at home were not enough, the larger world also presented difficulties unseen in over half a century.

In the year 2000, the euro was adopted, bringing a boom in Europe characterized by "wild speculation, doubling of wages for public employees, a boom in consumer spending and borrowing, real estate prices soaring sky high, and the abnormal growth of GNPs," in the words of the respected Italian economist and banker Lorenzo Bini Smaghi.[6] Following that euphoric moment, in 2009, "The paper castle crumbled." Ignited by the scandal of falsified financial reports, the European economy took the worst downturn since the Great Depression, bringing Greece as well as the Catholic countries of Spain and Italy to their knees.

Even as the European economy went into free fall, Europe remained the target for wave after wave of suffering migrants. Italy was the first stop for most. Initially the migrants arrived seeking jobs, but by the time Francis became pope, refugees from war and persecution swelled the numbers of asylum seekers. Many are believed to have been refugees from the failed Arab Spring of 2011. Whole families, not single young men, were now arriving; and on a single day in late August 2014, 450 refugees from Syria, Gaza, and Egypt—all places of conflict—landed near the town of Ragusa in Sicily. Of these, 81 were women and 133 were children, one clutching a pet cat. The number of arrivals continued to rise, from 60,000 in 2013 to almost 170,000 in 2014. On rickety boats, many more died at sea.

Sicily was, for most of these, their first port of call. Through Caritas, the Migrantes Foundation, and other Catholic organizations, the church was and is in the front line in receiving them.

Not long after his election, on July 7, 2013, Pope Francis made his first official trip outside Rome: a visit to the Sicilian isle of Lampedusa, only sixty miles from Tunisia. Accompanied by over one hundred local fishing boats, the pope, in a symbolic gesture, laid a wreath of yellow and white flowers (the Vatican colors) on the water in memory of those who had lost their lives during the crossing. Later he said a mass for them in a sports center that doubles as a reception point. Part of one of the sunken boats served as his altar.

Showing the impact on the whole church of such symbolic gestures, Boston Cardinal Seán O'Malley and twelve other bishops from three countries traveled to Nogales, Arizona, on the Mexican border to celebrate a mass April 1, 2014, in memory of the six thousand migrants found dead in U.S. deserts since 1998.

"The U.S.-Mexico border is our Lampedusa," said the bishops in announcing their project. In his homily on the border, Cardinal O'Malley quoted Pope Francis' comments about the "globalization of indifference" and the "culture of comfort, which makes people insensitive to the cries of others." After the mass, the impromptu congregation of three hundred crawled past barbed wire and cactus bushes to enter Mexico for a dinner at a *comedor*, a church-sponsored soup kitchen.

Continuing to show the impact of the pontiff's Lampedusa visit, Catholic teenagers in Arizona went to work staffing centers to help migrants in a program called the Kino Border Initiative. The project was founded by Catholic organizations on both sides of the border in order to promote binational solidarity and to "affirm the dignity of the human person," according to its executive director, Jesuit Fr. Sean Carroll. Kino also lobbies lawmakers to advocate for "more just" policies on immigration and deportation. The teens in the field serve meals to migrants and help with educational programs aimed at other youth. In recognition of their work toward showing that migration is more than "a source of illegality, social conflict and violence," the pontiff sent the teenagers a personal letter December 19, 2014.

In Europe, migration was bringing new interreligious tensions. As the situations in Pakistan, Nigeria, Kenya, Somalia, Tunisia, Libya, and Iraq degenerated, Christians were being slaughtered by Muslims, some of them former neighbors. Reverberations extended into Europe, where older waves of migration exploded with raging new tensions. Already in the EU countries in 1990 the Muslim population had risen to 4 percent, and in 2015, to 6 percent. In France as many as one out of ten is a Muslim.

Well before the *Charlie Hebdo* slaughter in Paris in January 2015, the pope had called for mutual respect of others' religions—their teachings, symbols, values, places of worship, and leaders, he specified—especially Christians and Muslims. "How painful are attacks on one or other of these!" he had said shortly after his election.

His traditional annual address to the members of the diplomatic corps accredited to the Holy See took place on January 12, only days after the terrorist murders in Paris. He mentioned that slaughter specifically only once, but implicitly by comparison with Albania, which he had visited the previous September. Despite the painful events of its recent history, said the pope, "Albania is marked by the peaceful coexistence and collaboration that exists among followers of different religions."

It was not always that way. Between 1945 and 1985, 111 Albanian priests, ten seminarians, and seven bishops had died in detention or were executed, and two thousand Orthodox and Catholic churches destroyed or converted into movie houses by the Communist regime.

Today's Albania is 60 percent Muslim. Although the Roman Catholic and Orthodox communities account for only 10 percent each, during the pontiff's daylong visit to Tirana tens of thousands of both Muslims and Christians turned out to greet him in the central Mother Teresa Square and lined the streets. Among those in the square was Muslim Hysen Doli, eighty-five, together with ten members of his family. "We belong to another religion but have come here out of respect to get the pope's blessing," he told a Western reporter.

Visiting Turkey in November 2014, the pope prayed in a mosque in Istanbul, and in a joint statement with Orthodox Patriarch Bartholomew I, spiritual leader of three hundred million Orthodox Christians in the world, he appealed to Muslims and Christians, who had lived together in peace for centuries but are now at war, "to work together for the sake of justice, peace and respect for the dignity and rights of every person."

Francis also praised President Recep Tayyip Erdoğan for his country's taking in more than two million refugees from Syria and elsewhere, and asked to visit a refugee camp near the Syrian border. Erdogan declined, on the grounds that a visit from the pope might be interpreted as support for the Kurdish separatist movement, the PKK, with whom the Turks have been at war for decades.

A hint of tension was evident therefore even before the pope arrived. On the eve of the visit, Erdoğan had said provocatively, "I speak clearly. Those who come from outside [the Muslim world] like only our oil, gold, diamonds, cheap labor, conflicts and disputes within the Islamic world. Believe me, they do not like us. . . . They like seeing us, our children die. How long we will continue to tolerate this?"

The war on Turkey's border with Syria, where ISIS and Kurdish fighters battle, remains high on the foreign policy agenda of Pope Francis. It can bring complications. When he called for a day of worldwide fasting and prayer for peace in Syria in September 2013, President Obama was threatening air strikes against Syria in retaliation for President Assad's alleged chemical weapons attacks against the civilian population. "How will Obama's visit with Pope Francis go?" asked *National Catholic Reporter* magazine when the two leaders met in Rome in March 2014. It turned out to be very friendly—but if the two discussed Syria, the Vatican's final communiqué made no mention of Syria or, for that matter, of poverty.

On the eve of a September meeting in 2013 of the G20, the club of the twenty wealthiest nations, at the Constantine Palace in St. Petersburg, the pope led a prayer vigil in St. Peter's Square on behalf of peace in Syria. He also sent Russian leader Vladimir Putin, G20 chairman for the year, a letter whose main focus was the conflict in Syria. The pope urged the G20 nations not to remain indifferent to the suffering of others, and appealed to "each and every one [of the leaders] . . . to lay aside the futile pursuit of a military solution. . . . The world economy will only develop if it allows a dignified way of life for all human beings," Francis wrote, "from the eldest to the unborn child, not only for citizens of the G20 member states, but for every inhabitant of the earth, even those in extreme social situations or in the remotest places."

Two months later Putin himself came to call upon Pope Francis in Rome, his fourth visit to the Vatican (two were audiences with John Paul II, one with Benedict XVI). After their thirty-five-minute private audience, Putin also met with Secretary of State Parolin. In the usual formal (and largely meaningless) language of diplomacy, the Holy

See declared the visit "cordial" with "satisfaction expressed for the good existing bilateral relations." The discussion included the "grave situation" in Syria, but was short on detail. (The Ukrainian conflict between pro-Western and Russian-backed separatists still lay in the future.)

The goal of the Vatican was also to smooth relations between the Catholic and Russian Orthodox churches. The latter accuses the Catholic Church of poaching Orthodox followers; Putin himself claims to be a practicing member of the Russian Orthodox Church.

Was the visit successful? Not so successful that Putin extended a return invitation to Pope Francis to visit Russia, as the pope had hoped. Nor did the pontiff's appeals for an end to the savage war in Syria show results.

A second visit by Putin to the Vatican in June 2015 proved similarly unproductive. Putin arrived at the Vatican an hour late for his appointment, but this time they met for a full fifty minutes and discussed the conflicts both in Ukraine and in the Middle East. Vatican officials said Francis told Mr. Putin that "a sincere and great effort" was needed to achieve peace. Francis also asked that Mr. Putin help guarantee access to humanitarian aid groups in the region.

In an effort to foster peace in the Middle East, a whirlwind three-day tour took the pontiff first to Jordan, then to Bethlehem, Tel Aviv, and Jerusalem in May 2014. In Jordan, Francis spoke of religious freedom as a "fundamental human right, the freedom to follow one's conscience in religious matters."

In Bethlehem, Palestinian territory, he said that the time has come for Israelis and Palestinians "to forge a peace which rests on the acknowledgment by all of the right of two States to exist and to live in peace and security within internationally recognized borders."

And in Jerusalem on May 25, where he met with Shimon Peres, the retiring Israeli president, Francis advocated dialogue with the Palestinians and expressed the desire that "those in positions of responsibility to leave no stone unturned in the search for equitable solutions to complex problems, so that Israelis and Palestinians may live in peace."

However noble his intentions, his words fell on deaf ears. As the right-wing *Jerusalem Post* commented acidly, the pope's lightning and "less than biblical" visit to Tel Aviv ended with a "less than exciting vibe." The event "lacked the buzz and glamor of Obama's more showy visit."

There was even a minor papal snub. When Prime Minister Benjamin Netanyahu mentioned that Jesus spoke Hebrew, Francis indelicately interrupted his host, interjecting, "Aramaic."

Worse still from Netanyahu's point of view, during the pope's remarks in Bethlehem, he had used the words "State of Palestine"; later, at the official welcome at Ben Gurion airport, he spoke more carefully, advocating peace, tolerance, and the two-state solution, all read in such a slow cadence in Italian that it suggested serious fatigue. The sole highlight for a number of the reporters present (most of whom had already received an embargoed copy of the pope's speech hours earlier) was the opportunity to take a pope selfie against the backdrop of the podium.

The fallout was less than positive. The *Jerusalem Post* headline read, "Pope Francis' unfriendly visit" because Francis had stopped at a section of the West Bank wall, which demarcates Israeli and Palestinian territories near Jerusalem, to look at pro-Palestinian graffiti. Among them one read FREE PALESTINE.

Photographs of the pontiff touching the separation barrier went viral on the Internet and were published on the front pages of newspapers worldwide, in an image that defined Francis' Holy Land visit. For the *Post*, this act "reinforced [the pope's] anti-Semitic position. . . . Alas, the Golden Age of Catholic-Jewish relations seems to have come to an end during Francis' visit to the Promised Land this week."[7] The incident overshadowed the pope's six hours inside Palestinian territory, where he met Vera Baboun, mayor of Bethlehem.

Reporting for the BBC, I noticed that among ordinary Israelis there was little curiosity about the visit. Security precautions were draconian, and relatively few Israelis turned out to see the papal motorcade sweep through the largely deserted streets of Jerusalem.

Pope Francis made his obligatory visit to the impressive Yad Vashem Holocaust History Museum, but stayed there for only forty-five minutes, clearly deeply moved during a brief meeting with some Holocaust survivors. Pope Francis' imaginative and dramatic gesture at the end of his visit to Jerusalem to invite the presidents of Palestine, Mahmoud Abbas, and Israel, Shimon Peres (on the eve of his retirement from public office), to the Vatican at the beginning of June 2014 to pray together with him for peace, stole world headlines very briefly, but failed to produce any softening of attitudes.

One place of significance was omitted from the papal itinerary for obvious security reasons; this was the blockaded enclave of Gaza, soon (July–August 2014) to suffer the resumption of seven weeks of no-holds-barred hostilities between Israeli forces and Hamas, which resulted in the deaths of over twenty-three hundred Palestinian men, women, and children and sixty-seven Israeli soldiers.

Each January since 1998, a delegation of English-speaking Roman Catholic bishops from around the world visits the Holy Land to support the dwindling Christian community there. Their goal is to try to witness for themselves the tragic failure of the international community to alleviate the suffering of the 1.5 million inhabitants of the enclave, and to comfort to the tiny surviving Palestinian community of three hundred or so Christians still living inside the Gaza strip.

I accompanied a group of sixteen English-speaking Catholic bishops from Europe, North America, and South Africa on a two-day visit there in January 2014. Our visit to Gaza began dramatically as we saw a desperately ill Palestinian man being rushed out on a stretcher into Israeli territory for hospital admission. This was a kindness, but otherwise there were only delays. At the Erez crossing point, where Israeli border guards in a large customs and border control building deliberately permit only a slow trickle of visitors to enter or exit the territory every hour, we (like everyone else) waited for hours before entering a long, narrow labyrinth of security barriers. Having passed through these, we then walked more than a half mile through a no-man's-land-like corridor to reach the Hamas border checkpoint.

When we were finally at the lone Catholic Church in Gaza, an elderly woman who attended the mass celebrated by the bishops turned to me to lament that the Israelis had denied permission for her to visit her dentist in Jerusalem to relieve the pain in her mouth. "We are all in prison here," she complained.

Here in Gaza, Pope Francis would immediately feel at home among the poor and the displaced families. One can only wonder what he would say if the Israeli authorities would allow him to see for himself this devastated cityscape and its impoverished inhabitants.

———

The biggest challenge facing Pope Francis is perhaps the future of his worldwide church in Asia, the largest continent, where two-thirds of humanity lives. After centuries of missionary activity, Christians make up only a miniscule percent of the total population (3 percent), and half of these live in a single country, the Philippines. Spanish explorers and missionaries first arrived there in the sixteenth century while searching for the Spice Islands. In January 2015, Pope Francis attracted perhaps the biggest congregation in history—some seven million worshippers— to his Manila mass.

As a young Jesuit priest, Pope Francis had wanted to be sent to Japan as a missionary, but was prevented from doing so by his fragile health after the removal of part of his lung. It was to be expected therefore that soon after his election Bergoglio would inform us: "I must go to Asia!" Pope Benedict never set foot in an Asian country during his eight-year pontificate.

During his brief stay in Sri Lanka en route to the Philippines, Pope Francis unexpectedly asked to see a Buddhist temple that was not on his scheduled program. While there he spent a half hour with Buddhist dignitaries, who explained to him their rituals and beliefs.

As the pope nears his eightieth birthday, a trip to Tokyo may be in his future. If so, the challenge he faces is how to make the Christian faith comprehensible to indigenous Asian cultures and religions such as Shintoism, Buddhism, Confucianism, and traditional Hindu worship, all of which predate Christianity.

Asian Catholicism, despite its minority status, displays a vitality and flexibility lacking in Europe. Although Asia's 130 million Catholics represent only 11 percent of Catholics worldwide, the church in Asia is growing faster than in any other continent with the exception of Africa. Almost half the population of Asia is under the age of twenty-five, and Asian youth are preoccupied by the same issues that trouble Pope Francis: poverty and income inequality.

Catholicism arrived in Korea not through the activity of foreign missionaries, but through the interest of a group of Korean Confucian scholars who during the eighteenth century had discovered in Beijing the Christian faith brought by Matteo Ricci and the Jesuits to China.

Ricci had dazzled the Chinese emperor and his court four centuries ago with his geographical and scientific expertise. A gilded statue of the Jesuit still stands in the compound of the South Cathedral in Beijing, the Catholic place of worship ten minutes from Tiananmen Square. The church, which caters to the Chinese capital's foreign residents, is normally packed with worshippers at its regular Sunday mass.

The Korean scholars set up an autonomous Catholic Church with their own bishops and priests upon their return home without asking Rome's permission. But they were soon wiped out when the ruling dynasty discovered that they opposed traditional ancestor worship; they were perceived as a threat to traditional social order. Thousands of Christian converts were executed near one of the main city gates of Seoul, and the first group of Korean Catholic martyrs was canonized by Pope John Paul during his visit to Seoul in 1984.

Catholic missionaries from France did arrive in Korea during the early nineteenth century, but the period of strongest growth has been since the end of the Korean War in the mid–twentieth century. Membership has peaked primarily among the middle classes and in wealthy areas as South Korea has grown into one of the world's most prosperous nations. So it may have come as a shock for them to hear Pope Francis during his visit to Seoul stressing above all the duty of today's Catholics to defend the poor and the marginalized. The number of Catholics in South Korea has grown by 70 percent during the past decade, although Protestant churches have attracted even more converts. Protestant churches now claim about 19 percent of the population in comparison with an estimate of 11 percent for the Catholic Church. (The fate of the former Christian population in North Korea remains largely unknown. As expected, the Communist authorities in Pyongyang turned down an invitation to send a delegation to Seoul to meet Pope Francis.)

Officially the Chinese authorities still regard the Vatican as a foreign power that tries to interfere in China's domestic affairs. Diplomatic relations between the Vatican and China had been broken after the Communist takeover in 1950, and today's Catholic Church inside China is split between an underground church that looks to Rome for the appointment of its bishops, and an officially tolerated "Patriotic Church" whose officials are government appointees.

After being granted permission to overfly Chinese territory on both legs of his flight to Seoul, Pope Francis held out an olive branch to Beijing. Permission had been refused when Pope John Paul II visited South Korea in 1984 and again in 1989.

Speaking to Asian bishops gathered near Seoul, Pope Francis insisted that the church is not present in Asia as a "conqueror" but as "a partner in dialogue." Father Lombardi explained that this applied not only to China but also to other Asian countries with which the Vatican does not have diplomatic relations: North Korea, Vietnam, Myanmar, Laos, Bhutan, and Brunei.

Yet official figures released in Beijing suggest that Catholicism is growing much more slowly than the Protestant churches in China. While Catholics have approximately doubled their flock since the Communist takeover, Protestant churches in China have increased their membership thirtyfold since Mao's revolution.

This makes the ruling Communist party nervous. In Zhejiang province authorities have removed rooftop crosses from more than four hundred Catholic and Protestant churches and this has sometimes led to violent clashes with congregation members. The authorities say building codes have been violated.

Returning to Rome, Pope Francis sent two Jesuit priests to Beijing with a personal invitation to President Xi Jinping to visit him in Rome. To date no reply has come.

Further currying favor with China, the pope rejected the Dalai Lama's request for a visit in Rome in December 2014. The Pope holds the Dalai Lama "in very high regard," said a Vatican spokesman, but declined the request "for obvious reasons."

In what became a coup for President Barack Obama, Pope Francis' most brilliant diplomatic initiative was to foster reconciliation between Cuba and the United States after fifty years of hostility. The Catholic Church had long been the sole outside power tolerated by Cuba, and, during Polish Pope John Paul II's visit in 1998, Bergoglio, already tipped as future archbishop of Buenos Aires, had attended a meeting between the pontiff and Fidel Castro. Shortly afterward, the future Pope Francis wrote a booklet entitled "Dialogues between John Paul II and Fidel Castro." In it Bergoglio assailed Cuban socialism, but also attacked the United States for imposing upon Cuba the embargo and economic isolation that had impoverished the island.[8]

In mid-2014, Pope Francis wrote to the leaders of both countries inviting them to a dialogue, and in October in the course of secret meetings held inside the Vatican, delegations from Cuba and the United States clinched a deal to reestablish diplomatic relations after a gap of more than half a century. A forty-five-minute phone call the following December between President Obama and Raúl Castro brought the release of a U.S. prisoner, Alan Gross, paving the way for further cooperation on the lifting of travel restrictions and easing of financial transactions.

A few sour notes were struck in Miami, ninety miles from Cuba. Greater Miami alone is home to 1.2 million Cubans, and many had lobbied for decades to avoid any normalization of U.S.-Cuban relations. Despite this, both Obama and Castro formally thanked Pope Francis for his brokering the deal. We "begin a new chapter among the nations of the Americas," President Obama declared. Even the U.S. Communist Party thanked the pope, Obama, and Castro for the "monumental shift" in relations between the two countries, "an historic sea-change in U.S. policy."

In April 2015, four months before embarking on his first-ever visit to the United States, Pope Francis surprised everyone by announcing that he would stop over in Cuba for three days before arriving in Washington.

Shortly afterward, Raúl Castro, Fidel Castro's brother, traveled to Rome to call in at the Vatican on his way back home to Havana from a visit to Russia. He spent nearly an hour in private conversation with Bergoglio, without the presence of interpreters to discuss arrangements.

He seems to have been very impressed with their face-to-face meeting. The Cuban president said he intended to go to all the pope's masses during the pontiff's visit. "If the pope continues to talk as he does," Mr. Castro said, "sooner or later I will start praying again and return to the Catholic Church."

"I am not kidding," he added.

Both the Castro brothers were baptized as Catholics, and were educated at Jesuit-run schools. For Pope Francis, brokering the restoration of relations between the United States and Cuba, conducted in secret inside the Vatican, has been a major diplomatic achievement.

———

Ever speedier communications steadily extend the global reach of the Vatican. The church itself is becoming something of a polyhedron, to borrow Pope Francis' metaphor. The church is a multifaceted organism whose management inevitably grows ever more complex.

The complexities are particularly visible in the church in the United States. The United States is a profoundly religious nation, with 76.7 million identifying themselves as Catholic in 2014, even though their weekly attendance at mass shrivels (down from 47 percent in 1974 to 24 percent in 2012). Catholic institutions run one out of twenty American schools and one out of ten of its hospitals. Despite the drop in church attendance, the Pew Research Center reports that eight out of ten American Catholics have a positive view of Pope Francis.

It is less simple for their bishops. As Jesuit priest and commentator Father Thomas Reese points out, most U.S. bishops had been appointed under previous popes. "[In] the last two pontificates, there was no room for discussion, and this makes [the U.S. bishops] nervous and confused."

Today the bishops of what is the wealthiest of any national Catholic church are divided between conservatives and progressives. Indianapolis archbishop Joseph Tobin has warned against a "Balkanization" within the U.S. church as rival ideological camps struggle to impose their differing points of view.[9]

The battlegrounds: priestly celibacy, liturgy, shortage of vocations, the ordination of women, the rights of those who divorce and remarry, and same-sex relationships. In September 2015, Philadelphia archbishop Charles Chaput, seventy-one, will host the pontiff's visit to Philadelphia to attend a global World Meeting of Families. Chaput admitted to being disoriented by the discussions within the church at the synod of 2014. Even the presynod discussion, he said in a lecture in Manhattan in October 2014, sent a confusing message, and "confusion is the work of the devil."[10]

The blog chatter evokes the mood and the contrasts. In a discussion on Vatican reform that ran in the online magazine *Crux*, a Francis enthusiast urged the pope to "Continue cleaning the barn!" Another, expressing disappointment with conservative church leaders, said, "Our bishops have thus far not boarded the Francis Express and moved themselves closer to the Gospel." Yet another expressed impatience: "When will Francis walk the talk?"

Speaking for the opposite camp, albeit politely, New York's Cardinal Timothy Dolan, sixty-four, wrote in an op-ed for the *Wall Street Journal* his own capitalist-leaning version of the pope's social thinking. "From media reports, one might think that the only thing on the pope's mind was government redistribution of property, as if he were denouncing capitalism and endorsing some form of socialism," wrote Dolan.[11]

"The pontiff also had recently warned African bishops against new forms of 'colonization' such as the pursuit of success, riches, and power at all costs," he wrote.

Cardinal Francis George, the late archbishop of Chicago, told Laurie Goodstein of the *New York Times* that Pope Francis says "wonderful things," but what he expects the church to do remains mysterious. "I'd like to sit down with him and say, 'Holy Father, first of all, thank you for letting me retire. And could I ask you a few questions about your intentions?'" Elsewhere George said that he would like to ask Francis if he fully grasps that in some quarters he has created the impression that Catholic doctrine is up for grabs.

In the meantime, the very nature of the U.S. Catholic Church is undergoing change. All told, approximately 30.4 million people in the United States identify themselves as Latinos and their religion as Catholic; by 2020 the figure is expected to rise to over sixty million, predicts the Pew Research Center. Already, the majority of American Catholics younger than thirty-five are Latino. Despite the fact that many Latinos are leaving the church, those who remain are now important financially to the church. In the Latino community today, 47 percent give regularly to their parishes, by comparison with 44 percent of non-Hispanics; previously their surplus income had been sent home.

Can Pope Francis impose his views? This is the crucial question, and obviously not only for the United States. One answer comes from Father Reese: "Do we really want [Francis] acting like a CEO with the bishops as branch managers?" Would you want more conservative popes to have that concentration of power? Reese asks.

If the U.S. Catholic world is not only the wealthiest but also the most discussed in the media, the church in sub-Saharan Africa is the least publicized and, it is safe to say, the least known to non-Africans. But it is also a church with skyrocketing membership, now about 16 percent of the world's Catholics. This was the background to Pope Francis' appointments in January 2015 of two cardinals from sub-Saharan Africa, Archbishop Berhaneyesus Demerew Souraphiel of Ethiopia and Bishop Arlindo Gomes Furtado of Cape Verde.

A study of African religion and economics by Santa Clara University's Markkula Center for Applied Ethics, located in Silicon Valley, reported that although "Africa ranks low on economic and communication system development" (the vast Democratic Republic of the Congo has only three hundred miles of paved roads), it is rich in oil and other natural resources, and vital "for the future of religion in the world system." In its composite of religions, Islam is strong in the north of the continent (up to 87 percent of the population of over 190.5 million) and in West Africa (46.3 percent), where Christians are 35.5 percent. In Central Africa, the Christian population is high (81.5 percent) by comparison with the Muslim (9.2 percent). And in East Africa, with its population of over 282 million, Christians are 61.4 percent and Muslims, 21.6 percent. In South Africa eight out of ten are Christian.

During the nineteenth century, the Vatican gave Portugal a monopoly on administration of Catholic Church interests in sub-Saharan Africa. But the Portuguese proved singularly inept, with the result that the Catholic Church lost ground. In 1910, Africa's 1,220,000 Catholics accounted for only 1 percent of the worldwide Catholic population (another 1 percent were Protestants).

Since that time the Catholic share of the total population of sub-Saharan Africa has risen a stunning 21 percent. Today, the Catholic Church remains on the move, and, with 171,480,000 Catholics in 2010, the region shows the fastest growth anywhere in the Catholic world.[12]

Their largest numbers are in the Democratic Republic of the Congo, whose over thirty-one million Catholics comprise almost half (47 percent) the entire population of sixty-eight million.

Some of its appeal is the result of the African church's commitment to providing and improving social services and even the justice system, say Western experts like Professor Paul Gifford of the SOAS at the University of London. But this success is not unalloyed.

Pope Benedict had fumbled in the eyes of many during his visit to Africa in 2011, when he insisted that to use condoms to address the HIV/AIDS epidemic would "increase" what was an "ethical problem." It is most definitely a problem, but not only ethical; in 2014, sub-Saharan Africa was home to two-thirds of people living with HIV, and adolescent girls and young women were up to five times more likely to acquire HIV as were young men. HIV remains the leading cause of death of women of reproductive age in low- and middle-income countries, according to The Global Fund.

When the Tanzanian bishops paid their *ad limina* visit (mandatory five-yearly visit to report to the pope) in April 2014, Pope Francis dodged the issue, praising "all those who strive diligently to educate people in the area of sexual responsibility and chastity." By comparison with Benedict's, his words were gentle in tone, but the substance was the same. For Pope Francis, a change in church policy on condoms is not a priority: chastity, not condoms, continues to be the way to prevent the spread of HIV. But in this way Francis chooses to ignore that of the almost twenty-four million in sub-Saharan Africa living with HIV, fully half are women and one out of ten is a child; and that the use of condoms could reduce the transmission to wives, and hence to the children they bear.

A second key issue bedeviling the church in sub-Saharan Africa is the spread of Islamic extremism, which has drastically increased the persecution of Christians. In May 2013, in the town of Arusha, the safari capital of northern Tanzania, extremists threw grenades into the brand-new St. Joseph's Catholic Church, killing three and injuring sixty-seven. One month before this a bomb tossed into a Catholic church in Arusha had injured thirty. A factor: Arusha is the chief drawing card for Western tourism, the country's second largest money-earning industry.

In Zanzibar the previous Christmas day, a Catholic priest was shot and wounded by two men on a motorcycle, who then trashed his church; that conflict was over rules governing the slaughter of meat. Tribal differences also matter; during the Hutu-Tutsi genocide in Rwanda, some three hundred priests who were either Tutsi or considered Tutsi protectors died.

The slaughter increases. In northern Nigeria, the Islamic terrorist group Boko Haram had killed almost twenty-five hundred Christians by February 2015.[13]

The fact that Christianity has become the dominant religion on the African continent is a disturbing factor for other religions, and fosters extremism. Speaking at a conference on "Religion in a Globalized Context," organized by the Center for Studies on New Religions (CESNUR) at Morocco's El Jadida University, the center's founder, sociologist Massimo Introvigne, said that the figures showing that there are now more practicing Christians in Africa than in Europe have a "profound historical, cultural and political significance."

In the long run, this will change not only Africa, but Christianity as well. Of course, not everyone is happy about this development. Some Islamic ultrafundamentalists consider it scandalous that there are more Christians than Muslims in Africa and proceed to persecute and kill Christians in countries such as Nigeria, Mali, Somalia, and Kenya. Ultrafundamentalists believe that today the battle that will determine whether the world will be Muslim or Christian is being fought in Africa.[14]

According to Dr. Anna Bono, "Many Christians [in the Zanzibar archipelago] are now afraid to attend church and are planning to move to the mainland." But the mainland itself is also unsafe as extremism is expanding there as well. Professor Bono, who teaches the history of Africa and its institutions at the University of Turin, lists other danger points as well: Central African Republic, Chad, Sudan, and Algeria. She predicts that the future of Christians living in sub-Saharan Africa will be partly decided beyond the shores of the continent: "It depends very much on the global determination to counteract radicalism and on how successful will be the war against local and international terrorist groups."

Of all these, says World Watch, Somalia topped the list of the most dangerous places for Christian persecution in 2015.

A third knotty problem the Vatican is called upon to address in sub-Saharan Africa is the socially approved and respected cultural tradition of polygamy. Catholic doctrine will not tolerate polygamy, and this becomes a problem when polygamists convert to Catholicism.

"Polygamy poses a major problem to the Church's evangelizing mission," writes Father Prosper Balthazar Lyimo, an Oblate and diocesan priest from Arusha. Lyimo studied canon law at the Urbaniana University in Rome. He also holds a doctorate in canon law on the culture of traditional polygamy from Saint Paul University and the University of Ottawa. "Pastoral prudence" is required, and "respect and concern" for the other wives, who are dismissed upon the husband's conversion, and their children, says Father Lyimo.[15]

The growing trend toward anti-Christian and anti-Catholic violence has become evident even in India, where priests and pastors say that in recent months nuns and priests have been brutalized by police. Four Catholic churches were vandalized and one burned down in New Delhi in December 2014 and early January 2015. At the Church of the Resurrection at Rohini near New Delhi, statues and a Christmas crib were burned on January 3, 2015. Earlier two Christian men had been murdered, one bludgeoned to death while returning from his son's baptism in a village in Rayagada, Orissa, the other stabbed to death near Hyderabad when Hindu extremists broke into his home. In March 2015, a nun was raped in West Bengal.

Police appear uninterested: "In the one case where there were arrests, the Church and the community have cast doubts on the police version of the motives of the suspects, whose images were recorded in the CCTV cameras installed in the church," said a joint letter from a group of Christian clergymen sent to Rajnath Singh, home minister, on February 5, 2015.

———

As this kaleidoscopic view of the universal church shows, Pope Francis—any pope—would be hard put to succeed in all the multiple tasks he faces. He conducts administrative policies including oversight of a bank. He defines religious doctrines and is expected to be a model pastor. He maintains relations with all the world's other religions. He undertakes diplomatic initiatives on the global stage. And he makes personal telephone calls to countless individuals who appeal to him for help.

He is himself a polyhedron. Small wonder then that he concludes every public speech with the words, "Please pray for me." No previous pope has ever adopted this touching trademark farewell greeting.

He was elected because he promised at the same time fidelity to the ancient traditions of the Catholic Church, but also a whole different slant on the way Catholics in every part of the world practice their religion in the twenty-first century.

Finally we shall examine how far the sometimes exaggerated expectations, the promises about the future detected by the cardinal electors when they chose Jorge Bergoglio to lead the church in March 2013, have been justified. If Pope Francis' election was neither a "miracle" nor a "revolution"—as some of his newer biographers and hagiographers have argued—how is his reign likely to be assessed by historians of the future? And is there a danger of the Vatican returning to the ossifications of the past when he decides to retire, or he dies?

The jury is still out.

9

—⚜—

Whirlwind

I am a little old and a little sick—but not too much.
—POPE FRANCIS, MAY 3, 2015, PARISH VISIT,
ROME SUBURB OF OSTIA

The toughest pressure on Pope Francis today is time.

At this writing, nearly two and a half years after his election, Francis is seventy-eight years old. Age is on his mind: as he told Mexican journalist Valentina Alazraki on the second anniversary of his election, March 13, 2015, "I have the feeling that my Pontificate will be brief: four or five years—I do not know, even two or three. Two have already passed. It is a somewhat vague sensation. Maybe it's like the psychology of the gambler who convinces himself he will lose so he won't be disappointed and, if he wins, is happy. I do not know."[1]

He went further during his regular early morning private mass on May 19, reminding worshippers that "each of us should reflect on our own final farewell from this life." He was speaking of the persecuted in the Middle East, but added these words: "I'm thinking of the great farewell, my great farewell, not when I must say 'see you then,' 'see you later,' 'bye for now,' but 'farewell.'"

If Francis is able, or does choose, to go on for five years, this would take him beyond the retirement age of eighty, which he himself imposed as obligatory. This applies not only (as before) to cardinals, who already lose voting rights in a conclave at that age, but also to all officeholders, who are now forced to resign.

"I think what Benedict so courageously did was to open the door to Popes Emeritus," Francis said on Mexican TV. "Benedict should not be considered an exception, but an institution. Maybe he will be the only one for a long time, maybe he will not be the only one. But an institutional door has been opened; today the Pope Emeritus is no longer a rarity, since a door has been opened, allowing him to exist as a figure." Elsewhere, Francis has said, "There are no lifetime leaders in the church."[2]

Pope Francis has already set in motion an ambitious plan to streamline and overhaul the central government of his church. If he were to decide to retire while former Pope Benedict is still alive, there could even be three popes living inside the Vatican. A new constitution is being drawn up by his advisory council of nine cardinals to replace the fifteen-year-old *Pastor Bonus* (Good Shepherd) constitution enacted by his predecessor John Paul II. But to combat Roman centrism has been hard going. Francis had hoped to conclude the new constitution within a couple of years, but work on it could drag on for several more years at the present slow pace.

Initial expectations by liberal Catholics that Pope Francis would agree to modify some church doctrines, particularly those on human sexuality which seem to run counter to modern social mores, have also been dashed.

Vatican insiders hold two completely opposing points of view regarding whether, under the papacy of Francis, doctrine can be changed on relaxation of the church's hitherto rigid rules on admission of divorced couples to the sacrament of communion. The first, expressed by Cardinal George Pell, is that no change is possible. Speaking at an annual "March for Life" held in Rome in early May 2015, Cardinal Pell addressed a gathering of antiabortion Catholic activists from Italy plus several cardinals from Africa and, from the United States, Cardinal Raymond Burke. Pell predicted that at the concluding session of the yearlong synod, slated for October 2015—immediately after the pontiff's return from the United States—there will be no change in the Catholic practice and teaching about marriage, divorce, and receiving communion. The church, said Pell, will "massively endorse" its traditional teachings. "I do not anticipate any deviation from that at all."

A diametrically opposed point of view is expressed by prelates like Archbishop Victor Manuel Fernández, rector of the Pontifical Catholic University of Argentina. Archbishop Fernandez is an old personal friend of Francis and helped to draft the pope's highly praised keynote document *Evangelii Gaudium*. In an interview with journalist Massimo Franco for the Italian daily *Corriere della Sera*, Fernández predicted that "there is no turning back."[3]

"If and when Francis is no longer pope, his legacy will remain strong. For example, the pope is convinced that what is already said or written cannot be condemned as an error," said Fernández, who is particularly close to Francis.

The people are with Pope Francis and not with his few adversaries. This pope first filled St. Peter's Square with crowds, and then began changing the church. He has a wide circle of people from whom he seeks advice on various issues. He listens to people outside the Vatican hierarchy, and in this way he is closer to the diverse voices in the church and in society. That is why, today, in international debates the church is more present than in the past, and world leaders listen more attentively to the church.

The pope goes slowly because he wants to be certain that the changes have a deep impact. The slow pace is necessary to ensure the effectiveness of the changes. He knows there are those hoping that the next pope will turn everything back around. If you go slowly, it is more difficult to turn things back.

But, when Francis speaks of a "short pontificate," does this not help his adversaries?

"The pope has his reasons: he knows very well what he is doing. He must have an objective which we do not necessarily understand yet. He is aiming at a reform that is irreversible. If one day he should sense that he is running out of time, you can be sure he will speed up."

Is there a risk of a schism—a split within the church?

"No. There is a schism when a group of important people share the same sensibilities that reflect those of a vast section of society. Luther and Protestantism came about that way, but now the overwhelming majority of the people are with Francis, and they love him. His opponents are weaker than one may think. Not to please everyone does not mean to provoke a schism."

These two opposing points of view color the remaining months or years of the pontificate of Francis. But it is already clear that by intimating that his reign will be a short one, Francis is encouraging his opponents inside the Roman Curia to apply delaying tactics to his reforms. Pope Benedict kept his abdication plans secret until almost the last minute. No one inside the Vatican would be surprised were Francis suddenly to announce that he had decided to step down.

Just as political analysts in the United States or United Kingdom look ahead to the next presidential or parliamentary election, so the crucial moment in determining the legacy of Pope Francis will be the conclave called to elect his successor, whenever that may be. Already, several cardinals who share his vision of the future of the church are in pole position. One possible candidate is Cardinal Luis Antonio Tagle of the Philippines. Youthful (he is fifty-eight) and charismatic, he enjoys singing in public, and has even performed at a festival of sacred music in Manila. Tagle was also recently elected president of the international charitable organization Caritas Internationalis, succeeding another possible *papabile* (as Italians call possible future popes), Cardinal Óscar Maradiaga, seventy-two, of Honduras.

The cardinals who will vote in the next conclave will be divided between those appointed by his deeply conservative predecessors, John Paul II and Benedict XVI, who can be expected to seek a return to the past, and Francis' own appointees, who represent parts of the world hitherto generally marginalized and excluded from positions of power. After Francis' innovative pontificate, these forces are bound to clash in the conclave when it comes to setting a path for the church to follow. Three batches of new cardinals have already been chosen by Pope Francis in 2014 and 2016, but his forty-two appointees still represent only just over a third of those who will be eligible to take part in the balloting for his successor.

Already, a split has developed and widens between what insiders call the Santa Marta crowd (that is the pope and his kitchen cabinet) and the official curial structure quartered mainly on the other side of St. Peter's Basilica, amounting indeed to a physical separation. The pope may now claim the allegiance of about 20 percent of the church's upper echelon, while he is opposed by 10 percent. Knowing that Francis will not last forever, the vast majority are holding back, many believe, to wait and see until the next papacy. In speaking of a short papacy, he has played into their hands.

Opposition to Francis is echoed on a lower hierarchical level of parish priests, including many among the newly ordained. Hundreds from the United Kingdom, the United States, and Ireland have sent petitions to the Vatican requesting that the Synod on the Family leave traditional church teaching unchanged. As Archbishop Diarmuid Martin of Dublin said in a speech in Melbourne, "Pope Francis' courage is causing disquiet among those with a very conformist and closed Catholicism."[4] Martin pointed out that in the Irish church, the few new young priests tend to be locked into a past model of the priesthood—in the way they dress, celebrate mass, and express their views.

As a result, the next conclave promises to be the mother of all conclaves.

In the meantime Pope Francis has had a very busy travel schedule. In September 2015 he visited the United States, addressing both a joint session of Congress in Washington and the United Nations General Assembly in New York. On his way to America he stopped over for a few hours in Havana, Cuba, for a first-ever meeting with the head of the Russian Orthodox church, Patriarch Kirill, who happened to be visiting the Caribbean island. In November 2015 Pope Francis travelled to the Central African Republic and to Uganda. Back in Rome he called upon millions of pilgrims to celebrate a Jubilee Year of Mercy in churches throughout the world during 2016.

Other rapid foreign journeys in 2016 took him to Greece, Armenia, Poland (for another World Youth Day), Georgia, Azerbaijan, and Sweden.

For a pontiff who originally told colleagues that he intended to avoid extensive foreign travel it was an intimidating program. In 2017 further visits were already planned to Portugal, India, and Bangladesh.

———

Not surprisingly, given the extent of his public worldwide exposure, a favorite working phrase is "the Francis effect," but precisely what is that? During an interview in 2014 with an auxiliary bishop in Rio De Janeiro, I asked just this. His reply was that a year after Pope Francis had attracted three million young people from 175 countries to Copacabana beach on July 28, 2013, for World Youth Day, mass attendance by young people and confessions were up on past figures. (Joyful Brazilian economists had noted that the pilgrims shelled out 1.8 billion Brazilian reales [about $800 million] during the event.)

As the mammoth crowds in Rio and later in Manila confirmed, Pope Francis is almost uniquely popular, and his popularity has brought new respect to the Vatican. His sense of humor has contributed to this popularity. Speaking in the Nervi Audience Hall at the Vatican to five thousand members of the Cursillos, an international Catholic leadership movement, he apologized for changing the date on short notice. "What confusion!" he said jokingly. "I know you had to change your plans, transport, and such. But you know that the pope is infallible when he makes dogmatic definitions, something one does rarely. But even the pope has his defects, and these defects have nothing to do with infallibility. This pope is not very well organized. He's also a bit lacking in discipline."[5]

At the same time, he has made the Catholic Church a dominant political and intellectual force. Under his guidance, Vatican diplomacy stands taller than in the past in world affairs—for example, his mediation helped foster the rapprochement between Cuba and the United States after a half century of hostility. In May 2015, he announced the first formal accord between the Vatican and the "State of Palestine," the term used in their new treaty. This de facto recognition of Palestinian statehood came despite strong publicly expressed criticism from Israel. He was similarly fearless in using the word "genocide" in referring to the massacre of up to 1.5 million Armenians a century ago, while fully aware that this would offend Turkey, which he had only shortly before visited.

He has steered a skillful course in what is an increasingly fragmented and complex geopolitical world, in which the various ideologies are less clearly defined than in the days of his long-serving predecessor John Paul II, when the world was more neatly divided between Communism and the West.

He has been careful to avoid taking sides on some hot-button issues like the conflict in Ukraine, seat of the Uniate or Greek Catholic Church. Part of the church of Rome for four centuries, only twenty-

three years ago it reemerged after decades of persecution under Stalin-
ism. Francis has retained his credibility in Russia and Syria, where in
this way he hopes to protect their Catholic communities.

In his native Latin America, Francis has led the church into a complete about-face toward liberation theology, reviled as "Marxist" in the
days of John Paul. This radical change in attitude is a hallmark of the
church leadership today even though, at the time when he was the "provincial" or head of the Jesuits in Argentina, Jorge Bergoglio himself had
opposed liberation theology on grounds that the church had no business
in direct participation in politics, especially when tainted with Marxism.

Showing the extent of the change, Father Gustavo Gutiérrez,
the Peruvian theologian considered the founder of the movement,
was invited to speak at a Vatican press conference in Rome in May
2015. Gutiérrez himself had never been disciplined by the Vatican, but
acknowledged that there had been "difficult moments" in his attempts
to have a dialogue with the Holy See. Now, however, "the wall has
fallen," he said.

The wall Gutiérrez was referring to was Vatican foot-dragging in
honoring the martyrdom of Archbishop Óscar Romero of San Salvador,
murdered by a death squad while celebrating mass at the altar of a chapel
in a cancer hospital in 1980. When appointed by John Paul only three
years previously, Romero had been considered a reliable conservative, but,
especially after a U.S.-supported right-wing military takeover in El Salvador in 1979, he became a deeply committed apostle of social justice and
a champion of the poor. For his defense of human rights and opening
church doors to campesinos fleeing persecution in the countryside, Romero's enemies called him a "Marxist guerrilla clothed in a clerical cassock."

On March 23, 1980, Romero challenged the military government
to end their abuses of civilians. "In the name of God and this suffering
population, whose cries reach to the heavens more tumultuous each day,
I beg you, I beseech you, I order you, in the name of God, cease the
repression," he said.

The very next day he was gunned down. His funeral, attended by a quarter million people, became a scene of dramatic confrontation between the military and Romero's flock. Snipers fired on the crowd, and a bomb exploded during the funeral, killing scores of people. No one has ever been brought to trial for his murder. Still, his tomb rapidly became a place of pilgrimage.

Archbishop Romero was already venerated locally as a saint when, three years later, I was traveling with Pope John Paul during his first whistle-stop tour of Central America. Just before our plane landed at San Salvador, a sudden change of plan was announced. John Paul had personal experience of Nazi occupation and Communist repression in eastern Europe, but was unfamiliar with Latin American politics and the plight of the poor and the exploited. Albeit hostile to liberation theology because of its allegedly Communist connections, he desired to make a gesture to the martyrdom of Óscar Romero even though the military junta had made it clear beforehand that a visit to Romero's tomb was not welcome.

Unexpectedly Pope John Paul made his own decision. With our small group of journalists in tow, he was whisked away in a heavily guarded motorcade to the cathedral where Romero is entombed. Since no one expected a visit from the pope, the cathedral was locked. While a feverish hunt went on for the key, for a half hour before the doors were opened the pope and we of the press paced back and forth in the hot sun.

We were all in a state of high tension. The officials accompanying us and a contingent of soldiers were as nervous as we were, and on the rooftops we spotted snipers. There were audible sighs of relief among the papal party when the sacristan finally turned up with the key. The pontiff's unexpected arrival to honor the martyred Romero was something of a breach of protocol because, for the military authorities, Romero remained a cleric who had incited the poor to violence. Even some within the church in Rome accept this view to this day. Their hostility delayed his official recognition as a martyr to the faith for no less than three decades. But finally on May 23, 2015, Romero was beatified before a crowd estimated at 350,000. The next step, formal sainthood, seems inevitable.

As pope, Francis formally recognized Romero's martyrdom, confirming that the Salvadorean archbishop was murdered mainly out of hatred for social justice, not only out of hatred for the faith. Henceforth Romero will no longer be regarded as a radical and marginal; he has become mainstream. In the words of the English Catholic weekly *The Tablet*:

> *Many conservative Catholics, including clerics in high places* [*are*] *profoundly uncomfortable. It means they have misread the Gospel. They want Romero to be seen as a saint only because of his holy life, or as a man who lived and died exceptionally in exceptional circumstances. They do not want his example to be a vindication of the central truth of liberation theology—that the church cannot stand aside from historical processes such as the struggle of the poor for justice.*
>
> *Yet plenty of church leaders . . . have allowed such political struggles to pass them by, concentrating instead on the state of people's souls and aligning themselves with tyrannical regimes because that served the Church's interests.*[6]

I have dwelled on this at length because the shift in the attitude of the church regarding Romero under Pope Francis synthesizes the so-called Francis effect.

Closer to home that effect has shown in his more tolerant attitude toward gays, and in his (perhaps belated) crackdown on the formerly extensive cover-up of the pedophile scandals among the clergy. He has made overtures to Protestants, including evangelicals, and to Orthodox Christians, showing his conviction that, in his words, "Christian unity does not depend upon unanimity." He has also reached out to Judaism and to the moderate Muslim world.

Among the most significant and potentially long-lasting of the Francis effects is his decision to issue a papal encyclical—the highest form of Catholic teaching—on the controversial subject of climate change and the obligation of humanity to protect the environment. Entitling his document *Laudato Si'* (Praised Be), Francis borrowed words first uttered by his medieval namesake Saint Francis of Assisi in his famous poetic prayer *Canticle of the Sun*, in which the saint praises God for creating "Sister Water," "Brother Wind," and "Mother Earth."

He addressed the United Nations Special Summit on Sustainable Development in New York in September 2015. Speaking in Rome beforehand, he said, "We must remind the powerful of the earth that God will call them to judgment one day if they fail to protect the environment so as to ensure that the world can feed its population."[7] In December 2015 world leaders gathered at a conference in Paris on climate change, at which crucial decisions were made over global warming. His UN speech therefore had unusual political significance. He in effect joined those lobbying for the environmental movement.

Although Pope Francis has opened countless doors to genuine change (though often through carefully crafted ambiguities), many of his positions have come under attack. Some poorer developing countries now claim that they have a right to pollute because it is unfair that their interests be sacrificed after the developed world exploited the environment. Within the church the climate change deniers accuse him of meddling. Others argue that environmentalism and population control are intrinsically linked; they fear that the church, by cooperating with the UN, is quietly approving population control while appearing to talk about something else.[8] These opponents believe that the Catholic Church will lower its guard against abortion, contraception, and other population control measures. In their view, the church will be joining a secular-led "ecological chorus" that is convinced that human overpopulation is the main threat to the environment.

Italian Catholic journalist Riccardo Cascioli is the author of *Le bugie degli ambientalisti* (*Lies of the Environmentalists*), whose aggressive subtitle is *The False Alarmism of the Environmentalist Movement.* "It's the usual story: in order to eliminate poverty, all you have to do is to physically eliminate the poor," Cascioli warned a decade before Francis was elected pope. President of the Italian-based Centro Europeo di Studi su Popolazione, Ambiente e Sviluppo (CESPAS), Cascioli also predicted that, should the Catholic Church officially embrace the crusade against climate change, it is bound later to regret its decision.

The conservative American Catholic writer George Weigel, best-selling biographer of Pope John Paul II and former theology teacher, believes that Pope Francis is the victim of a successful climate-change industry of spin. "He [Francis] has become a global Rorschach blot, onto whom are projected an extraordinary number of hopes and fears, fantasies and anxieties," he wrote in a blog. "This Rorschaching of the Pope has gotten to the point where, now, it is very difficult to find the real man and his authentic teaching amidst the pre-spin, the spin, and the post-spin."

Francis' papacy furthermore happens to coincide with a particularly dramatic moment in twenty-first-century history: the exponential rise of Islamic terrorism, which represents a threat everywhere, including in Rome. The Islamic State (ISIS) propaganda has already faked a photograph, widely circulated on the Internet, of their black flag fluttering over St. Peter's Square.

Among the serious consequences already is the heightened persecution of Christians in the Middle East and sub-Saharan Africa, and the worsening hemorrhage of the Christian presence. The fallout effects of war in Syria, Iraq, and elsewhere means that the southern tier of

Europe attracts growing hordes of desperate migrants prepared to risk their lives to cross the Mediterranean in search of safety.

Monsignor Domenico Mogavero is the bishop of Mazara del Vallo, at the southernmost tip of Sicily, a port city only a hundred nautical miles from the North African coast. According to Mogavero, "Two-thirds of the migrants we see arriving are coming to avoid war. In making their risky crossing in overcrowded, leaky rubber boats, they are choosing probable death over certain death." From twenty thousand to twenty-five thousand have died en route, Mogavero added in an interview in Rome in mid-May 2015.

The church in Italy is in the forefront in attempting to address the immense problem of these refugees, who include numerous deeply traumatized pregnant women, victims of repeated rape by the traffickers, and hordes of unaccompanied children; one Sicilian town alone, Augusta, houses 180 such minors.

The twin problems, the rise of Islamic terrorism and the pressures of migration upon Europe, are linked. The war of religion creates on the other hand an onslaught of needy human beings. So far the response of the politicians has been to ask for impractical solutions like bombing the boats, criticized by Bishop Mogavero, among others; Mogavero blames the arms dealers, including in the United States, for contributing to the problem.

New pressures arrive from traditionally Catholic countries like Ireland, where a referendum on same-sex marriage on May 22, 2015, led to a surprising victory for gay marriage. Even in the supposedly staunchly Catholic countryside, voters opted for this change to be introduced in the Irish constitution. With a 60 percent turnout, almost two-thirds voted in favor, demonstrating the extent to which the authority of the church has been seriously undermined. The solid majority voting in favor of gay marriage, ignoring Irish church leaders' appeals to hold fast to traditional values, shows the waning influence of the church, caused in good measure by a decade of revelations of the systematic cover-up of clerical pedophile scandals.

"I think this is a social revolution," said Archbishop Diarmuid Martin of Dublin, who urged the church to "move out of denial and take a reality check."

Back in the Vatican there was silence for forty-eight hours while feverish consultations took place among top officials about how to express their dismay. It was left to the Italian Cardinal Pietro Parolin, as secretary of state, Pope Francis' number two, to intimate just how upset Francis was at the result. "I think we can speak not only about a defeat for Christian principles, but also a defeat for humanity," he said.

Some twenty countries have already legalized same-sex marriages, beginning with the Netherlands in 2001. Even the pope's native Argentina was among these, by an act of Parliament in 2010.

In its foreign policy, the Vatican's frustrating relations with China—with between twenty million and thirty million Catholics, many of them practicing their religion clandestinely—loom large. Their presence is divided between the officially tolerated church subservient to the Communist authorities, and an underground church, which has managed to survive the long hiatus in diplomatic relations between the Vatican and China dating from the Communist takeover in 1949.

Like his predecessors, Pope Francis has attempted to reestablish relations with the now rich and powerful Chinese government, which however continues to demand complete control over what it calls the "patriotic" Catholic Church there. In this state-controlled church, the government, not the Vatican, appoints bishops; occasionally the Holy See has rubber-stamped these appointments, but normally China brushes off Vatican efforts to assert the pope's right to appoint his bishops as "interference in its domestic affairs."

Despite this, on his way to South Korea in August 2014, Pope Francis received formal permission from Beijing to overfly Chinese territory; when John Paul had visited South Korea back in 1984, he had been obliged to make a long detour to avoid flying over China. From his charter plane Francis also sent cordial telegrams to the leadership in Beijing. But these mild overtures seem to have been ignored.

Retired Hong Kong cardinal Joseph Zen, eighty-three, originally from Shanghai, is the only cardinal actually to have been born in mainland China. Zen is openly angered by what he considers the failure on the part of Pope Francis and his secretary of state, Cardinal Pietro Parolin, to grasp the reality of Chinese politics.

"I see no reason for optimism: there is no religious freedom in China. Speculation by the Chinese media in Hong Kong—that relations are improving between the Vatican and Beijing—is unjustified," said Zen in a recent interview with a French Catholic magazine.[9] "The Chinese authorities manipulate the so-called election of new bishops, and Beijing then asks the Holy See for approval. But there are no true elections in China!"

Perhaps the largest problem of all is that at the same time the church is failing to make inroads in China, and despite the pontiff's personal popularity, his papacy coincides with the harsh reality of a diminished church in the West.

What is to be done with the growing number of empty church buildings, whose spires still define both urban and country landscapes in Europe? In Germany alone, the Roman Catholic Church has shut more than five hundred churches during the past decade. While visiting Rome in December 2013, the head of the Netherlands Catholic Church, Cardinal Archbishop Willem Eijk, told the pope that by the year 2025, at the present rate of attrition two-thirds of the churches in his country—that is, around a thousand Catholic churches—must be shut down or sold.

One Dutch church already closed is St. Joseph's at Arnhem, where Sunday masses once attracted over a thousand worshippers. Today it is a spacious arena for skateboarders, but even this lease is not working out. To quote the *Wall Street Journal*, this "once-stately church is streaked with water damage and badly needs repair; the city sends the skaters tax bills; and the Roman Catholic Church, which still owns the building, is trying to sell it at a price they [the skaters] can't afford.... The Skate Hall's plight is replicated across a continent that long nurtured Christianity but is becoming relentlessly secular."[10]

The Catholic Church is not the sole victim of secularization, of course. Nearly half the population (42 percent) of the Netherlands already claims to have no religious affiliation. Seven hundred Protestant churches there are also due to close within the next four years. In Great Britain, the Church of England now shutters some twenty churches every year. Among those was the late-eighteenth-century St. Paul's Church in the heart of Bristol, the seaport from which thousands migrated to America. This handsome, Georgian-style Anglican church fell into disrepair from rusting ironwork and water damage that eroded the ceiling and was shut down in 1988. The church was reopened only in 2005, when, albeit still consecrated, it was taken over by a circus school called Circomedia. From the rafters trainee trapeze artists work through their aerial paces. It now also sports a wooden dance floor.

In the United States too, Catholic churches as well as schools are being shuttered. One-quarter of the American population had been Catholic in 2007, but eight years later, the figure has dropped to one-fifth (20.8 percent).[11] Pew survey results the previous year showed Catholicism registering a higher rate of decline than any other religious denomination; for each new convert welcomed into the church every year, six left. The result is that 13 percent of Americans today describe themselves as "former Catholics." The religious communities of Jews, Muslims, and Hindi all have higher rates of retention.

In Philadelphia alone, sixteen of forty-six local churches are being closed and their parishes merged with others.[12] Cardinal Timothy

Dolan has advised that the same is happening in New York. "The arch-diocese of New York is merging thirty-one parishes into fourteen new parishes as part of consolidation." Speaking on New York TV in May 2015, Dolan said, "We are still working in an infrastructure that was great for the thirties, forties, and fifties, when we had tons of priests and families with eight and ten kids."[13] The process, said Dolan, is "gut wrenching"; distressed Catholic parishioners who had been baptized and married in those churches use the term "heartbreaking."

The crisis applies to many Protestant as well as Catholic churches. Banks are foreclosing as lenders lose patience with financially distressed churches and religious schools that have defaulted on mortgages. Their plight was worsened by the severe recession of 2008, and within only two years, 270 U.S. churches had to be sold as bankrupt.

To what extent is Francis concerned with this decline of religion in the West? For him, the future of the church lies in the developing world—Asia, Africa, and his own Latin America—home to the major-ity of today's Catholic believers. Central to his vision is the "church of the poor," rather than the shrinking Christian communities of the West.

Pope Benedict was no less aware of the problem, but he accepted the concept of retrenchment—"a simpler and more spiritual entity," to use his words from over forty years ago, when he was still a young profes-sor of theology in Regensburg, Germany. In his view, a redimensioned church is acceptable. The church "will become small and will have to start pretty much all over again," Ratzinger said in 1969. Social privi-leges will be lost, and the process will be long, "but when all the suffer-ing is past, a great power will emerge from a more spiritual and simple church." Priests should not be reduced to social workers, he also said.[14]

This is distant from the position of Pope Francis, who is more pas-tor than theologian, and whose focus is consistently on the practical rather than on the theoretical. Indeed, in his third year, Pope Francis has come under attack for being too much the pastor and too little the theologian, and in this way, has sown confusion among the faithful. His leadership style is "too authoritarian, too sophisticated" and he neglects "matters of doctrine," according to Walter Mayr, author of a highly critical article published in the German weekly *Der Spiegel*.[15]

Cardinal Cormac Murphy-O'Connor, the retired archbishop of Westminster, took part in the conclave that elected Bergoglio. Shortly after the election, the new pope, speaking privately with Murphy-O'Connor, chided him, exclaiming, "You are to blame!"

The back story is that during the conclave, Murphy-O'Connor had been part of a small group that included not only Bergoglio, but also cardinals from New York, Turin, Lisbon, and Lvov in the Ukraine. Former Pope Benedict had handed all of them their red hats at the same ceremony in the same year, 2001. Tending to huddle together at conclaves and related meetings, they joshingly called themselves "the Team."

The day after the election, Francis greeted Murphy-O'Connor— who has told this story—saying affectionately, "Where's the Team?" The new pope then asked the cardinal to gather their group together for a photo. For Murphy-O'Connor, the phrase "you are to blame" was slightly embarrassing, for it implied that the now-retired cardinal had voted for Francis. This violated the very serious rule of conclave secrecy.[16] Later Murphy-O'Connor admitted at least that "the cardinals had certainly voted for change. But none of them expected the whirlwind that was to follow."

———

Who are the other members of the pontiff's top administrative team? After over two years in office, he still keeps his own appointment book, makes his own telephone calls, and has dispensed with the "gatekeepers" who jealously guarded the privacy of his two immediate predecessors. He has two multilingual private secretaries. Argentinian Monsignor

Fabián Pedacchio Leaniz, fifty-one, is a canon lawyer who also has a second job in the Vatican department that appoints bishops worldwide. His second secretary, Monsignor Yoannis Lahzi Gaid, forty, born in Cairo, is a Coptic rite Catholic priest who speaks fluent Arabic, French, Italian, and English, and is a Vatican diplomat with experience in both the Middle East and Africa. Gaid is also the author of a book published in Italian as *Grazie, Gesù: La mia conversione dall'Islam al Cattolicesimo* (*Thank You, Jesus: My Conversion from Islam to Catholicism*).

As secretary of state, Cardinal Parolin occupies the second most powerful post in the Vatican. Parolin is a seasoned diplomat who under Pope Benedict had carried out secret negotiations in both Vietnam and China, but was then shunted off as papal nuncio to Venezuela by Benedict's secretary of state, Cardinal Tarcisio Bertone. In recent papacies that role has been compared to that of prime minister, but when Pope Francis installed Parolin as head of Vatican diplomacy, he downgraded the post to some extent in order to keep tighter personal control over key foreign policy decisions.

It was Parolin who was apparently deputed by the pope to state the official thumbs-down on the same-sex marriage vote in Ireland, in effect overruling Archbishop Martin's view that the church had become out of touch with reality. Parolin also was ignoring the views of Pope Francis' own favorite theologian, the eighty-two-year-old German Cardinal Kasper. For Kasper, "The result of the Irish referendum is emblematic of the situation in which we find ourselves, not only in Europe, but in the entire West. Looking reality in the face means recognizing that the post-modern idea, that we are all equal, goes against church teaching. We can't accept that [same-sex unions] are the equivalent of marriage, but it is a fact that many Irish faithful voted in favor, and my impression is that a similar atmosphere prevails elsewhere in Europe."

Previously the pope had famously said of homosexuality, "Who am I to judge?" Now, with Parolin calling the Irish vote a "disaster for humanity," the U.S. *National Catholic Reporter* asked, "Are Francis and Parolin playing good cop–bad cop on same-sex marriage?"[17]

Another particularly influential member of the papal "Team" is German archbishop Georg Gänswein, fifty-nine, Prefect of the Papal Household. Gänswein, who plays tennis, skis, and holds an amateur pilot's license, has been described as the Vatican's George Clooney; his photograph once appeared on the cover of the Italian edition of *Vanity Fair*. Gänswein's style, as opposed to substance, is distant from the simplicity of Francis. Gänswein clings to the traditional pectoral cross of gold, relatively larger and more ornate than the pope's plainer silver one. His cassocks are custom made by Gammarelli, Rome's leading ecclesiastical tailor for two centuries. Gammarelli also clothes the pontiff, but on occasion Francis has been seen with sleeves frayed from wear.

Gänswein is the aide normally seen hovering by the side of the pope during official ceremonies, especially when welcoming heads of state and other VIP visitors. In addition, Gänswein enjoys unique daily access, not only to Pope Francis but to former Pope Benedict, who lives out his retirement within walking distance across the manicured Vatican gardens from Francis' residence in the Casa Santa Marta. This is also Gänswein's residence, and he and the former pope dine together there every evening. In an extraordinary dual role, Gänswein also retains his longtime job as Benedict's private secretary, making him one of the Vatican's best-informed (and also most discreet) insiders.

Archbishop Giovanni Angelo Becciu, the Vatican's "Substitute for General Affairs," is another veteran diplomat, now on Pope Francis' team as second-in-command to Parolin. Born in Sardinia in 1948, he served under both Pope John Paul II and Benedict. Today he is the top manager of the Vatican and the equivalent of a presidential chief of staff, a role that brought him into the limelight during the scandal of an alleged gay lobby, an accusation brought by a former deputy commander of the Swiss Guard in January 2014.

"All too facile," said Becciu in an interview with an Italian daily.

"Like other times, no names were given. The former Swiss Guard can come into my office any time." At any rate, Becciu continued, "I believe that, because lobbies are not good, one must distinguish between the fact of being gay and the fact of being part of a lobby. In short, there are those who speak of a 'gay lobby' but no one yet knows just where that lobby might be."[18]

As demonstrated in his reform of Vatican finances, a defining characteristic of Francis' papacy has been his willingness to consult widely outside customary Vatican channels. In this spirit, in an effort to communicate the church's message more efficiently and effectively, particularly to youth, the pope called upon Chris Patten, former head of the BBC Trust and the last governor of Hong Kong before the colony was handed back to China in 1997.

For six months beginning in September 2014, Patten chaired an advisory committee appointed by Pope Francis to devise a radical overhaul of Vatican media. On the committee were six laymen from outside the Vatican and five insiders, including the pope's official spokesman Father Federico Lombardi, seventy-two. Still somewhat on the periphery of the Francis team, the friendly, overworked Jesuit father (see chapter 6) has remained the public face of the Vatican under two popes, running Vatican Radio as director general since 2005, while also heading the Vatican press office since 2006.

Lord Patten's committee has since been replaced by a new committee. In an unusually candid report in May 2015 on his experience as a Vatican insider, he told a London audience why he believes that Francis' attempts to reform the Vatican media structure are doomed until and unless the prevailing culture is reformed: "It resists changing long-established work practices and adapting to new institutional settings."[19]

Lord Patten apparently encountered exactly the same obstacles that face and frustrate Pope Francis in his daily battle with existing Vatican power structures. Patten explained that he had been asked to suggest financial savings in an annual budget of nearly €70 million ($77 million). "We quickly realized that major savings would only be possible through cutbacks in the staff of six hundred, but this was judged to be 'not ethically appropriate.'"

In other words, the Vatican, having accepted strong measures and a policy of following best banking and management practices to reform Vatican finances, accepts waste in its media operations, choosing not to apply normal commercial criteria. This, said Patten, amounts to a "bizarre" manner of managing Vatican media "with its eyes closed."

Moreover, he continued, "Those who work for Vatican media are its most important resource, with all their professional skills, but they cannot expect, and should not want, the job assurances they enjoy to become guarantees to do exactly the same jobs in the same way forever.

"We are now living in a digital world. The Holy See has to respond rapidly to a twenty-four-hour news cycle in more than twenty different languages. It requires rethinking; what is needed now is a more visual, multimedia content, especially if one wishes to reach younger people." Instead, 85 percent of Holy See communications expenditures goes to old media: to the daily newspaper *L'Osservatore Romano*, with its circulation of only fifteen thousand, and to Vatican Radio. Whereas television and social media services provided by the Vatican are highly professional, they are, he says, seriously underresourced; print, voice, and images should be converged into multimedia content, but instead remain fragmented.

"The lack of coordination has resulted in the duplication and, at times, the multiplication of certain core activities such as translation services, accreditation, rights management, media relations, technological innovation, and social/digital media engagement," he said. "These duplications and multiplications are wasteful, and make it difficult for external media to know how to engage the Holy See. A phrase often used in the world outside is that of 'one-stop shops'; there is not much chance of sighting one in Rome."

The conclusion of his now-dissolved committee was that if ever a reform is feasible, it must be under the guidance of Pope Francis, and there is no time to waste.

"If not now, when?" Patten asked.

———

As archbishop of Buenos Aires, Jorge Bergoglio often appeared somber and could on occasion seem even sour. Federico Wals, his press secretary there for six years, recently and surprisingly revealed that his role had been to keep the cardinal's name out of the newspapers as much as possible. In religious processions Cardinal Bergoglio similarly avoided the limelight, choosing to walk among the crowd and mingle with other participants, rather than in the lead. "If he was by any chance invited to an important big event, he made only a brief appearance. His main concern was with people who were out of the mainstream." [20]

"To him it is a necessity to be with people who are suffering," Wals said in an interview with Australian TV. "That is why a few days after he was elected pope, he compared the church to a hospital—a field hospital in wartime."

If this was the past, just who is he today? Has he changed during this time and if so, how and to what extent? For a man who for most of his life dodged the limelight, he now seems to enjoy giving interviews, particularly in Spanish (he still appears somewhat uncomfortable in English). He smiles in public. He kisses babies. He is unfazed when a child removes his white skullcap, the *zucchetto*, and frequently swaps his own for a pilgrim's souvenir replica. He delights in spontaneous personal contact, however brief, while being driven through a crowd of tens of thousands at his weekly general audience in St. Peter's Square.

"Psychologically, I cannot live without people—I would be no good as a monk," he said in a remarkably candid interview with the Argentinian journalist Juan Berretta, who writes for *La Voz del Pueblo* (*The Voice of the People*) in Buenos Aires.[21] This, he said, is why he enjoys living in the Vatican guesthouse.

"Forty of us who work in the Holy See live here, and we have other guests—bishops, priests, visiting laity who stay here. Coming here, eating in a dining room where there are other people, saying mass four days a week for people coming from outside and from parishes—I like that a lot. I became a priest to be with the people. I give thanks to God that this has not left me." What he really misses, he continued, is being able to go out for a walk on the streets of Rome and to "eat a pizza in a pizzeria."

The interviewer cut in: "You could always order takeout . . ."

"Yes, but it isn't the same. The point is to go there. I was always a person of the streets. As a cardinal I loved walking down a street, and traveling by bus and subway. I love the city."

What he does not enjoy is watching television, unlike his predecessor Pope Benedict, who still follows Italian TV nightly news. "I gave it up twenty-five years ago," Francis told Berretta rather proudly. "I read only one newspaper—*La Repubblica*." (This amounted to a gaffe; when recounted in the Italian press, the *Repubblica* editors were overjoyed—only to be told a few days later by the pope himself that he had been mistaken, having meant to say his daily favorite was *Il Messaggero*, a rival Roman newspaper.)

Then their discussion took a serious and more intimate turn.

Asked if he feared a possible attempt on his life, such as that which had almost killed John Paul II in 1981, Pope Francis replied that he is in God's hands. "I speak to the Lord and say, 'Look, if this has to be, then let it be.' I ask only one grace: that it not be painful. I am cowardly about physical pain. . . . I find it hard to tolerate, probably this [fear] has stayed with me ever since the lung operation I had when I was nineteen."

How would he like to be remembered—as the pope of the poor?

"Yes—if they add another word, like *pobre tipo* [poor guy]," he said, only partly in jest. "Poverty is at the heart of the Gospel. Jesus came to preach to the poor. If you take poverty out of the Gospel, you understand nothing.

"Let me simply be remembered as a *buen tipo*—so that people will say, 'He was a good guy, who tried to do good.'"

———

The international media have latched on to the breaks with papal protocol and magnified their significance, but the issues at stake go far beyond that, and there are still more questions than answers. Among the most crucial is whether or not the promise of the "Vatican Spring," as it has been called, which arrived two years after the "Arab Spring," has been fulfilled.

In a *New York Times* op-ed article printed on the eve of Pope Benedict's resignation in February 2013, the eminent Swiss Catholic theologian Hans Küng boldly coined the term. The Arab Spring, he said, has shaken a whole series of autocratic regimes.

With the resignation of Pope Benedict XVI, might not something like that be possible in the Roman Catholic Church as well—a Vatican Spring?[22] His conclusion was not very comforting.

"If the next conclave were to elect a pope who goes down the same old road," he wrote, "the church will never experience a new spring, but fall into a new ice age and run the danger of shrinking into an increasingly irrelevant sect."

Well, his fellow cardinals did choose Jorge Mario Bergoglio. But were they in fact handing him a poisoned chalice?

Perhaps. And at any rate, the honeymoon is now over. Europe's mainstream media criticism is becoming less inhibited than during the first flush of popular enthusiasm after his election.

Consider this recent comment from *Der Spiegel*, the German news magazine, one of Europe's most influential periodicals with a weekly circulation of more than one million.[23]

"Amidst all of this pomp and patina, Bergoglio, an Argentinian, still seems strangely alien to this day—like a big, exotic bird beating its wings in a golden cage.

"When he's sitting at his desk in the Apostolic Palace, the pope—a man who has assiduously dedicated his church to serving the poor—only needs to push a golden button to set off a ringtone and summon a servant from the neighboring room."

Francis himself speaks of "the God of surprises" who moves in mysterious ways. He is spontaneous and unpredictable, and some in the Catholic press, while appreciating this, increasingly fault him for inconsistency and spreading confusion among the faithful. For example, where exactly does the pope stand on the vexed question of Paul VI's much criticized encyclical *Humanae Vitae* of 1968, which banned artificial contraception for Catholics?

On the return flight to Europe from his Asia trip in January 2015, Pope Francis made seemingly contradictory statements about Catholic teaching on birth control, praising his predecessor for "having the strength to defend openness to life," but at the same time suggesting that Catholics have a moral duty to limit the number of their children.

Nearly half a century has now passed since Paul VI published his controversial encyclical on birth control. Pope Francis must take into account the Vatican's own opinion surveys among the faithful. Commissioned for the Synod on the Family in 2014 and 2015, they reveal that few Catholics anywhere in the world pay heed to that ban on contraception.

To what extent do twenty-first-century popes consider their role as teachers to be their primary function of leadership? Or as they travel around the globe should they instead be learning from the experiences of other believers?

I was once able to ask Pope John Paul in person this key question as we flew across the Pacific Ocean during one of his intercontinental journeys, which left ample time for informal interviews in the back of the papal plane.

He fudged the answer. "I teach learning, and I learn teaching," he replied in a slow drawl in heavily Polish-accented English.

Pope Francis appears to have called into question not only the church views on homosexuality but the very concept of papal infallibility with his lapidary statement about gays in the church: "Who am I to judge?" But at the same time he takes very seriously his role as teacher and essential guardian of church doctrine, whether he happens to be talking off the cuff to children during a parish visit in Rome, or giving his regular homily full of biblical wisdom at his morning mass in the Santa Marta chapel.

No timetable is laid down for the most important and crucial decision that Pope Francis must make when the second and final session of the Synod on the Family ends in October 2015. Are there to be exceptions to the church's traditional ruling that marriage is indissoluble despite the fact that most countries, even predominantly Catholic ones, now allow divorce? Should divorced Catholics be allowed to remarry in church and to receive communion if they wish?

Francis' promise and vision will not be realized if he loses a whole generation of Catholics by continuing to impose upon them a teaching, such as the failed ban on artificial contraception, that they have already clearly rejected. If that happens, he will have lost esteem, and not only in the Catholic community.

———

Early in the pontificate of John Paul II, Hans Küng was officially silenced by the Vatican and punished for rejecting the doctrine of papal infallibility, despite the fact that during the Second Vatican Council, he and the future Pope Benedict XVI had been the youngest theological advisers. *Can We Save the Catholic Church?* is the title of Küng's latest book.[24]

In a devastating analysis of the crisis facing the Catholic Church in this century, Küng uses medical terminology to diagnose what he sees as a potentially fatal disease and suggests suitable treatment and therapy. Küng argues that the Catholic Church is undergoing its deepest crisis of confidence since the Reformation. He traces what he calls the "seeds of a chronic illness" and argues that the church must go back to basics. Although officially banned from teaching at Catholic universities, Küng sent a copy of the Spanish edition of his book to Francis, who sent a handwritten note in reply thanking him and indicating his interest. It was signed "Fraternally, Francis."

It is surely no coincidence that Pope Francis employs similar medical metaphors. He has compared the church to a field hospital giving urgent first aid to the wounded and practicing triage.

Nowhere is first aid more necessary than saving the planet. Published in June 2015, *Laudato Si'* is his much anticipated and groundbreaking encyclical letter on climate change, an eclectic mix of scientific observation, biblical teaching on the duty of humanity to protect the environment for the benefit of future generations, and lyrical poetry by his namesake Saint Francis of Assisi.

The encyclical is addressed to everyone, not just to the world's Catholics. Our common home, the earth, is turning into an immense rubbish dump, Pope Francis argues with passion. Cities are becoming unlivable through air pollution, sea levels are rising, extreme weather events are increasing. The increase in greenhouse gases in the atmosphere is due to human activity, and governments must act. He takes as a given that there is a solid scientific basis for global warming, anticipating opposition from lobbyists and some conservative Catholics in the United States. He wanted to place his views on the record well in advance of his planned keynote speech to the United Nations in New York in September 2015 and of the crucial environmental conference in Paris three months later, where government negotiators tried to hammer out an international deal to reduce greenhouse gases to an acceptable level.

The force of the whirlwind caused by Francis' election may have abated somewhat, but the pope from Argentina continues to fascinate and interest Catholics and non-Catholics alike. The outcome of the task that he has set himself—nothing short of changing the very mindset of the Vatican—demands both a long- and short-term strategy. Considering his age and state of health, there may not be time enough for long-term plans.

Within my lifetime I have seen a stunning metamorphosis of the pope from a hieratic and static figurehead of the church into a media-friendly, baby-kissing, cap-swapping crowd-pleaser who preaches tenderness and mercy, not hell-fire.

Henry James was impressed during his first visit to Rome in 1868 at seeing Pope Pius IX huddled inside his ornate carriage as he was driven through the city. On his return a few years later, James lamented that, following Italian unification, the pope had become in fact a prisoner of the Vatican. "After 1870 ... you'll not ... meet the Pope sitting deep in the shadow of his great chariot with uplifted fingers like some inaccessible idol in his shrine."[25]

I personally remember very clearly, as a student on my first visit to Rome in 1950, being astonished at the sight of Pope Pius XII being carried through St. Peter's Basilica on his swaying sedan chair, the *sedia gestatoria*. This pharaonic scene reminded me not so much of an inaccessible idol as of the Egyptian stage-set for Giuseppe Verdi's opera *Aida*, which I had just seen performed in the Baths of Caracalla. The origins of the pope's gestatorial chair, a sort of portable throne carried on the shoulders of twelve red-clad footmen, flanked by attendants holding ceremonial fans of huge white ostrich feathers, may well go back to ancient Rome, when newly elected consuls were carried through the city on a similar throne.

John Paul II consigned the portable papal throne to a museum on his accession in 1978 and replaced it with the popemobile. After an attempt on the Polish pope's life in 1981 a bulletproof version of the modern mechanized *sedia gestatoria* was substituted, but Pope Francis has reverted to an open-top popemobile which allows him to have direct contact with the crowds that flock around him whenever he appears in public.

Beyond crowd scenes, the Francis effect is visible in Rome itself, where attendance at mass has soared since his election. A report published in June 2015 by the authoritative pollster Censis showed that 62.2 percent of Catholics in Rome now regularly attend mass and 23.2 percent go on religious pilgrimages. For the daily *La Repubblica* July 8, this marks a return to popular devotion. In a climate of fear of Islamic extremism, "The present pope has given new life to the popular dimension of faith."

Jorge Mario Bergoglio has not only become the most accessible pope of modern times; he has also restored prestige to the voice of the Catholic Church. Beyond that, in a world where, in his words, the Third World War has already begun, he has already established himself as the single most influential and—in his way—powerful moral voice of the century.

EPILOGUE

"There has also been some malevolent resistance. . . ."
—POPE FRANCIS, ADDRESSING VATICAN CARDINALS,
BISHOPS AND DEPARTMENT HEADS. DECEMBER 22, 2016

"Prayer is not a magic wand."
—GENERAL AUDIENCE, VATICAN, MAY 2016

"[Christianity] must not become a colonial enterprise."
—INTERVIEW WITH INTERNATIONAL CATHOLIC
NEWS AGENCY LA CROIX, MAY 2016

Four years have passed since white smoke gushed from the Sistine Chapel smokestack. As the smoke cleared, we learned that his fellow cardinals had chosen Jorge Bergoglio from Argentina as Bishop of Rome, the third successive non-Italian pope to reign at the beginning of the new millennium.

Yet although he continues to be universally hailed as an inspiring global moral leader in an increasingly destabilized, cruel world, a sense of ambiguity and puzzlement still prevails about how Pope Francis will go down in history. Is he a true revolutionary and a reformer? Or has he just sown confusion among the Catholic faithful with his off-the-cuff remarks and his tendency, annoying to some aides, to put aside prepared speeches and to speak straight from his heart without getting his doctrinal statements fact-checked? Will he eventually be declared a saint for stretching out a helping hand instead of wagging a threatening finger at Catholic couples who have divorced and remarried? Will future popes judge his lapidary question about gays in the church— "Who am I to judge?"—a cop-out? Or could his reformist pontificate exactly five centuries after Martin Luther nailed his protests to a church door in Wittenberg, sparking the Protestant Reformation, lead to a new twenty-first-century counter-reformation papacy with conservative traditionalists once more in command in Rome?

On the one hand, "liberation theologians" such as Leonardo Boff from Brazil, the former Franciscan priest once castigated for heresy by Joseph Ratzinger, the future Pope Benedict XVI, are enthusing about changes that have already taken place at the Vatican (see pp. 46–47).

I vividly remember interviewing Father Boff, as he then was, in 1985, as he walked across St. Peter's Square, having emerged aghast from the Holy Office. He was clearly shaken by his four-hour inquisitorial interrogation by the Catholic Church's highest ecclesiastical tribunal. He had just been informed that he must maintain silence about his allegedly heretical beliefs for a whole year, and he seemed distraught. Later, he left the priesthood and started a family, although he continues to teach religion, write articles, and even exchange correspondence with Pope Francis from Rio de Janeiro.

On the other hand, a relatively small group of conservative cardinals continues to snipe at Pope Francis' reforms. Among the most prominent of these is American Raymond Burke, removed by the pope from his former prestigious post as head of the Vatican's supreme court in November 2014.

Cardinal Burke, together with three other fellow cardinals—two Germans and an Italian—accused the pope of confusing and disorienting loyal Catholics with Francis' publication in April 2016 of his teaching document on the family, *The Joy of Love*. This document was the pope's personal distillation of more than two years of public and private discussions on Catholic teaching on sexuality, marriage, and the family, which took place both at grassroots level and at two Vatican synods.

These four cardinals wrote confidentially to Pope Francis, quoting chapter and verse of their objections to what they regarded as his unduly "soft" approach to the vexed question of the rights of divorced and remarried Catholic couples. They accused the pope of ignoring traditional Catholic teaching on the indissolubility of marriage. After failing to get a reply, they released their letter to the media.

Pope Francis refused to rise to the bait, and, although he was reportedly angry at this internal challenge to his authority, said he was "not going to lose any sleep" over it.

In an interview with *Avvenire*, the official newspaper of the Italian bishops, the pope accused the dissenters of "fomenting divisions" and "acting in bad faith."

In 2014, back in the second year of his pontificate, while delivering his traditional Christmas greetings to more than one hundred cardinals and bishops of the Roman Curia, he stunned his audience of top Vatican administrators by diagnosing no fewer than fifteen different ailments from which he said they were suffering, including "spiritual Alzheimer's." These included careerism, putting ecclesiastical promotion ahead of Christian humility, living double lives, and wallowing in the wealth and power entrusted to them by their church.

Only the tiniest ripple of polite applause greeted the pope at the end of his damning discourse.

The following year, at Christmas 2015, Francis listed the virtues that he expected his heads of department to display: honesty, sobriety, respect for others, and humility. Again, the cardinals continued to ask themselves: at whom was he pointing his finger?

Addressing the assembled cardinals and bishops holding senior posts inside the Catholic Church's Rome headquarters just before Christmas 2016, for the third consecutive year he voiced his criticism of the behavior of some of the men who have been running the Holy See. He did not mince his words. He explained that his reform program for the Holy See was more than a simple face-lift. He even hinted that the devil could be at work among some prelates holding high-ranking positions.

Francis complained that his previous calls for a change of mentality among Vatican bureaucrats were still meeting what he called "malevolent resistance [that] germinates in distorted minds and presents itself when the devil inspires wicked intentions, often in lambs' clothing."

"Dear brothers, it's not the wrinkles in the church that you should fear, but the stains!" he added.

And he castigated the engrained habit of Vatican human resource administrators of kicking upstairs staff lacking the necessary qualifications for their jobs, or causing internal friction. "This is a cancer!" he admonished them.

When Pope Benedict resigned suddenly in February 2013 citing reasons of ill health, he decided to give himself the title of "emeritus," an honorific normally bestowed on retired university professors (which, of course, he was). But he also decided to retain his former title of "pope" and to continue to wear the white cassock marking his former office, although he promised to take a backseat in church government, leaving a completely free hand to his successor.

The unprecedented experience of two popes cohabiting inside the Vatican has on the whole been quite successful; Pope Francis has generously described the continuing presence of Pope Emeritus Benedict as being like having a "wise grandfather" around. "He is the man who protects my shoulders and back with his prayer," he told journalists flying back with him from a visit to Armenia in June 2016.

Although the two clerics visit each other from time to time and consult by telephone, and Benedict has very occasionally been present at Vatican ceremonies, the former pope lives the secluded life of a monk among his books in his specially converted new home, a former convent a quarter of a mile down the road from Pope Francis' Santa Marta residence.

However, Archbishop Georg Gänswein, Benedict's longtime personal secretary, raised an interesting point in a May 2016 interview with German journalist Paul Badde.

Gänswein continues to fulfill a key double role as the official papal go-between in the Vatican. He lives and sleeps in the same residence as the Pope Emeritus and shares meals with him. But at the same time he enjoys the title of Prefect of the Papal Household, appearing regularly in public at Pope Francis' side at all his official papal functions.

In the interview, Gänswein suggested that the two popes living inside the Vatican in fact exercise a joint ministry, one "contemplative" and the other "active." Gänswein was later forced to explain and justify what he called this "new step in the history of the papacy," insisting that he never meant to question the authority and legitimacy of Francis' overall leadership of the church.

Pope Francis is aware that were he to decide to retire at some time in the future like his predecessor, Benedict—as he is fully entitled to do under church rules—there could be as many as three popes living together at the same time inside the walls of the Vatican.

There are two reasons why, in December 2016, after reaching the compulsory retirement age of eighty, which applies to all Vatican employees (the normal retirement age for bishops is seventy-five), Pope Francis may no longer be thinking of following Benedict's path of abdication in the near future. Church historians look back in horror at one precedent, the confused period at the end of the fourteenth and the beginning of the fifteenth century when there were three rival claimants to the papal throne, in Rome, Avignon, and Pisa. Although it is highly unlikely that Benedict, Francis, and Francis' eventual successor would argue over questions of papal legitimacy, the overriding policy point would be the decision over how to provide adequate security for two retired popes and one reigning pope inside the Vatican in an age of growing international terrorism. Until Pope Emeritus Benedict dies (he is ten years older than Pope Francis), this is a strong argument why Pope Francis should remain in his post for the foreseeable future rather than follow his original plan of spending his old age in a retirement home for priests in his native Argentina, where Vatican security cannot guarantee his protection.

The second reason why Pope Francis may have changed his mind about early retirement during the past four years is that he perceives he needs extra time to complete his planned constitutional reforms at the Vatican. He wants to ensure that an eventual successor is not going to renege on his pledge to transform the headquarters of the Catholic Church from what has become over centuries an increasingly anachronistic and sclerotic monarchical institution into a real church of the poor. What he would like to do, he says, is to invert the pyramidal structure of the present church hierarchy by putting the pope at the bottom, not at the apex of the pyramid. The summit becomes the base. He also wants what he calls "a healthy decentralization" of decision-making, giving local bishops all over the world new powers and responsibilities in order to encourage them to make their own policy decisions for their own flocks without necessarily referring every controversy to higher authority in Rome.

Pope Francis has so far replaced only just over one-third of the members of the electoral college of cardinals who will eventually choose his successor. The cardinals who used to run the Vatican under the two very different popes whom he succeeded, John Paul II and Benedict XVI, still outnumber his own nominees to top posts. Italians also still outnumber any other nationality, with 46 out of a total of 227 electors and non-electors.

Proportionally their membership of the Sacred College still far exceeds that of any other nation. At current rates of attrition, as older members lose their voting rights at age eighty or die, creating new vacancies, Pope Francis could have to wait as long as 2020 before cardinals of his choice, who reason along the same lines as he does, outnumber the slowly diminishing old guard appointed under previous popes.

At the time of writing, 110 cardinals—slightly fewer than half the members of the College—are "emeritus" or retired, which is to say they are over the age of eighty just like Pope Benedict, and therefore are disqualified from voting in any future conclave. There are currently 227 living cardinals, of whom only 117 are under the age of eighty and entitled to vote in the next conclave; 32 are Vatican officeholders and live and work in Rome, while 85 more head dioceses in major cities around the world. Pope Francis has attempted to spread his red-hat appointments more widely than before to such distant shores as Tonga and Papua New Guinea in the Pacific, and he has also given predominantly Muslim countries such as Bangladesh and Malaysia their first top-rank appointments in the church.

Pope Francis inherited a church in a state of crisis, with declining attendances at mass and ever-fewer vocations. Many Catholics optimistically predicted that his election would have a positive effect on mass attendance worldwide, but this has not so far been fulfilled. Millennials and baby boomers in the United States, and also younger believers in predominantly Catholic Brazil and in Poland, formerly bastions of the faith, are showing progressive disinterest in the future of the church.

The latest opinion poll statistics (2016) provided by the Center for Applied Research in the Apostolate (CARA) at Georgetown University suggest that weekly or monthly mass attendance among all U.S. Catholics has remained almost static at 43 percent since the last survey in 2008. There was a perceptible increase in weekly mass attendance following the 9/11 Twin Towers disaster, but that soon leveled out, and there has been no similar increase during the present decade as a result of any "Francis effect."

Older U.S. Catholics pray more than millennials, although the practice of regular confession, despite Francis' appeals to return to the confessional box, is still on the decline.

In Poland a general decline in mass attendance has become notable. In 1991 Pope John Paul attended World Youth Day celebrations in Częstochowa, Poland. This major Catholic youth festival was created by Pope John Paul in 1985 and has since been held in a different part of the world every two or three years. One and a half million people attended John Paul's final mass. At that time the Vatican claimed 95 percent church membership and said 80 percent of Poles went regularly to Sunday mass.

By 2016, when Pope Francis attended a similar gathering in Kraków, local opinion polls revealed that their faith was declared to be important by only 48 percent of Polish women and 38 percent of men questioned. The "John Paul effect" has worn off, and there has been an 80 percent decline in daily mass attendance during the last decade. Two million Poles have stopped going to mass altogether, although 60 percent still follow Catholic traditions and practices.

In Brazil, nine million former Catholics, or 6 percent of Brazilians over the age of sixteen, have decided to leave the church during the past two years, according to a December 2016 opinion poll carried out by the São Paulo newspaper *Folha de S. Paulo*. These statistics contradict the optimistic picture (p. 260) drawn by an auxiliary bishop of Rio de Janeiro whom I called on in June 2014 and asked about the "Francis effect." It was just one year after the new pope's triumphal visit, which had drawn three million young people, including many foreigners, to his mass on Copacabana beach.

The newspaper estimated that 75 percent of Brazilians had declared themselves members of the Catholic faith in 1975. By 2013, this had declined to 60 percent at the time of Pope Francis' first foreign visit after his election, and to only 50 percent today.

———

Pope Francis appears to be in good health, despite his having lost a lung through illness when he was young. He suffers from sciatica, and leans on the arm of his master of ceremonies when officiating at Vatican masses, but when you meet him and see him close up, he seems vital as well as gregarious. He rarely takes time off, even during the Vatican's traditionally long summer holidays. He abandoned the roomy penthouse apartment used by popes for the past century in favor of a small three-room suite in the Vatican guesthouse and turned his back upon the palatial papal summer residence at Castel Gandolfo much loved by Pope Benedict and his predecessors, which Francis ordered opened to visitors as a museum.

———

Desperate times demand desperate remedies. There was no mistaking the sense of desperation inside the Vatican following the surprise resignation of Pope Benedict in February 2013. The papacy had suddenly run out of steam.

Anyone who had carefully read Pope Benedict's book-length interview with his German journalist friend Peter Seewald, *Light of the World*, published two years previously, should have been prepared for this possibility.

"If a pope clearly realizes that he is no longer physically, psychologically, and spiritually capable of handling the duties of office, then he has a right and, under some circumstances, also an obligation to resign," Benedict told Seewald.

But if Pope Benedict had declined to resign at the height of the crisis in the early spring of 2010, when some accused him of personally mishandling cases of pedophile priests in Germany and the United States, it is hard to imagine what sort of crisis Pope Francis might deem disturbing enough to compel him to resign.

As Benedict told Seewald later that same year: "When the danger is great, one must not run away. For that reason, now is certainly not the time to resign. Precisely at a time like this one must stand fast and endure the difficult situation. That is my view. One can resign at a peaceful moment or when one simply cannot go on. But one must not run away from danger and say that someone else should do it."

So far there's no evidence at all that Pope Francis is preparing to run away from danger in Rome despite the fact that progress on reviewing and redrawing the Vatican's current organizational chart has been proceeding painfully slowly. Several former separate offices have, it is true, been telescoped into a single administrative body, or "dicastery" in church jargon, but relatively few heads have rolled at the Vatican during the first four years of Francis' pontificate. Pope Francis has been reluctant to clear the decks of personnel he considers inept, too old, or lacking the necessary qualifications for their job.

His committee of nine cardinals from around the world—what I earlier called his "kitchen cabinet"—continues diligently to meet at the Vatican once every three months under his chairmanship. But the committee's proposals for change are plainly sometimes blocked or simply ignored by the Roman Curia, the permanent ecclesiastical bureaucrats, mainly Italians, who have made successful careers inside the Vatican.

Pope Francis has publicly stressed the need for bringing more lay women and men into top jobs at the Vatican—"the insertion of women is very weak in the decisional processes. We must go forward"—but so far there have only been relatively low-level appointments. An exception is the newly promoted director of the Vatican Museums, still one of the most visited sites in the world, with over six million entry tickets sold in 2015. In December 2016, Pope Francis appointed Barbara Jatta, a fifty-four-year-old Italian art curator specializing in antique engravings, to replace the retiring Antonio Paolucci, seventy-seven, a former culture minister in the Rome government with vast previous experience in running the state-owned museums of Florence.

Although Pope Francis' decision in 2016 to set up a committee to look into the historical evidence of the role of women in the early history of the church has been welcomed as a hopeful sign that one day he might authorize the ordination of women deacons, there is not much optimism in Rome that a new feminist dawn is about to break and that the historical ban on the ordination of women priests is to be overturned. Pope Francis has in fact publicly excluded any such development.

Meanwhile, the total number of nuns in the world—who still outnumber the men ministering to the Catholic faithful—continues to fall. It decreased by over ten thousand in 2014 alone according to the latest edition of the Vatican yearbook, published in 2016. The biggest falls were in North and South America and in Europe, although numbers in Africa and Asia continue to rise.

The question remains in the end: can we already define the Francis effect, or is it too soon? Has he restored credibility to an institution that, it could be argued, passed him a poisoned chalice in 2013? All too evidently, the forces within the church that oppose him have gathered strength over the past few years. But on the other hand, his stewardship has changed the way countless Catholics, and also people of other faiths, view the church. He has raised its profile and even its moral stature in a world whose political leaders are seen to lack moral authority.

With vigor and humanity, he has thrown open doors, evoked new possibilities, and created new pathways to thinking about the role of his church in the twenty-first century.

Courtesy of Osservatore Romano

ACKNOWLEDGMENTS

This book has taken shape since the surprise election of Pope Francis in March 2013, but was honed by four decades of reporting for the BBC from my base in Rome. During this time I was privileged to observe and analyze the breadth and variety, and the contradictions, of the Catholic church through worldwide travels with three successive popes—a Pole, a German, and an Argentinian—which took me to more than eighty different countries.

Longtime residence in Rome led me to join the ranks of the "Vaticanisti," the correspondents who try to penetrate the secretive papal bubble, and read between the lines of "popespeak."

I am not a professional student of theology, and the views expressed here are strictly my own.

Shaping these views have been countless conversations and consultations with innumerable cardinals, bishops, priests, nuns, and Catholic laymen and -women, who have shared with me their joys and frustrations in belonging to the world's oldest international organization. Some have now, alas, passed away. These include Peter Hebblethwaite, who left the Jesuits to marry, teach, and have a family, but maintained warm relations with his former order; and Cardinal Agostino Casaroli, papal Foreign Minister during the Cold War, and later Vatican Secretary of State.

Among the diplomatic and academic fraternity, I am particularly indebted to Francis Campbell, former British Ambassador to the Holy See, now Chancellor of St Mary's University, Twickenham, London, for his insights; to Monsignor Fortunatus Nwachukwu, former Vatican chief of protocol, who is currently papal nuncio in Nicaragua; and to Professor Eamon Duffy, Professor of the history of Christianity at Cambridge University.

Journalist friends who also study the runes of the Vatican warrant special mention: Catherine Pepinster, editor of *The Tablet;* John Wilkins, who used to occupy the editor's chair of that lively British Catholic weekly; Robert Mickens, of the *Global Pulse* internet magazine; Paddy Agnew of the *Irish Times;* Phil Pullella of Reuters, who shared so many grueling papal journeys with me; and Massimo Franco of *Corriere della Sera.*

I would like to thank Father Eduardo Drabble, an Argentinian priest ordained and inspired by Jorge Bergoglio who now works in the slums of Buenos Aires, for sharing his thoughts with me and showing me megacity realities; Cardinal Cormac Murphy O'Connor, former head of the Catholic church in England and Wales and emeritus Archbishop of Westminster; Cardinal Walter Kasper, former president of the pontifical council for promoting Christian unity; Walter Freyburg, former president of the Vatican bank, the IOR; Father Gerald O'Collins, SJ, from Australia, retired theology professor at the Gregorian University in Rome, who taught many of today's bishops; Dr. Joanne Cayford of BBC News, who encouraged me on the long haul; Father Thomas Rosica, founder of Salt and Light TV, Toronto, and assistant to the Vatican Press Office, and, of course, Father Federico Lombardi, SJ, Director of Vatican Radio and official papal spokesperson.

I owe special thanks to Michael Carlisle and David Forrer of Inkwell Management in New York for their support and encouragement.

My gratitude also goes to William Grey Harris of Los Angeles, whose intelligent research and interest in my project went well beyond the call of duty.

A big thank you also to Mitchell Ivers, vice president of Simon and Schuster, for his patience and advice in putting this book together in record time.

And finally a glittering halo for Judith Harris, for her professional editing skills. Without her inspirational help this work could never have been completed.

Trevignano Romano, Italy, July 2015

NOTES

— ❧ —

INTRODUCTION: The Challenge of Change

1 Pope Francis interview by Father Antonio Spadaro, "A Big Heart Open to God," *La Civiltà Cattolica*, September 2013.

2 *Palabra Nueva*, the magazine of the Archbishopric of Havana directed by Orlando Marquez, published the notes that Cardinal Bergoglio gave to Cardinal Ortega. March 26, 2013.

3 Austen Ivereigh, *The Great Reformer* (New York: Henry Holt, 2014), 110.

4 Pope Francis interview by Ferruccio de Bortoli, Editor, *Corriere della Sera*, "Benedetto XVI non è una statua (Benedict XVI is not a statue)," March 5, 2014.

5 Annuarium Statisticum Ecclesiae, Vatican City, 2015.

CHAPTER 1: The Bishop of the Slums

1 Pope Francis homily, Chrism Mass, April 17, 2014.

2 Pope Francis interview by Father Antonio Spadaro, *La Civiltà Cattolica*, February 2014.

3 Ibid.

4 Francesca Ambrogetti and Sergio Rubin, *El Jesuita* (Buenos Aires: Ediciones Javier Bergara), 2010.

5 Ivereigh, *The Great Reformer*, 61.

6 Gustavo Gutierrez, *A Theology of Liberation* (New York: Orbis, Maryknoll, 1971).

7 *The Economist*, August 20, 2014.

8   Leonardo Boff, *Church, Charism and Power: Liberation Theology and the Institutional Church* (New York: Crossroad, 1985).

CHAPTER 2: Peter's Pence

1   Fiona Ehlers, "Vatileaks Scandal: Documents Expose Pope's Frail Leadership," *Der Spiegel,* June 4, 2012.
2   Father Filippo Di Giacomo, "Il Papa della porta accanto," *Il Venerdi,* July 11, 2014.
3   *Annual Report,* IOR, December 2014, www.ior.va/content/dam/ior/.
4   "The Francis Effect, The Pope as Turnaround CEO," *The Economist,* April 19, 2014.

CHAPTER 3: A Deeper Theology of Women

1   G. Galeotti and L. Scaraffia, *Papa Francesco e le donne* (Milan: *Il Sole 24 Ore,* 2014), 128–29.
2   "The Church Needs More Female Theologians, Says Pope Francis," *Catholic Herald,* December 6, 2014.
3   Franca Giansoldati, *Il Messaggero,* July 2, 2014.
4   Phyllis Zagano, *National Catholic Reporter,* July 2, 2014.
5   Melinda Henneberger, "Pope Francis to Nuns: Don't Be Old Maids," *Washington Post,* May 8, 2013.
6   Michelle A. Gonzalez, "Pope Francis, Gender Equality and the Idea of Machismo," *National Catholic Reporter,* September 26, 2013. Gonzalez is associate professor of religious studies at the University of Miami.
7   www.lauramcalister.com/2014/12/09/female-theologians-strawberries -cake, December 9, 2014.
8   Nora Galli de' Paratesi, *Le brutte parole: semantica dell'eufemismo* (Milano: Mondadori, 1973), and *Lingua toscana in bocca ambrosiana, Tendenze verso l'Italiano standard: un'inchiesta sociolinguistica* (Bologna: Il Mulino, 1984).
9   Michele Mancino and Giovanni Romeo, *Clero criminale: L'onore della Chiesa e i delitti degli ecclesiastici nell'Italia della Controriforma* (Laterza: Bari, 2013).
10   Galeotti and Scaraffia, *Papa Francesco,* 43.
11   NRVC/CARA, National Religious Vocation Conference, Report, 2009.

12   Francis X. Clooney, SJ, "Sister Laurie Brink OP and the CDF," *America*, April 22, 2012.

13   David Gibson, "Vatican's Doctrinal Chief Renews Criticism of US Nuns," *National Catholic Reporter*, September 2, 2014.

14   Patrick Craine, Lifesitenews.com, March 7, 2011.

15   www.bustle.com, January 18, 2015. Catherine Hornby, "Women Stage Pink Smoke Protest in Rome as Men-Only Conclave Begins," Reuters, March 12, 2013.

16   www.univision.com/interactivos/openpage/2014-02-06/la-voz-del -pueblo-portada-en.

17   FutureChurch, press release, January 15, 2013.

18   *National Catholic Reporter*, January 13, 2015.

19   Francis X. Rocca, "Why Not Women Priests? The Papal Theologian Explains," Catholic News Service, January 31, 2013.

20   Cristina Odone, "For the Sake of the Priesthood's Future, Catholics Need to Talk about Women Priests," *Daily Telegraph*, January 21, 2015.

21   Hornby, "Women Stage Pink Smoke."

22   Robert McClory, "A Greater Role for Women in the Church," *National Catholic Reporter*, February 18, 2014.

CHAPTER 4: Execrable Acts

1   Father Thomas P. Doyle, O. P., "How Survivors Have Changed History," Chicago SNAP Convention, August 2 2014.

2   "Child Abuse Scandals at the Heart of the Catholic Church," Agence France Presse, February 5, 2014.

3   Sir Anthony Hart, retired judge, currently directs official inquiry into institutional child abuse in Northern Ireland.

4   McKenzie, Baker, and Lee, "Church's Suicide Victims," *Canberra Times*, April 13, 2012.

5   *Dan Rather Reports,* July 30, 2013.

6   *La Repubblica*, letter to Professor Giorgio Odifreddi, September 25, 2013.

7   Alan Zarembo, "Many Researchers Taking a Different View of Pedophilia," *Los Angeles Times,* January 14, 2013.

8   Ibid.

9   Jon Henley, "Paedophilia: Bringing Dark Desires to Light," *Guardian,* January 3, 2013.

10   Ibid.

11 Jorge Maria Bergoglio and Abraham Skorka, *On Heaven and Earth* (New York: Random House, 2013), 50.

12 See: www.bishop-accountability, July 2014.

13 Vatican audience, April 11, 2014.

CHAPTER 5: Family Matters

1 Francesco Viviano, "Noi, la famiglia che ha salvato dalla morte in mare 3,000 migranti," *La Repubblica*, November 11, 2014.

2 Father Robert Dodaro, *Remaining in the Truth of Christ: Marriage and Communion in the Catholic Church* (San Francisco: Ignatius Press, 2014).

3 Ibid.

4 Juan Perez-Soba, *The Gospel of the Family: Going Beyond Cardinal Kasper's Proposal in the Debate on Marriage, Civil Re-Marriage and Communion in the Church* (San Francisco: Ignatius Press, 2014).

5 www.people-press.org/2012/02/14.

6 *Center for Applied Research in the Apostolate*, Georgetown University, 2014.

7 www.mycatholicfamily.org, January–February 2014.

8 *Tablet*, July 5, 2014.

9 Thomas Reese, *National Catholic Reporter*, October 17, 2014.

10 Erasmus, "Catholicism and the Family," *Economist,* October 6, 2014.

11 *Economist*, October 25, 2014.

12 UCANews.com, November 4, 2014.

13 Press bulletin, Vatican, November 5, 2014. *Papal speech at the Tribunal of the Roman Rota.*

CHAPTER 6: @Pontifex

1 Beppe Severgnini, "Che cosa fare se telefona il Papa, Nove consigli se al telefono c'è Sua Santità," *Corriere della Sera*, August 23, 2013.

2 Ferruccio De Bortoli, *Corriere della Sera*, interview May 9, 2014. De Bartoli is editor-in-chief of the Italian daily.

3 British Pathe YouTube version: https://www.youtube.com/watch?v=GVCfktdcMXM.

4 www.stayathomepundit.com/2013/05/new-at-the-broad-side-pope-francis-on-religious-tolerance/#sthash.bHd0PL8w.dpuf.

5   Clay Ziegler, www.ideagrove.com/blog/2013/03/heads-up-what-the
     -new-pope-is-teaching-us-about-marketing.html.

6   "The PR Genius Who Helped Make the Pope Popular: Francis's Mar-
     keting Mastermind," *Mail Online,* November 21, 2012.

7   Vladimir Polchi, "Libri, francobolli o braccialetti, Papa Francesco
     vende benissimo," *Il Venerdi di La Repubblica,* October 24, 2014.

8   Stefano Ronchetti, interview with the author, February 1, 2015.

9   Polly Toynbee, "On Charlie Hebdo Pope Francis Is Using The Wife-
     Beater's Defence," *Guardian,* January 6, 2015.

10   For the full text, see www.dmi.unipg.it/~mamone/sci-dem/contri
     /capone.htm.

11   Andrew Brown, "Vatileaks: Secret Conspiracy, or a Butler Covering
     His Back?" *Guardian,* April 30, 2013.

12   Miguel R. Camus, "Tweets on Pope Francis' PH visit break Twitter
     records," *Philippine Daily Inquirer,* January 30, 2015.

13   "Francis''Boom' on Twitter," *Vatican Insider,* November 4, 2013.

14   Nick Squires, "Rabbit Breeders Tell Pope Francis: 'Rabbits Do Not
     Have a Rampant Sex Drive,"January 20, 2015.

15   *Independent,* May 23, 2014.

16   Paul Tighe interviewed, Oct. 27, 2015, www.vatican.va: www.pccs
     .va/index.php/en/news2/attualita/item/2635-monsignor-paul-tighe
     -discusses-how-the-vatican-has-embraced-digital-platforms.

CHAPTER 7: Saving the Sistine

1   Lucetta Scaraffia, "Elogio del direttore dei musei Vaticani,"
     L'Osservatore Romano, June 17, 2011.

2   Antonio Spadaro S.J. "A Big Heart Open to God," *America,* Septem-
     ber 30, 2013.

3   Rabbi Noam E. Marans, "Pope Francis, Marc Chagall and the Jews,"
     (Missouri: Religious News Service, March 3, 2014).

4   "Archeologia: a giugno annunciate nuove scoperte dalle catacombe
     di Santa Tecla a Roma" (Rome: ADNkronos agency, February 27,
     2014).

5   Nick Squires, "Catholic priests urged to liven up sermons," *Daily Tele-
     graph,* November 6, 2011.

6   Natalia Aspesi, interview, *La Repubblica,* July 24, 2012.

7   "A treasury of talents" (editorial), *Osservatore Romano,* June 17,
     2011.

8   Vittorio Zincone, www.vittoriozincone.it, June 30, 2011.

9   Philip Pullella, "Vatican Marks Anniversary of 1972 Attack on Michelangelo's Pieta," Reuters, May 21, 2013.

10   Antonio Paolucci, "The Restoration of the Pauline Chapel," June 30, 2009, http://mv.vatican.va/3_EN/pages/z-Info/Stampa/pdf/Ultima _opera_Michelangelo_pittore.pdf.

11   Galeotti and Scaraffia, *Papa Francesco*.

12   Judith Harris, "Debating a Vatican Cover-Up," *ARTnews*, January 1, 2010.

13   Pope Julius III, in *The Catholic Encyclopedia* (New York: Robert Appleton Co., 1910), accessed August 8, 2014, www.newadvent.org /cathen/08564a.htm.

14   Paolucci, "Restoration of the Pauline Chapel."

15   Anna Tahinci heads the Art History Department, Glassell School of Art, Museum of Fine Arts, Houston.

16   Loren Partridge, Fabrizio Mancinelli, and Gianluigi Colalucci, *Michelangelo the Last Judgment: A Glorious Restoration* (New York: Abrams, 1997).

17   See: http://msopal29.myweb.uga.edu/AntiRestoration.html.

18   Holland Cotter, "James Beck, 77, Art Scholar and Critic of Conservation Is Dead," *New York Times,* May 29, 2007.

19   See: www.ariasrl.net/2014/06/16/aria-celestiale-nella-cappella-sistina -a-ottobre-nuovo-impianto-di-climatizzazione.

20   Nicole Winfield, "Sistine Chapel Pollution Levels Threaten Michelangelo Frescoes," Associated Press, October 17, 2013.

21   See: www.catholicculture.org/culture/library/view.cfm?recnum=3067.

22   Concordat Article 33: "The disposition of the existing Catacombs in Rome and other parts of the territory of the Kingdom are reserved to the Holy See, with the consequent honour of keeping, maintaining and conserving them. The Holy See can, with the observance of the law of the State and saving the eventual rights of third parties, proceed to future excavations and the transfer of the bodies of the saints."

23   Sandro Orlando, "Inchiesta sulle proprietà immobiliari del Vaticano," *Il Mondo*, May 18, 2007.

24   *Ibid.*

25   *Ibid.*

26   Orazio La Rocca, "Sembrano Magazzini," *La Repubblica*, May 16, 2013.

CHAPTER 8: The Pope of the Periphery

1   Lucio Brunelli and Gianni Valenti, "Lo spazio e il tempo di Papa Francesco" (Pope Francis' Concept of Time and Space), *Limes*, March 2014.

2   Neil Swidey, "The Promise of Francis," *Boston Globe*, February 23, 2014.

3   *On Heaven and Earth: Pope Francis on Faith, Family and the Church in the 21st Century* (London: Bloomsbury, 2013). Originally published in Spanish in 2010.

4   Tina Beattie, "Part of the Solution, Not Part of the Problem," *Tablet*, May 10, 2014.

5   Andrea Tornielli, *Pope Francis: This Economy Kills* (Milan: Edizioni Piemme, 2015).

6   Lorenzo Bini Smagh, *La Repubblica*, February 6, 2015.

7   "Pope Francis' unfriendly visit," *Jerusalem Post*, May 27, 2014.

8   "Pope Francis Wrote Cuban Book in 1998 between John Paul II and Fidel Castro," Huffington Post, December 20, 2014. Details of the booklet were published by Austen Ivereigh in his 2014 biography *The Great Reformer.*

9   Michael Sean Winters, "US Church Divided on How to 'Read' Pope Francis," *Tablet*, June 12, 2014.

10 David Gibson, "Archbishop Chaput Blasts Vatican Debate on Family," *National Catholic Reporter*, October 21, 2014.

11 Timothy Dolan, "The Pope's Case for Virtuous Capitalism," *Wall Street Journal*, May 22, 2014.

12 Pew Research Center statistics, 2013.

13 David Curry, "Persecution of Christians a Significant Indicator of Future World Chaos," Fox News, February 9, 2015.

14 Anna Bono, "The Predicament of Christians in sub-Saharan Africa," published online by the Italian Atlantic Committee.

15 John Barker, "St. Lawrence Priest Awarded PhD in Canon Law for Study of Polygamy in Sub-Saharan Africa," *Thompson Citizen*, June 13, 2012.

CHAPTER 9: Whirlwind

1   Valentina Alazraki, interview with Pope Francis, Televisa News, Mexico, March 13, 2015.

2   Pope Francis speech, interdenominational rally, St. Peter's Square, July 3, 2015.

3   Massimo Franco, interview with Archbishop Victor Manuel Fernandez, *Corriere della Sera*, May 10, 2015.

4   Sarah Mac Donald, " 'Conformist' younger clergy wary of Francis," *Tablet*, August 4, 2014.

5   Cindy Wooden, "When It Comes to Scheduling, Pope Says He's Definitely Not Infallible," Catholic News Service, May 1, 2015.

6   *Tablet*, editorial, May 23, 2015.

7   Pope Francis, opening remarks, General Assembly of Caritas Internationalis, May 12, 2015. Caritas is a confederation of 165 Catholic charity and aid organizations operating in two hundred countries.

8   Riccardo Cascioli, La Nuova Bussola Quotidiana (www.lanuovabq .it, Italian Catholic journalists' website), May 2015.

9   Sandro Magister, *China, Cardinal Zen against Saint Egidio*, http:// chiesa.espresso.repubblica.it/articolo/1350164?eng=y, February 9, 2012.

10 Naftali Bendavid, "Europe's empty churches go on sale," *Wall Street Journal*, January 2, 2015.

11 According to a Pew Research study released May 12, 2015.

12 NBC-TV, June 1, 2013.

13 ABC News, May 8, 2015.

14 Vatican Insider website, managed by La Stampa, Turin (www.vatican insider.stampa.it), February 18, 2013.

15 Walter Mayr, "Where Is Pope Francis Steering the Church?" *Der Spiegel International*, May 29, 2015.

16 Cardinal Cormac Murphy-O'Connor, "Cometh the hour, cometh the man," *Tablet*, May 7, 2015, citing his memoir: *An English Spring* (London: Bloomsbury, 2015).

17 Jamie Manson, *National Catholic Reporter*, May 28, 2015.

18 Angelo Becciu, *La Repubblica*, January 21, 2014.

19 Lord Patten, lecture at World Communications Day, St. Patrick's, London, May 27, 2015.

20 Rachael Kohn, interview with Federico Wals, Australian Broadcasting Corp., May 15, 2015.

21 Juan Berretta, interview with Pope Francis, *La voz del pueblo*, May 2015. See: www.lavozdelpueblo.com.ar/nota-27095-aoro-ir-a-una-pizzera -y-comerme-una-buen.

22 Hans Küng, "A Vatican Spring?" *New York Times*, February 27, 2013.

23   Walter Mayr, "Where Is Pope Francis Leading the Church?" *Der Spiegel International,* May 29, 2015.

24   Hans Küng, *Can We Save the Catholic Church?* (London: William Collins, 2013).

25   Henry James, *Italian Hours,* 1909.

SELECT BIBLIOGRAPHY

John L. Allen, *Against the Tide: The Radical Leadership of Pope Francis* (Liguori, Mo.: Liguori Publications, 2014)

John L. Allen, *The Francis Miracle: Inside the Transformation of the Pope and the Church* (New York: Time Publishers, 2015)

Jason Berry, *Render Unto Rome: The Secret Life of Money in the Catholic Church* (New York: Crown Publishers, 2011)

Leonardo Boff, Francis of Rome and Francis of Assisi (New York: Orbis, 2014)

Roberto Calderisi, *Earthly Mission: The Catholic Church and Development* (Conn.: Yale University Press, 2013)

Massimo Franco, *The Crisis in the Vatican Empire* (Milan: Arnoldo Mondadori, 2013)

Austin Ivereigh, *The Great Reformer: Francis and the Making of a Radical Pope* (New York: Henry Holt, 2014)

Walter Kasper, *Mercy: The Essence of the Gospel and the Key to Christian Life* (New Jersey: Paulist Press, 2014)

Hans Küng, *Can We Save the Catholic Church?* (Glasgow: William Collins, 2013)

Ivan Maffeis, *Cronisti dell'invisibile. Informazione religiosa: 15 protagonisti si raccontano* (Milan: Ancora, 2015)

Michele Mancino and Giovani Romeo Clero, *Criminale: l'onore della chiesa e i delitti degli ecclesiastici nell'Italia della Contrariforma* (Bari: Laterza, 2013)

Selina O'Grady *And Man Created God: Kings, Cults, and Conquests at the Time of Jesus* (New York: Atlantic, St. Martin's Press, 2012)

Marco Politi, *Francesco Tra I Lupi* (Bari: Laterza, 2014)

Paolo Rodari, *Il Progetto di Francesco: Dove Vuol Portare la Chiesa* (Bologna: Editrice Missionaria Italiana, 2014)

Paul Vallely, *Pope Francis: Untying the Knots.* (London: Bloomsbury, 2013)

INDEX

—⁓—